THE OLD TESTAMENT LIBRARY

General Editors

A. H. J. GUNNEWEG

UNDERSTANDING THE OLD TESTAMENT

THE WESTMINSTER PRESS
Philadelphia

Translated by John Bowden from the German
Vom Verstehen des Alten Testaments. Eine Hermeneutik,
Das Alte Testament Deutsch, Ergänzungsreihe Band 5,
published by Vandenhoeck & Ruprecht, Göttingen 1977

Published by The Westminster Press®
Philadelphia, Pennsylvania

PRINTED IN THE UNITED STATES OF AMERICA

Library of Congress Cataloging in Publication Data

Gunneweg, Antonius H   J
   Understanding the Old Testament.

   (The Old Testament library)
   Translation of Vom verstehen des Alten Testaments,
eine hermeneutik.
   Bibliography: p.
   Includes index.
   1. Bible. O.T.—Criticism, interpretation, etc.
I. Title. II. Series.
BS1171.2.G8613   221.6′3   78-6696
ISBN 0-664-21371-5

CONTENTS

I

INTRODUCTION: THE OLD TESTAMENT AS A HERMENEUTICAL PROBLEM

The concept of hermeneutics is an evasive one. It is concerned with the process and the result of understanding, with the ability and the failure to understand, but is not itself so closely defined as to exclude misunderstanding. This situation makes it necessary to give a preliminary definition of the sense in which 'hermeneutics' and 'hermeneutical' will be used in the present book. This volume does not set out to present hermeneutics as understood by Friedrich Schleiermacher and Wilhelm Dilthey as an aesthetic theory of how we understand the Old Testament. Those looking for an introduction to exegetical method may be referred to the works by Otto Kaiser et al., Hermann Barth and Odil Hannes Steck, Georg Fohrer et al., Wolfgang Richter and Klaus Koch (all cited in the bibliography, IA). Nor is there any intention of writing a theology of the Old Testament: that has been done elsewhere. Equally, I have not tried to write a complete history of the acceptance of the Old Testament in the church: this can be found in books by Ludwig Diestel (Ic) and Emil G. Kraeling (Ic) – the former a large work which is still indispensable, even though it is out of date in many respects, and the latter a study which is limited to the period after the Reformation. Finally, Hans-Joachim Kraus has produced a key work on the history of biblical theology (Ic). No, the task I have set myself here is a different one, namely, to describe and give a critical evaluation of the different and often contradictory possibilities of understanding the Old Testament as part of the Christian canon – or even of rejecting it altogether.

This concern is a hermeneutical one, because it involves an overall understanding of the Old Testament and the presuppositions on which that is based. It is also theological, because any theology of the Old Testament, like theology generally, begins from particular pre-conceptions and a particular overall understanding of the canon of the Old and New Testaments and their interrelationship. Indeed, it would be no exaggeration to understand the hermeneutical problem of the Old Testament as *the* problem of Christian theology, and not just as one problem among others, seeing that all the other questions of theology are affected in one way or another by its resolution. If the interpretation of holy scripture is an essential task for theology, and if the Bible is the basis of Christian life, the foundation of the church and the medium of revelation, then it is of fundamental importance for the theologian to ask whether and why the collection of Israelite and Jewish writings to which the Christian church has given the name Old Testament are part – indeed the most substantial part – of the canon of scripture and what their relevance is. This question affects the extent and also qualitatively the substance of what may be regarded as Christian. No more fundamental question can be posed in all theology; providing an answer for it defines the realm in which theology has to be done.

The hermeneutical and theological task with which we are con-fronted here is also, of course, a historical one. The many different and often contradictory possibilities of understanding the Old Testa-ment as part of the canon or even of refusing to acknowledge it as being un-Christian were expressed long before the various outlines of theology which are to be found today; they have developed in the course of a long history. Some of them recur during this history in more or less different forms and at different levels of reflection. Others become more pointed or reappear as a consequence of the changed situation and approach to the question which developed out of the Reformation and especially out of the rise of historical criticism. Thus if an account and evaluation of the various possibilities of understand-ing the Old Testament is not to remain completely abstract and theological, it cannot avoid taking account of history. That does not, of course, mean that we have to resort to a purely chronological presentation and an approach similar to that of L. Diestel or E. G. Kraeling (both Ic); both these writers set out to depict the various attempts at and outlines of hermeneutics in chronological sequence. A problem-oriented treatment seems much more suitable for the task to be accomplished here, a treatment which is con-cerned to do justice to both the diachronic and the synchronistic aspects, i.e., not only to historical developments but also to those questions and answers the substance of which remains the same. Several considerations would seem to support the approach. First, the history of hermeneutical problems is so long and so many people have been involved in attempts to solve them that no account could present a complete picture (as has been demonstrated by Diestel, Kraeling and Kraus). Secondly, different and often contradictory or even conflicting approaches to hermeneutics may well appear at the same time – we need only think of Marcion's polemical rejection of the Old Testament or present-day theological pluralism. Another reason in favour of a systematic rather than a chronological approach is the way in which some sets of questions and conceptions tend to recur in history, albeit with certain modifications.

The reappearance of the same or similar problems and solutions is a clear indication that the hermeneutical problem of the Old Testament in its varied aspects is not a matter of historical coincidence or theological whim; it arises from the very content of the Old Testament itself. The basic problem is that the Old Testament is a collection of Israelite and Jewish writings. These writings are the religious national literature of the people of Israel and the holy book of the Jewish community, the synagogue. Without doubt and beyond question they are not of Christian origin, but are older than Christianity. Nor were they first collected and made into a canon of holy, unassailable – sacrosanct – and, as was taught, divinely inspired writings by the Christian church. The compilation and completion of the Hebrew canon was the work of the synagogue of about AD 100, a synagogue which was strongly influenced by the Pharisaic movement in Jewish theology. Moreover, not even the Greek translation, first of the five books of Moses, the Torah, and then of the rest of the Old Testament writings, which became generally binding on the Christian church, was of Christian origin; it was a Jewish work, originally intended for the Greek-speaking Jewish diaspora and not for the Christian church. Furthermore, the Greek arrangement of books (historical books, didactic books, prophets, corresponding to past, present and future) which differs from the Hebrew canon and became normative for the church, was originally Jewish and not Christian (this includes the books which from the time of Jerome, c. AD 350, or at least from Karlstadt and Luther, are known as the Apocrypha: III Ezra (I Esdras), Maccabees, Tobit, Judith, the Prayer of Manasseh, additions to Daniel and Esther, Baruch, the letter of Jeremiah, Jesus Sirach and the Wisdom of Solomon). Presumably the early Christian churches depended upon Jewish collections of writings which will have differed from place to place.

Thus in every respect the Old Testament is a *legacy* from the pre-Christian period. And at this point the hermeneutical problem arises. Is the Old Testament pre-Christian and therefore non-Christian simply because it comes from the period before Christianity? Can the recognition of non-Christian writings as part of the Christian canon make them Christian after the event and thus so to speak baptize them? Furthermore, within the Christian church the collection of Israelite and Jewish writings is called the Old Testament. But what is meant by the adjective 'Old'? Does the word simply indicate the temporal dimension – something that is older, earlier, prior to the new, or does it have connotations of being of an inferior quality, even obsolete?

This problem arose at a relatively early stage. It became even more acute as a result of the Reformation and was further intensified with the rise of historical criticism and its consistent application to the biblical writings. If scripture was to be the sole source of revelation and the foundation of the church of the Reformation, unsupported by the tradition and the teaching authority of the church, then the correct exposition of scripture was of prime theological importance; and if there was to be a return to the literal sense of scripture, as the Reformers desired, it was inevitable that the Old Testament would appear in a different light. Once it was understood literally and not allegorically it would demonstrate not only its own independent character, which had been concealed over the ages, but also its *alien* nature. This alien nature became increasingly evident to the steadfast gaze of historical critics whose eyes had been freed from the blinkers of dogmatism. The old hermeneutical problem posed by the Old Testament as a legacy handed down to the church was now felt in all its force. Is the Old Testament not primarily '*law*', as it was termed in Judaism and even among the early Christian communities? Is it still binding as law, or has it been abrogated for Christians? Is this Israelite and Jewish legacy not the expression of an *alien religion*? Might it not have been possible to conclude from the historical fact that after the time of Paul the Christian community withdrew from the synagogue and formed its own religious fellowship that the legacy of the synagogue should have been abandoned along with the synagogue itself? For one reason or another that may not have happened then, but might it not now be time and indeed high time to put into effect what had been inconsistently neglected previously? And if we are not to draw such a consequence, and if the Old Testament is to continue to remain as the first part of the canon, despite the recognition of its pre-Christian origins, how are we to explain its significance, not merely historically, by referring to the tradition, but also in theological terms?

Of course, there is also a quite different way of understanding and evaluating the Old Testament: its supposedly alien nature can also be an expression of the *totaliter aliter*, the wholly otherness of the one true God who revealed himself first as the God of Israel and thereafter in Jesus Christ. The first and most extensive part of the Bible, at one time the only sacred scripture for the early church, would even now be holy scripture proper, and the New Testament would merely be the correct interpretation of it in the light of Christ's birth, death and resurrection. Even the law would remain in effect in so far as it was not specifically intended for Israelite and Jewish times and circumstances, if not as the human way to divine salvation then at least as God's unchanged will. Woe to anyone who works on sabbath or feast day or allows manservant, maidservant or even animals to do the same!

Putting the Old Testament in such a prominent position and valuing it so highly does not necessarily mean, however, that the Old Testament law has to be placed in the foreground and accentuated. Such a procedure can also bring out the often incomplete character of this collection of writings and the fact that the promises of its prophetic and apocalyptic sections have not been fulfilled. In that case the Old Testament is understood as the book of a *history* which moves on *from promise to promise*: the conclusion is its fulfilment in Christ, but this in turn has the character of promise – the exodus from the land of slavery has still to be accomplished, the promised land has not yet been reached.

Another possibility of incorporating the Old Testament into Christianity and doing justice to its quality as the Old Testament, in polarization with the New, is to see it as a prelude to the New Testament not only in time, but even more in terms of content. It may be thought that the prophecies or promises of the Old Testament are fulfilled in the New or that the types which are prefigured in a shadowy way in events, persons or institutions of the Old Testament emerge into full light in the New Testament and are there – as antitypes – considered to be fulfilled. This approach, which takes the two testaments together while at the same time being concerned to keep the Old old and the New new, is termed typological. But is there not a danger of utter arbitrariness if Christians from a later period seek to interpret typologically events, persons and institutions of ancient Israel which were by no means simply prefigurements and types pointing forward beyond themselves? Does not exegesis turn into eisegesis here?

This suspicion is avoided by those who seek to understand the Old Testament and indeed the New primarily as the written record of *patterns of life and conduct* which are poles apart in their opposition one to another. On the one hand is the polarity of the law which leads to death, and on the other that of the gospel which brings salvation and life. There is an opposition between the cultic community in Jerusalem and in the diaspora, still bound by the law, which does not abandon its ties with the Jewish people and sets itself apart from other nations, and the Christian community, which understands itself as the true eschatological people of God. In this view the Old Testament has been done away with by the New. However, the fact that it is done away with does not mean that it is good for nothing. On the contrary, the Old Testament retains permanent validity as an indication of a wrong possibility for men in general and even for the Christian: it is a book which presents the Christian with his *failure* as though in a mirror, a failure which is constantly overcome by the grace of the gospel. Thus in this pregnant theological sense the Old Testament is seen to be old, the evidence of the old man who needs to be won over and put to rights every day by means of the gospel. Such a conception of the Old Testament allows it to be the *Old* Testament in a strictly theological sense, as the New Testament is new, without having to abandon the Old Testament as an obsolete book; at the same time, however, it does raise the further question whether the whole of the Old Testament can really be seen as a document of the law and of man's failure. To an approach which makes more precise distinctions, identifying various strata and culminating points within the Old Testament, must not such an overall understanding appear to be a vague generalization? The New Testament itself, after all, continues to presuppose the continuing validity of essential parts of the Old Testament, if not of all of it, and cannot be understood at all except on the basis of the Old Testament. This is the reason why Old Testament texts were used to interpret the gospel even after the birth, death and resurrection of Christ: the proclamation of the gospel in the teaching and preaching of the Christian church used them as a basis.

For all its provisional character, this sketchy survey of the various possibilities of understanding the Old Testament already indicates that one approach does not always rule another completely out of court. Some concerns may be expressed too one-sidedly, but they are nevertheless justified, and questions emerge which prove insoluble partly because of the limited possibilities at man's disposal. While it would indeed be wrong to want to reconcile the irreconcilable (for example, a Marcionite repudiation and a Calvinistic over-estimation of the Old Testament are mutually exclusive), possible ways of understanding the Old Testament which seem to be ruled out because of their one-sidedness can nevertheless conceal true insights which are not to be ignored. The long and wide-ranging discussion over the right way to understand the Old Testament and its place in the canon is not – or not only – a consequence of theological disputatiousness. Rather, it is a reflection of the competing and conflicting positions and counter-positions, not only religious but often manifestly secular, within that varied thousand-year-old collection of Israelite and Jewish writings which is called the Old Testament. Often the only thing that they seem to have in common is the canonicity which Jews and Christians have assigned to them all. This common feature can easily mislead the reader – as was the case even more in the past than it is now – into looking for a single miraculous hermeneutical key with which to open up the multiplicity of the tradition in a consistent and reliable way. Some have even been confident that they have found a reliable way, a key that fits, until someone else has come along with a new key, shifting the centre around which everything in the Old Testament is supposed to turn, and attempting to open it up in a different way. Past one-sidedness should be a warning here. It is also worth remembering that from the beginning the New Testament – and that means the earliest Christian churches – was aware that the Old Testament could be read at many levels: attempts at a one-sided, one-level approach only came at a later period. This is the situation which we must now investigate.

II

THE OLD TESTAMENT AS A LEGACY

1. *The canon of the fathers*

It is often said that the Christian church accepted, or took over, the Old Testament. To talk in such terms, however, is not really correct or appropriate, for the simple reason that in the time of Jesus and even later in the first century AD the Hebrew Old Testament had not been finally completed. By and large, the contents of the Jewish, Hebrew canon were only established round about AD 100. The Greek translation of the Old Testament – the so-called Septuagint – remained an incomplete and variable entity for even longer, being distinguished from the Hebrew not only by the different arrangement of its individual parts (historical books, poetic and didactic books, prophetic writings), but also by the fact that it contained apocrypha. This Greek canon with a variable form, incomplete and open to begin with, became the holy scripture of the Christian church. At this point its completion and demarcation was no longer a matter for the Jews; Judaism rejected the Greek translation of the Septuagint for which it had been responsible and turned to the *veritas Hebraica*, the Hebrew truth, or to new literal translations. Thus it was a task for the Christian church to define the extent of the Greek canon of the Old Testament; however, even today there is still no agreed solution.

Jerome (*c.* AD 400), who made the Latin translation of the Old Testament known as the Vulgate, failed in his attempt to make the Jewish canon of Hebrew books the sole norm for the church. At a later date Luther classed the books which had found a place in the Vulgate but not in the Hebrew canon as apocrypha. He defines them as 'books which do not have the same rank as holy scripture but which are useful and good to read'. The Lutheran churches have never made a definitive decision on this question. Among the Reformed churches, article 6 of the Belgic Confession (1559) makes the distinction between canonical and apocryphal books more precise: the church may read the apocryphal books and learn from them in so far as they correspond with the books which are in the canon. Thus they are not a guide-line and a basic norm (*norma normans*). In the official Dutch translation (*Statenvertaling*) they find a place as an appendix to the New Testament, preceded by a warning which expressly declares that they are not part of holy, divine scripture. Consequently later editions omit them altogether. Thus the Reformed church has recognized only the Jewish, Hebrew canon as canonical. The Roman Catholic church only arrived at a definitive demarcation of the canon at the Council of Trent in 1546, making the (apocryphal) books of Wisdom, Jesus Sirach, Tobit, Judith, I and II Maccabees deuterocanonical and adding them to the valid canon. The Eastern church left open the question of the validity etc. of the apocryphal books for an even longer period. The books of Wisdom, Jesus Sirach, Tobit and Judith were recognized as canonical at a synod in Jerusalem in the year 1672.

This brief historical survey is itself enough to show that we cannot really talk of the Old Testament being accepted or taken over by the church. The church itself has had a hand in defining the canon; to leave the canon open or to fail to come to a decision was *ipso facto* to be involved. Instead of speaking of the church taking over the Old Testament, we would do better to think of the Old Testament as a *legacy*. Then it can be made clear that while the writings of the Old Testament are not a literary product of Christianity (they are pre-Christian), they are not an arbitrary collection of the literature of an alien religion which early Christianity took over from outside, for whatever reason, in the course of its formation. These writings were understood as a legacy which had come down from the Israelite and Jewish ancestors whose legitimate successors the early Christians understood themselves to be. Indeed, they themselves were born Jews and in their own ways followed the religion which was made known and proclaimed in the ancestral writings.

In this respect the Christians were no different from other groups or sects which emerged from the bosom of Judaism. Members of the Qumran community, that Jewish sect whose writings were discovered in the neighbourhood of the Dead Sea in the years after the Second

World War, looked upon themselves in the same way; they believed that they were the legitimate heirs to the ancestral writings of Judaism, while putting their own particular works alongside this legacy or even attaching more importance to them.

Thus the hermeneutical problem is not simply a matter of asking whether the early church was justified or even well advised in taking over the Old Testament; the Old Testament had been its holy scripture right from the very beginning. The question, rather, is whether it was possible and necessary to continue to hang on to the legacy of the Old Testament as it had been handed down. Might it not have been better to leave it to those who laid exclusive claim to it, namely the Jews? True, this question did not arise immediately, but it was implicit in the very fact that the church had inherited the Old Testament.

Polemic can illuminate an opponent's weak spots. So it is no surprise that the question whether Christians could rightly appeal to the scripture they had inherited came first from Judaism. The Greek translation of the Septuagint had been the work of Jewish scribes. Since this translation had now become the holy book of Christianity, a dispute was inevitable. It was apparently no more than a dispute over the correct interpretation of individual passages. The best known is the discussion of the understanding of Isa. 7.14. The Greek translation used by the Christians reads the word *parthenos* here, meaning virgin, whereas the Hebrew text means 'young woman'. Now as Isa. 7.14 was interpreted from the Christian side as a prediction of Christ, the Christian church thought that it had here scriptural proof for the virgin birth, the birth of Christ from the Virgin Mary. This was disputed by the Jews, who appealed to a better text and a better interpretation. Of course the Jews could hardly challenge the point that the translation on which the Christians based their case had been made by the Jews themselves. Ultimately, controversies of this kind led the Jews to abandon the Septuagint and to condemn it as being at variance with the true Hebrew. In the end, Pharisaic and rabbinic orthodoxy recognized only the Hebrew canon, containing the writings of the earlier, classical period, as being the truth. The Hebrew canon is itself a piece of polemic against all Hellenistic and apocalyptic innovations, and at the same time a polemic against the 'sect' of the church with its proclamation of Christ. The dispute might have seemed to have been about individual questions of interpretation, but whether those involved were aware of the fact or not, what was at stake in the last resort was the validity of the Old Testament for Christians and their right to be allowed to appeal to it at all.

Christians, who were Jews believing in Christ and as such felt that they were the true Israel, initially had no doubts about the legitimacy of their appeal to the scriptures which they had inherited. It is also very probable that, quite apart from all the other factors and from the problem of interpretation which at this stage had yet to emerge fully, the love of the status quo which is to be found in all religious matters also played its part here. There was a reluctance to give up the religious heritage of the past unless it was absolutely necessary.

2. *The attitude of Jesus*

This is also the case with Jesus. Sufficient sayings of Jesus of indubitable authenticity have come down to us to show that Jesus too, like the scribes, recognized the authority of the Old Testament *law*. The man who asks him about the supreme commandment is referred to the Old Testament and its demands: 'The most important commandment is: "Hear, O Israel: the Lord our God, the Lord is one; and you shall love the Lord your God with all your heart, and with all your soul, and with all your mind, and with all your strength." The second is this, "You shall love your neighbour as yourself"' (Mark 12.29–31). This answer given by Jesus quotes Deut. 6.4f.; Lev. 19.18. When he is asked, 'What must I do to inherit eternal life?', he replies, 'You know the commandments', and then quotes the Decalogue: 'Do not kill, Do not commit adultery, Do not steal, Do not bear false witness, Do not defraud, Honour your father and mother' (Mark 10.17–19).

As well as legal prescriptions, Jesus cites other passages, as biblical authority. For the resurrection of the dead he refers to Ex. 3.2ff.: 'Have you not read ... how God said to him (Moses), "I am the God of Abraham, and the God of Isaac, and the God of Jacob?"' (Mark 12.26f.). In defence of the laxity with which he and his disciples regard the sabbath he refers to I Sam. 21.7, which tells how in an emergency David consumed the temple 'shewbread', which normally only priests were allowed to eat. We shall have to discuss at a later stage the fact that these passages do not serve the purpose for which they are quoted and are interpreted in a way which goes against their original meaning. The primary point of interest here is that Jesus recognizes the authority of the passages which occur to him and stands by it. In this respect he is no different from the scribes who were his contemporaries. That he can quote legal statements and passages from historical books or prophetic writings by way of proof shows only that for him, as for contemporary Judaism, the different parts of the scriptures on the whole represented an undifferentiated unity and therefore were no longer fully comprehensible in their original sense. The reference to a passage from I Samuel cited above in order to justify a particular mode of conduct suggests that for Jesus, as for Judaism, scripture was primarily understood as law and that passages other than the strictly legal ones were understood as law (see also ch. IV below).

By and large it was typical that the Judaism of Jesus' time should understand the scripture as law and the prophets as interpreters of the law. This indicates that it was not only Christianity which found its legacy a problem and incomprehensible without special interpretation: the same was already true for Judaism. During the period of Roman rule, as in earlier days under other foreign powers, when Israel had become a cultic community, the older laws had lost their original applications to state, people and tribe and no longer expressed specific political and social requirements. Consequently they must have seemed to be an alien heritage, and keeping them faithfully despite this alien character could only have the aim of maintaining the people as a superior, elect and alien group. Moreover, in so far as history was understood as something more than a collection of examples of right and wrong conduct under the law, it must have seemed to be something over and done with. Its written expression also needed interpretation and was inaccessible without it. This hermeneutical problem which had already emerged in Judaism was so important that those who were responsible for dealing with it – in name if not in fact – became important also. Even in the time before the rise of Christianity the priests and those responsible for temple worship had retreated into insignificance in comparison with the scribes and their work. The figure of Jesus must also be viewed in the light of the problem of hermeneutics. His concern with inherited tradition is also a matter of interpretation – even if by modern standards this may be a matter of reading in something that is not there. The difference between Jesus and the scribes who were his contemporaries lies elsewhere. For them it was the formal authority of scripture that was binding as the will of God, in other words, *the fact that* the law commands and forbids, even though God's will may seem utterly incomprehensible to men. Thus a rabbinic saying runs: 'Death does not make unclean, nor water clean. But the Holy One has said, I have established a Law, have fixed a decree; you are not to transgress my decree, which is written; this is the distinguishing mark of my law' (quoted from R. Bultmann, *Jesus and the Word*, IIA, 55).

Jewish hermeneutics were less concerned with understanding than with obedience, even without insight, because Judaism saw the divine as being incomprehensible. For Jesus, however, the authority of scripture – which he also recognized – was not only grounded in but also derived from the will of God. He therefore differed from the scribes who were his contemporaries in regarding its substance as more than an incidental matter. The important thing was to seek the true content or the true understanding of the divine will. For Jewish interpreters, the law was of equal force in all its different and even contradictory parts, and interpretation was concerned not least with the harmonization of contradictions. Jesus, on the other hand, can make a clear distinction between one commandment and another, between what is important and what is unimportant, and also between the basic essentials and elements which have been added later. The will of God is not unrelated to scripture, but scripture is less important than the will of God.

A well-known instance of this kind of interpretation is Jesus' understanding of the divorce procedure provided for in the law. The law allows divorce (Deut. 24.1), but we also read (Gen. 1.27): 'God made them male and female. For this reason a man shall leave his father and mother and be joined to his wife, and the two shall become one flesh.' His conclusion from a comparison of the two passages is: 'What therefore God has joined together, let not man put asunder.' In other words, God's true will is concerned with the indissolubility of marriage; divorce is simply an emergency measure 'because of the hardness of man's heart', and does not correspond to the real will of God (Mark 10. 2–9).

Thus despite the reference to scripture, its formal authority is surrendered in favour of the will of God which can be ascertained from scripture. Here we have the beginnings of *a distinction between the letter and the spirit*.

It is evident that even with Jesus we have the possibility of a fundamental conflict with the Old Testament heritage. Whereas for Jewish scribes interpretation of the content of the law is less important than the formal authority of what is written, in practice the opposite is now the case. If the important thing is to perceive and to do the will of God, and if God's will is concerned for the whole man, his obedience and his surrender, then it is possible not only to discard individual elements of the written law as having been introduced because of the hardness of man's heart but also to reject them altogether, as running contrary to the will of God. Jesus' remark that nothing going into a man from outside can defile him but the things which come out of a man are what defile him (Mark 7.14ff.) completely undermines the laws of purity and everything connected with them in Jewish ritual. Jesus may recognize the authority of the Old Testament, but this does not prevent him from making positive use of only a selection of it. Here we already have the beginnings of the Christian use of only a particular selection from the Old Testament.

Selection also means rejection, and indeed an antithesis between the old and the new. This is expressed above all in the so-called 'antitheses' of the Sermon on the Mount (Matt. 5.21ff.). The mere fact that Matthew has Jesus proclaiming these words from a mountain signifies an antithesis to the law of Moses, which was promulgated from Mount Sinai. The message now runs: 'You have heard that it was said to the men of old ... But I say to you ...' What Jesus now has to say to 'the men of today' is opposed to what was said to 'the men of old', their forbears, who were under the old law. It derestricts what was enjoined upon 'the men of old', intensifies it and makes it more radical. Whereas the law of Moses, which was given to the men of old, prohibits murder and homicide, adultery and perjury, Jesus proclaims to the men of his time that God's will even rules out anger, malicious taunts, evil covetousness and lies. God's will cannot be encompassed by legalistic formulae which leave men room for evil; it requires man's complete self-surrender. Jesus' words 'But I say to you ...' already indicate the opposition between the old and the new. In the light of the new element which dawns with Jesus, the legacy of tradition acquires the character of being old in the sense of past, transitory, provisional and even obsolete.

Of course, not everything that was said to the men of old is old in this sense. The way in which Jesus places strong emphasis on God's work of creation and his rule can be shown to be in the Israelite and Jewish tradition even without explicit quotations from the traditional writings. God's fatherly care for flowers, animals and even more for men (Matt. 6.25–34) can be read out of the thought-world of the Old Testament. The new element in such an interpretation is, however, that God's present care and gracious presence is proclaimed to a generation to whom – as in the Judaism of the time – God seemed inaccessibly remote, removed from history into some other-worldly heaven. Thus this new interpretation assigns new validity and truth to the ancient material.

However, Jesus is not first and foremost an interpreter of scripture, like the Pharisees or the Teacher of the Qumran sect. By his words 'But I say to you ...' he makes the claim that he can discern, indeed has discerned, God's will directly, and not just from the law. This divine will is indeed a matter of claims and demands which make the written law even more radical, but in addition it is a promise which holds out the prospect of forgiveness and new creation and deliverance in the kingdom of God which is soon to come. Consequently the Old Testament, understood as law, retreats into the background in favour of the gospel, the good news of the imminent salvation of God. But as in the stress on God's present activity as Creator and Lord, so too new force can be given to the promise, assurance and affirmation of the saving nearness of God and his salvation which is certainly also known to the Old Testament, as in the promises to Abraham (Gen. 12.1ff.) or the revelation of the divine name: 'I will be for each one of you what I shall be' (Ex. 3.14). To the Judaism of Jesus' time, dominated by an understanding of scripture as the law and the prevailing feeling that the history of God's saving dealings with his people had long since come to an end and lay in the distant past, remarks like this now sounded quite new; indeed they were made without any express quotation of the scriptures. Their hearers were now free from the law which had 'come after' (Rom. 5.20; Gal. 3.19). Jesus' preaching also proclaimed that the New Testament gave even more force to the forgotten truths contained in the Old.

Above all, we should note that here the legacy of the Old Testament is neither endorsed nor rejected in a one-sided way; it is completely reinterpreted and understood afresh. There is no one hermeneutical key, and the lack of such a key is in no way a deficiency; there can be no single key because the heritage is such a varied one. At the same time, however, we can also understand why at this stage there was no hermeneutical reflection on the need for different approaches to the traditional material and the intrinsic problems which it presented.

3. *The Old Testament in the earliest churches*

To begin with, the situation in the earliest churches was no different. For these churches, too, the Old Testament was at first an obvious heritage. Jewish Christianity hung on to the ancestral law as it hung on to the temple and its worship, the temple tax and the rulings of the synagogue (cf. Acts 6.46; Matt. 5.23f.; 17.24–27; Mark 13.9; Matt. 10.17). Jewish Christians understood themselves as the true Israel, and in historical terms an outsider might well describe them as an eschatological sect within Judaism, distinct and then formally separated from the mainstream of Judaism by their awareness of being eschatological Israel and their belief in the saving significance of the crucified and risen Jesus Christ.

The honorific titles which the earliest church bestowed upon Jesus are without doubt of Jewish origin: Messiah, Christ, Son of man, Son of God, Servant of God. However much they may have undergone inward change by their application to the crucified and risen Jesus – not only 'Jesus is the Messiah', etc., but also 'the true Messiah is the crucified and risen Jesus' – they give the new element which has appeared in Jesus Christ a setting in the old. The ancestral heritage provides the language which makes it possible to express and proclaim the new revelation.

In so far as the Jewish Christians in the early church in Palestine did not break with Judaism, their fidelity to their religious and ethnic origins meant not only that they held fast to the law, the Old Testament, as an ancestral heritage, but also that non-Jews who wanted to enter the Jewish-Christian church had to submit to the law and undergo circumcision as a token of their seriousness. To become a Christian it was necessary to be prepared to become a Jew. If the Old Testament was the law for Gentiles who had become Christians, it was even more so for those who were Jews by birth. The philosopher Hegel was wrong in teaching that reality is always rational. For this attitude was by no means rational, seeing that Jesus had already shown a variety of different attitudes towards his ancestral heritage. His remarks directed against legalism and the Pharisaic notion of reward, and even against the ritual of worship, may have been remembered and handed down, but at the same time there was a reversion to legalistic thinking. A saying was ascribed to Jesus that he had not come to do away with the law but to fulfil it, and that neither an iota nor a dot would pass away from the law until the end of days (Matt. 5.17f.). There are already hints in the earliest church and in the New Testament of Christianity as a new and not always better legalism on the basis of an unqualified under-standing of the Old Testament as a valid law. Of course this expression and direction of Christian belief was not to be found in the period immediately following. After the fall of Jerusalem in AD 70 it lost its significance and was embodied only in the sect of the Ebionites. At the same time, it is worth noting that even this sectarian, legalistic form of Christianity did not retain the Old Testa-ment in an unaltered form, but followed a 'purified' Pentateuch without sacrificial worship or priests, also rejecting the prophets who were born only of women (Diestel, Ic, 27f.).

Far more important for the developing church and for its acceptance and understanding of its ancestral heritage was the Hellenistic move-ment, which goes back to those groups which originated in the diaspora. Their greater freedom towards the law was in no way diminished by their transition to Christianity. Caught up in the toils of Judaism and situated in the sphere of its ancestral heritage, the Jewish-Christian church in Jerusalem was unable to carry on a mission among the Gentiles. This grew out of Hellenistic Christianity, and among the Gentile-Christian churches which began to develop it was no longer essential to recognize the law and to adopt circumcision (cf. Acts 8.4ff.; 11.19ff.; 15; Gal. 2.1–10). The so-called Apostolic Council (Gal. 2.1–10; Acts 15) expressly recognized a Gentile Chris-tianity which did not observe the law and thus confirmed a situation which was already existing *de facto*. The question which the Council discussed was only superficially concerned with church law. The basic theological question was whether Christianity could be or could remain Jewish by nature, whether the traditional law and the ancestral heritage could continue to remain valid without change, indeed whether the salvation which had appeared and had been offered in Christ was adequate in itself without being bound up with the condition of fulfilling the law. Here it made no difference whether the whole of the law was to be a necessary precondition or only part of it (e.g. circumcision).

It was Paul who had an acute theological perception of this problem and who brought about a solution. In his view, while the law was promulgated by God in order to be fulfilled, men had perversely made it the means of achieving their own righteousness through their own works. They had thus made their own existence godless, instead of living by God's grace, which alone could bestow life (Gal. 2.15–21; 3.21–25; Rom. 3.19–28; 7 etc.). Paul's theology and indeed the theological polemic and disputes in which he was involved centre on this cardinal question: in the end, does man create his own salvation, does he redeem himself and make himself righteous, or does he only live rightly ('righteously') when he lives by the grace of God? This question, which has been of central importance right down history and to the present day, was the subject of the first theological dispute in the early church. It was a controversy over the *law* and over the *Old Testament understood as law.*

Whereas for Paul the dispute was decided theologically in favour of grace alone (*sola gratia*), the 'apostolic decree' (Acts 15.20, 28f.; 21.25), which prohibits the Gentile Christians from eating meat offered to idols, meat from animals which have not been killed according to the precepts of Jewish ritual law, food which has been prepared with blood in it and 'unchastity', i.e. marriage within the degrees of affinity which according to Lev. 17.8, 10ff., 13; 18.6ff. are also binding upon Gentiles, shows that the law was not disregarded to such a degree everywhere. Thus this decree allows Gentile Christians to be free from the law only to a degree which is in conformity with the law of Moses. Therefore the decree, which represents a compromise solution and was presumably intended to make it possible for Jewish Christians and Gentile Christians to live together and to share the same table, lies midway between a strict Jewish Christianity which maintains the ground of the traditional law and for which Christian converts must first become Jews, and Pauline Christianity which is free of the law.

4. *The break with the Jewish past*

Despite all this, neither freedom from the Jewish law nor Paul's fundamental theological polemic against the law amount to a repudiation of the legacy of the Old Testament. Of course this must have been a hermeneutical problem in the actual carrying out of the Christian mission among the Gentiles and even more clearly in theological reflection on the law or on the Old Testament, understood in traditional Jewish terms as the law. The dispute over the validity of the law for Gentile Christians implied the question of the validity of the law for Christians generally, and this in turn inevitably developed into the problem of the validity of the Old Testament within the sphere of the Christian church. Moreover, freedom from the law, either in its entirety or in its ritual elements, inevitably opened men's eyes to the fact that the legacy handed down by the fathers which had now also become the holy scripture of Gentile Christianity contained not only laws, but also histories and narratives, instructions and prayers, prophecies and promises. How far were these still valid? How far were they valid for the new Christian community? Differences with Judaism which had far-reaching practical consequences were given characteristic expression first in the teaching of Jesus, then above all in the theology and preaching of Paul, and finally in Gentile Christianity which after the destruction of Jerusalem in AD 70 soon began to become much more important than Jewish Christianity. These differences also made it clear how far removed Jewish Christianity was from its religious origins. A gulf had opened up between fathers and sons, between the legacy and those who administered it and indeed claimed it exclusively for themselves. The question now was not only how justified those who no longer observed the demands of ancestral law were in laying claim to this ancient heritage, but even more whether the Old Testament could still have any real meaning at all, even if it was an ancestral heritage and the Bible of Jesus. After all, with the cross and resurrection of Jesus Christ the last days had dawned and the new community was grounded on this fact alone (I Cor. 3.11); 'The old has passed away, behold the new has come' (II Cor. 5.17).

As is well known, the Christian church understood itself to be God's true Israel (Gal. 6.16) as opposed to the empirical people which made up Israel after the flesh (I Cor. 10.18). They saw themselves as the true sons of Abraham (Rom. 4.12–15; 9.6–8; Gal. 4.22–28). Now if the church made up of Jews and Gentiles believing in Christ is, according to its own understanding of itself, the true, eschatological Israel, then the ancestral heritage is in truth an integral part of Christianity and all the promises and assurances, the warnings and admonitions, apply to the community of the last days. By means of this hermeneutical approach the first Christians affirmed and accepted their heritage, but failed to resolve the hermeneutical problem. And what applies to the early church applies equally to modern theological justifications for the retention of the Old Testament by Christians. It is not enough simply to refer to the heritage as such and to claim the title of the new, true Israel. For the new Israel, or the true Israel, *was not and is not the historical continuation* of the old Israel, any more than it was and is a sect within the complex of Israelite and Jewish religion, even if that is what to all outward appearances it may have seemed to be. No historical development leads from Israel to Judaism and from there directly to Christianity, however many historical links there may seem to be between Israel and Judaism on the one hand and Christianity on the other (indeed there are so many that it is impossible to understand Christianity properly without these historical connections). However, at this point we are concerned not so much with historical understanding as with an outline and definition of the nature of Christianity. There is more to confessing that Jesus, who died and rose again, is the anointed Christ and Lord, than saying that the Messiah whom the Jews await has already come; important as the dating of the coming of the Messiah may be, the difference lies deeper than that. To believe in Jesus Christ who died and rose again is also to believe in the eschatological (i.e. the ultimate and final) action of God which puts an end to all that has gone before and relegates it to the past (II Cor. 5.17), which leads men from death to life (Rom. 5.12–21; 6.3–11; Gal. 2.20; I Cor. 15.21f.; II Cor. 4.10; 13.4; Col. 3.3f.) and constitutes the new Israel as a qualitatively new, eschatological community which is already participating through faith in ultimate salvation. Now if God's eschatological action in Jesus Christ distinguishes the old Israel from the new and sets it apart, indeed 'calls it forth' from the old Israel and the rest of the world, the question inevitably arises whether this new Israel has anything more in common with the old than a name. How can the *Old* Testament, addressed to the old, historical Israel, which presupposes a tribal alliance, a state and ultimately an ethnic community centred upon distinctive worship and the observance of the law, have any further significance for the new Israel which God has 'called forth' in the last days in Christ? Christian faith may have inherited a belief in the scriptures, but there is more to it than that: it does not arise from the scriptures, even from the scriptures interpreted in a new Christian way, but rather is belief in Christ who proclaims himself in the testimony of Christian preaching.

Thus the problem of the law proves to be only part of the question. For obvious historical reasons it was the first to arise, but freedom from the law did not resolve the real problem. Then as now it was more than a *hermeneutical* problem, namely how the traditional heritage can be made comprehensible, i.e. be interpreted and understood, after a lapse of time, given that it is historically conditioned. This question arises in connection with all literature and every expression of human life. Rather, the problem is also and above all a strictly *theological* one, which arises here and not in connection with the writings of the New Testament: how can a heritage which is old in a qualitative sense still apply to the Christian church, an eschatological community which is the new Israel in the strict sense? This question was not put with sufficient urgency and precision in the primitive community nor, for instance, in Paul's markedly reflective theology. But it was there nevertheless, as is clear from the way in which the traditional heritage – and not just the law – was treated.

5. *Promise, prophecy and type*

The point made above can already be illustrated from the collection of sayings of Jesus which underlie the synoptic gospels and was incorporated into them, and which is usually designated Q (sayings source, cf. W. G. Kümmel, *Introduction to the New Testament*, IIA, 63ff.). Here it becomes clear that the Lord is the first and unconditional authority. He is more than Jonah and more than Solomon (Matt. 12.41; Luke 11.31f.); men's salvation depends on whether they confess him (Matt. 17.21, 24–27; 10.32f.). Jesus himself is the real authority and his appearance is the saving event; the scriptures, 'the law and the prophets were until John' (cf. Luke 16.16). At this point we already come up against the other approach which treats the traditional heritage of scripture not primarily as law but as *prediction* and *prophecy* and *promise*. It is an approach – and a hermeneutical key – which has continued to be important down to the present day. The earliest Christian confession of faith (kerygma) which is handed down by Paul, although it dates from before him, claims to be scriptural: 'that Christ died for our sins according to the scriptures, that he was buried, that he was raised on the third day in accordance with the scriptures, and that he appeared to Cephas, then to the twelve' (I Cor. 15.1–5). It is more important to note that 'the scriptures' in general are cited as a prediction and a proof that what happened to the Christ is in accordance with the scriptures than to ask which particular scriptures are meant here – the allusion seems to be to Isa. 53.4–6; Hos. 6.2. The central event of the crucifixion and resurrection was at an early stage narrated, reshaped and demonstrated to be in accordance with the scriptures with the aid of Psalm 22 (mockery, shaking of the head, division of the garments, cry of 'My God').

Mark, who was writing for Gentile Christians, did not regard the Old Testament heritage simply as law. In this 'book of secret epiphanies' (Martin Dibelius, *From Tradition to Gospel*, IIA, 230), Jesus is the eschatological Son of man, Son of David and Son of God who proclaims a new teaching and drives out demons with divine authority (Mark 1.27). In controversies with Pharisees and scribes Jesus condemns their legalistic and ceremonial understanding of the law (Mark 2.6–9, 23–28; 3.1–6; 7.1–13; 10.1–12). Although this polemic in fact does away not only with Jewish interpretation but also with the law itself, the one to whom the remarks in these controversies are ascribed has been foretold by the scriptures (Mark 1.2f.; 7.6f.; 12.10f., 36f.; 14.27). The passion narrative in particular is shaped 'in accordance with the scriptures' (15.24, 34, 36). As a whole, the gospel of Mark gives the impression of being dependent on a Gentile Christian tradition of dealing with the Old Testament which has yet to attain complete theological clarity. The law, and especially the ceremonial law, is a thing of the past, but the scriptural tradition still retains its force as a prediction which found fulfilment in Christ. But do the passages cited (Mal. 3.1, cf. Mark 1.2; Isa. 29.13, cf. Mark 7.6f.; Ps. 118. 22f., cf. Mark 12.10f.; Ps. 110.1, cf. Mark 12.36f.; Zech. 13.7, cf. Mark 14.27) really mean what they are supposed to predict and prove? We shall have to return to this question later.

The apostle *Paul* also testifies that the scriptures promise and predict the Christ event. They do so not so much by predicting individual events and experiences as by foreseeing the salvation which God has provided for the Gentiles in Christ (Gal. 3.6). True, Paul also bases belief in Christ on an encounter with the living Jesus Christ, and he did not 'learn' the gospel (Gal. 1.12), but for him his ancestral heritage is and remains holy scripture in the strict sense. Not only is the law contained in the scriptures given by God, 'holy, right and good' (Rom. 7.12); the whole scripture is divine. Indeed, according to Paul its holiness, its divine character and its truth are revealed through faith in Christ and become all the clearer in the light of this faith. Without Christ the real truth of scripture is concealed, and for the Jews it is as though it were covered with a veil (II Cor. 3.14). Apart from Christ the dominant factor is the 'letter' which kills, but now there is the spirit which brings life (II Cor. 3.6; cf. Rom. 2.29; 7.6). By the letter he means not only ossification in stereotyped formulae but also the fatal power displayed by the law apart from Christ. Proper exegesis is far more than an exegetical technique; it is the disclosure of divine truth in the light of Jesus Christ (II Cor. 3.7–18). The real truth of scripture is salvation in

Christ, righteousness through faith alone. Thus *before* any law, Abraham believed in God's promise, and this was reckoned to him as righteousness (Rom. 4.3; Gal. 3.6; both passages refer to Gen. 15.6). Here Paul cites scripture quite appropriately, and does not read the new confession of faith into the text in an artificial way. A new development from Judaism is, however, the hermeneutical principle which gives these passages a central place and sets them above the law, which was only promulgated 430 years afterwards (Gal. 3.17)!

Now if scripture remains in force, it also provides the *language* for proclaiming the gospel of Christ in its various aspects. This language is itself a prediction of Christ and of the last days. Paul's letters are steeped in quotations and allusions. All the predictions and promises contained in the Old Testament find their fulfilment in the Christ event (II Cor. 1.20); indeed, quite apart from prophecies and promises in the narrower sense, 'Whatever was written in former days was written for our instruction' (Rom. 15.4). Everything in scripture has only one aim and one end: the last days, which have dawned with Christ. Paul finds in Ps. 19.5, 'their voice has gone out to all the earth, and their words to the ends of the world', a prophecy of his own mission to the Gentiles (Rom. 10.18), and those who proclaim Christ's message may draw on the churches for their sustenance because according to Deut. 25.4 the ox who treads the corn is not to be muzzled. The exodus, the wandering of Israel in the wilderness, when Yahweh went with them in a cloud (Ex. 13.21f.), the manna (Ex. 16.4ff.) and the water from the rock (Num. 20.7–11) are prefigurements (types) of baptism and the eucharist (I Cor. 10.1–6). For Paul all the events which the Old Testament records from that time are 'typical' (I Cor. 10.11), types of what is happening in the last days. So here we do not have words or sayings which are interpreted as predictions or promises, but events, persons, institutions which become prefigurements of the future which has now dawned. Thus according to Paul the first Adam from whom disaster overtook mankind is the type of the future new Adam, who is to come and has now indeed appeared, namely Christ, from whom all salvation flows (Rom. 5.14).

We are not always told expressly that typological correspondences are intended. In I Cor. 5.7 Christ is described as the paschal lamb which is sacrificed for us, thus providing a kind of typological correspondence with the passover lamb and the crucifixion, just as in John 19.14 the hour of Jesus' death accords with the hour at which the passover lambs were usually slaughtered (cf. John 19.36; for the

New Testament cf. also Col. 2.17 and I Peter 3.21, where the term 'antitype' also appears: baptism is the antitype over against the type of Noah's ark; in John 3.14f., just as Moses lifted up a serpent, so the Son of man is lifted up; in John 6.31ff., Jesus is the true, eschatological bread as opposed to manna, which is the type; in Heb. 3.7–4.13 there is a typological correspondence between Israel's wandering in the desert and the existence of the Christian community).

Thus typology, with its combination of type and antitype, always begins from the antitype: the types are shown to be prefigurements and to have their real character as proofs only in the light of the antitype which has come into being and been realized. The new becomes the hermeneutical key to the old. At the same time, interpretation in terms of type and antitype also presupposes a distinction in time and a distinction between old and new, between the Old Testament and the New Testament, even if this is not as yet seen in terms of a distinction between two parts of the canon (II Cor. 3.6, 14). Here we have the beginnings of the possibility of retaining the old canon and of adding a new section.

Like understanding the Old Testament as prophecy, this typological method of interpretation has retained its significance from the time of Paul down to the present day.

If typology rests on the assumption of a particular kind of correspondence in which the antitype goes beyond the type, showing it to be a mere foreshadowing and itself putting the type in the shade, the understanding of the Old Testament as prediction and promise is based on a pattern of announcement and fulfilment. Old Testament passages are interpreted as prediction or promise in the light of their fulfilment in Christ. Whereas Paul was merely concerned to use this means of interpretation to show that the new salvation in Christ had already been announced in the Old Testament and was indeed its real theme, and for the pre-Pauline church the death and resurrection of Jesus Christ had happened according to the scriptures, the gospel of Matthew developed the proof from prophecy thoroughly and gave it full theological consideration. The holy scriptures prophesied the work of Jesus Christ and his fate even down to apparently unimportant details. 'All this took place to fulfil what the Lord had spoken by the prophets ...' (e.g. Matt. 1.22). But all the individual fulfilments and individual instances from scripture only show that the whole of Jesus' earthly life, his death, his resurrection and the salvation which he has brought, are a fulfilment of the prophecy and promise which have been given in the Old Testament. And despite the antitheses of the Sermon on the Mount, which contrast with and contradict what was said in the Old Testament, Jesus did not come to do away with the law, but to fulfil it completely and to require a fulfilment which would be manifest in a new life in surrender to God and in love for one's neighbour (Matt. 5.17ff.; 5.48; 7.12; 22.40).

In order to demonstrate the fulfilment of prophecies, Matthew does not just cite passages which were prophecies in their original sense (Isa. 7.14 in Matt. 1.23 as proof for the virgin birth; in the Hebrew text this passage does not of course speak of a virgin, though it does proclaim a symbolic and miraculous birth). More often passages are cited which were not originally meant to be prophecies or which had quite a different sense: according to Matt. 8.17, Isa. 53.4 is supposed to predict Jesus' miraculous healings; Jer. 31.15, 'Rachel weeping for her children' referred to the imprisonment of the exiles but is in fact connected by Matt. 2.17f. with the murder of the children in Bethlehem; in Matt. 21.5, Zech. 9.9 is meant to foretell the entry of Jesus into Jerusalem; the parallelism of Zech. 9.9, which describes the animal as an ass and a foal, but clearly refers to a single beast, is supposed to prophesy that Jesus entered Jerusalem on two animals; the invitation in Ps. 78.2 is interpreted in 13.35 as a prophecy of the discourse in parables; in 27.9f., Zech. 11.12 is supposed to prophesy the thirty pieces of silver which the traitor Judas received as a reward, but the passage originally had another reference and is wrongly assigned to the book of Jeremiah, where it does not in fact occur. These are only a few examples.

The early church in fact proclaimed the Christ event as a fulfilment of Old Testament expectations simply by bestowing on Jesus the honorific titles of Israelite and Jewish religion – Messiah, Christ, Son of man, Son of God, 'servant of God' – and by transferring to him the divine predicate 'Kyrios' (= 'Lord' in Christian manuscripts of the Septuagint, where Kyrios is a rendering of the divine name Yahweh). The reflective quotations which permeate the gospel of Matthew (perhaps better termed 'fulfilment quotations', cf. W. G. Kümmel, *Introduction*, IIA, 110) are an expression of what is now a systematic attempt to depict the Christ event as a whole in all its details as a fulfilment of Old Testament prophecy and of the scriptures in general. It is an attempt to appropriate the traditional heritage and come to terms with it, to allow its validity and indeed to give it new force, thus 'proving' that the Christ event is in accordance with scripture. In this context, that can only mean that it is in accordance with divine truth. There is dispute as to the controversy towards which this theological argumentation is directed – is it concerned with proving to Judaism that Christian faith is based on scripture or with understanding the traditional heritage in a truly Christian way (cf. W. G. Kümmel, op. cit., 113ff., where there is further literature)? But it is clear that the use of Old Testament texts sketched out here, which is not limited to the gospel of Matthew, no longer allows the texts to retain their original sense; they say what people want to hear and what they already know in advance. This obviously enormous theological attempt to come to terms with the heritage of the Old Testament is in danger of losing it completely, because it can no longer present the message which it has to give. We may allow that the new interpretation of the law is concerned to reduce the wealth of regulations to their essentials, to perceive the true will of God and thus to bring to light again the old truth of the law; we can also value the intention of typological exegesis to bring out the old in its relationship and its analogy to the new in the light of the Christ event, even in its character as proof and its significance which goes beyond the mere wording. Nevertheless, interpretation in terms of prophecy and the proof from scripture is often simply not interpretation, but a matter of reading in without heed to the original meaning or context. This conclusion is not altered by the mitigating circumstance that the wording of the texts quoted was not yet canonized as holy scripture, which was later the concern of rabbinical and indeed Christian doctrine, and that similar methods of interpretation were also used outside the sphere of the Christian church in Judaism and in the pagan world. Although the interpretation of the Old Testament in the gospel of Matthew stresses that Jesus did not come to do away with the law, it shows that in hermeneutical terms the emphasis had shifted away from the law towards promise and prediction. L. Diestel's remarks (Ic, 13) apply even to this gospel: 'Thus the deep difference between the Jewish use of scripture and the new Christian approach lay primarily in the fact that the focal point was no longer the law, but prophecy.'

This shift of emphasis can also be seen clearly in Luke's two books. The very first verse outlines their programme. They are to deal with a story which extends over history, a saving event which has taken place in a series of historical facts (*pragmata*). Pauline typology was already familiar with a distinction between old times and new, but this was in the qualitative sense of a polarization, a sharp contrast, between death and life (II Cor. 3.4–16). Luke is concerned with a temporal line, an earlier time and a later, the time of Jesus' ministry, the time of the missionary work of the church among the Gentiles. For the Gentile Christian mission the Old Testament law is no longer the acute problem that it was for Paul, for the gospel of Matthew and wherever else controversies with Judaism over faith and practice were inevitable. For Luke it belongs to a past age not only as a matter of fact, but also theologically, in terms of salvation history. This age lies before the 'mid-point of time' (cf. Hans Conzelmann, *The Theology of St Luke*, IIA), which Luke understands Jesus' earthly activity to be. The theological problem of the law as recognized by Paul, which is not connected with time, even though on occasions in history it is intensified, now becomes incomprehensible. In the new church order which has grown up after the fall of Jerusalem and the end of the temple and of sacrificial worship, the law has lost its significance, even if at an earlier stage it may have had its good sense. The problem of the law has, as it were, settled itself. For the Jews, of course, that means judgment and punishment, because they have failed to observe the law which was given to them and have killed the prophets and even Jesus (as Stephen puts it in his speech, Acts 7.35ff.). So if the question of the law is settled as far as Luke is concerned, the Old Testament is seen all the more as prophecy. Just as the 'mid-point of time', Jesus' ministry, is followed by the period of the missionary community to which it gives rise, so it is preceded by the period of Israel, whose testimonies point forward to Christ and his church. Here Luke, unlike the gospel of Matthew, is concerned less with detail than with the great decisive saving event.

Unlike the Jews, who killed their prophets and Jesus, the righteous Israelites such as the pious parents of John, Zechariah and Elisabeth (Luke 1.6), or Simeon, had longingly looked for salvation in Christ (cf. Luke 1.70–75; cf. 24.21; Acts 1.6). The fulfilment far exceeded their expectation, which to begin with was still limited and thought of in terms of the nation: Christ brings salvation to all people (Acts 2.30–32). It is the Jews' own fault if they do not share in the fulfilment; according to Isaiah's prophecy (Isa. 6.9f.) their heart is hardened, so now God's salvation is sent to the Gentiles, as we are told at the end of Acts (28.27f.). The hardness of heart among the Jews is in fulfilment of scripture, just as scripture generally is fulfilled in the activity and fate of Jesus Christ and the church and its preaching which develop out of it. The fulfilment of scripture in the dawn of salvation and the proclamation of the gospel is preached as early as in the sermon with which Jesus makes his first appearance (Luke

4.16–21). At the same time the reaction of the Jews to this sermon shows that they have been rejected in their failure to recognize Jesus and their lack of belief in God. This rejection, too, is in accordance with the scriptures. Just as God has predetermined this course of history (Luke 22.22; 24.26, 44), so too he has given the prophets a prior glimpse of what was to happen in the future (Luke 24.25–27, 32, 44–48; Acts 1.16; 2.31; 3.18; 7.52; 13.24). The truth of the Christian message derives from scripture and can be proved by scripture (Acts 17.11; 18.28). It is the risen Jesus himself who 'opens up' the scripture to the disciples (Luke 24.32).

It is indeed the case that the work of Christ and his disciples is done in the power of the spirit which was promised for the time of salvation (Luke 4.18, 21; 24.49; Acts 2, esp. vv. 14–21), and is more than just interpretation of scripture, but at the same time scripture acquires a heightened significance as testimony to God's plan of salvation and his direction of history. Christian preaching as Luke understands it cannot dispense with scripture as prophecy or with a prophetic interpretation of scripture which also serves as a confirmation of Jesus' work. The more the Christ event moves into the past and the eager expectation of the earliest community begins to fade, the more the span of time which 'has elapsed becomes a hermeneutical problem. The traditional Old Testament heritage, which is obsolete as law, has become a prelude, the significance of which lies in its character as a forecast. It contains a forecast and thus also testimony to the divine predetermination of individual events (*pragmata*, things, Luke 1.1), which in the meanwhile have also become past events, though they are continued in acts of the apostles. The testimony of scripture becomes the forecast of divinely directed events the significance of which cannot be recognized without the scriptures. This hermeneutical approach was also taken up often at a later date and developed into the conception of salvation history, in which the Old Testament finds a place as a book of prehistory: over considerable areas it can even be regarded as a dogma of normative church theology.

The gospel of John shows that there can be quite a different reaction to the problems which arise with the passing of time – it is just as far from the history of Jesus as Luke is. It does not present a history of early Christianity but proclaims the present significance of Christ to its own day, 'that you may believe that Jesus is the Christ, and that believing you may have life in his name' (John 20.31). The Christ of Johannine faith is from the beginning so opposed to the Jews that it has been assumed that the gospel's real intention is to present polemic against Judaism and to provide a defence against Jewish attacks on Christianity. Be this as it may, it is at all events clear how opposition to the Jews, who in effect personify the anti-Christian, godless world, also implies detachment from the Jewish law.

It is still said that Jesus breaks the law by healing on the sabbath (John 5.9; 9.14), but that leads to a discussion on the person and authority of Jesus rather than on the law (John 9.14ff.) or to the resolve to kill Jesus (John 5.9, 16). It is not said whether Jesus by acting in this way wanted to abrogate the law or to fulfil it rather along the lines of Matt. 5.17. According to John 7.19 the Jews themselves do not keep the law, but the gospel does not draw strict theological consequences from this fact for the significance of the law, as happens in the case of Paul. In fact, however, the exclusiveness of the salvation offered in Christ (John 14.6: 'I am the way, and the truth, and the life; no one comes to the Father but by me') makes any other order of salvation retrograde, and there can only be a 'new commandment' (John 13.34), the commandment to love.

Nevertheless, even in the gospel of John, scripture is not done away with as such, despite the rejection of the law. As in the earlier tradition, the Old Testament prophesies in particular the suffering and the death of Christ (John 12. 13–15; 19.24, 28f., 36f.), and this is often stated explicitly ('that the scripture might be fulfilled'). Because the scripture prophesies the Christ event, it can be said to contain eternal life; in that case people must perceive its true meaning, its testimony to Christ, and accept it in faith (John 5.39, 46f.). Just as in Luke it is the risen Lord who first discloses the true sense of scripture (Luke 24.25ff., 32, 45–47), so here the truth which hitherto had been obscured is only brought to light after Easter (John 2.22; 12.16). The faithful members of the old Israel had seen the pre-existent Jesus: Abraham looked on him with joy and Isaiah prophesied of him (John 8.56; 12.41), a fact which the blinded Jews cannot understand (John 8.57: how can Jesus, who is not yet fifty years old, have seen Abraham?).

For the most part the gospel of John corresponds to the earlier gospels and the still earlier tradition in this use of scripture, but it is also aware of another hermeneutical key. According to John 1.29, 36, Jesus is the lamb of God who takes away the sin of the world. This is an allusion to Isa. 53.7, where the servant of God is compared to a lamb led to the slaughter. Here the passage from Deutero-Isaiah is not really understood as prophecy in terms of the usual proof from scripture; rather, the significance of the Christ event is expressed with

the help of an Old Testament text and at the same time the truth of
the text is shown. This is not something announced beforehand which
happens at a later date – as is the case, e.g., in Luke; the truth of
the existing text is realized and manifested in Christ: 'Behold, there
is the lamb of God'. As has been said (above, 23f.), the use of
Num. 21.8f. in John 3.14f. is typological: as a serpent was lifted up to
heal the people of that time, so the Son of man is lifted up for the
salvation of all who believe in him; the fact that the cross and the
exaltation are a paradoxical unity is expressed with the help of a text
which spoke of a serpent – a creature that was both noxious and
healing at the same time. Here too it is not really a matter of prophecy
nor even of a typological correspondence, but of the exegesis of the
Christ event with the help of the scriptural language already in existence. Nevertheless, the gospel of John, which itself advances some of
the scriptural proofs which have become traditional, apparently recognizes what questionable theology such a procedure is. Quite apart from
the hermeneutical problem in the narrower sense – whether and to
what extent texts may be used against their original sense – proof from
scripture tends to secure faith. But is a faith that is proved still faith?
Furthermore, the essential element of the Christ event, the real content
of the message, namely the saving significance of cross and resurrection, cannot be proved from scripture. We can understand why the
argument from scripture and prophecy used in the earliest community
began here and was first developed here, for it was at this point, as
now, that the real stumbling block was to be found. The stumbling
block of a crucified Messiah proved to be stronger than all the proofs
from scripture, which ultimately fail here. So John undertakes to
demonstrate this very stumbling block with the help of scripture.

According to scripture the Messiah comes from Bethlehem, the city
of David (John 7.42, 52), but Jesus comes from Nazareth in Galilee.
Hence the question 'Can any good come out of Nazareth?' and the
answer, 'Come and see!' (John 1.45f.). Nevertheless Jesus is the one
who was prophesied by Moses and the prophets (John 1.45). But that
in turn is recognized only by the 'true Israelite in whom there is no
guile' (John 1.47). By contrast the false scribes misunderstand their
scriptures even if they have a correct understanding of the literal sense
which is in the foreground – in just the same way as the words of
Jesus are misunderstood: they certainly are the descendants of
Abraham, but they are sons of the devil (John 8.39–44).

Just as the paradoxical exaltation of the Son of man on the cross
can only be understood in faith, so too the paradoxical truth of

scripture can only be understood through Christ and in the light of his revelation. At this point, however, we have left behind the controversy with the Jews over their interpretation of the law; this is direct proclamation for Christians, so that they may believe even without seeing or being assured by proofs from scripture. As in the beginnings of the Christian community Christ himself is here once again the origin and ground of faith; in the light of this, scripture retreats very much into the background. This is different from what we find in Luke. The letters of John no longer have any quotations from the Old Testament in them. Since John does not recognize any course of salvation history, the scriptures cannot be arranged in any temporal order, and their continuing validity (which John never questions) is strictly speaking an inconsistency on the basis of this conception. The persistence of religious tradition and the dead weight of the legacy of tradition were stronger than theological reflection, and that is always a disadvantage.

6. *Allegorical interpretation*

We are confronted with very different attempts to master the problem which the legacy of the Old Testament presented to early Christianity: the Old Testament as a promise of the Christ event, as a prophecy of the life and death of Jesus, indeed as a prediction of biographical and other details, the Old Testament as law, as the pedagogue who leads us to Christ, as a previous testimony which bears witness to a salvation history and makes it recognizable, and as scripture the paradoxical truth of which is recognized in the light of the revelation in Christ. To begin with they are still more or less spontaneous attempts, the consequences of which cannot be systematically drawn. Those who were convinced of the truth of the revelation in Christ and the validity of scripture felt that the scripture had to bear witness to Christ. Things could not be otherwise. The new meaning of scripture was its old true meaning. To begin with, there was still no awareness of the difference between this 'true' meaning and the literal meaning. But realization of the problem began to dawn where specialist interpretation was needed to bring out the true meaning. Exegesis, even when it is in fact only eisegesis, first comes about when the immediate sense of a passage is no longer understood – or seems to be no longer usable. Whereas modern historical critical exegesis is concerned to discover the old original meaning and its possible relevance for the present, such exegesis is not concerned with the original historical sense but always with the significance for the present of a scripture whose authority is quite simply taken for granted. If the scripture is authoritative, it must have a meaning for the present. Exegesis has to bring this to light.

The fact that in such exegesis texts may be detached from their original context is as much a Jewish legacy as other features of method, e.g. the argument by analogy (Mark 2.21–24: what was permissible for David must by analogy also be allowed to the disciples), etymological interpretation (Matt. 2.23: because Jesus lived in Nazareth he was called a Nazarene; this designation and the place name have nothing to do with each other), the argument *a minori ad maius*, from the lesser to the greater value (II Cor. 3.10f.: if the ministry of the law had glory, how much more so must the ministry that preaches the justification of the sinner).

In talking of typological interpretation as it was practised by Paul and from then on we can hardly think of a developed method of interpretation which rests on quite definite hermeneutical presuppositions (see above 23ff.). That is even more the case with allegorical interpretation. This method, which in the biblical sphere was first applied to the subsequent interpretation and application of the parables of Jesus (Mark 4.13–20; Matt. 13.36–43, 49f.) begins from the presupposition that the *text* interpreted in this way *itself* has a *different meaning* from the direct literal sense. In fact there is a mode of speech termed allegory, which through the accumulation of metaphors in all its individual features has a figurative sense which to this degree is something other than direct and literal (cf. already in the Old Testament e.g. Ezek. 16; 17; 19; 23; 31; 34; Pss. 23; 80.9–20). But allegorical interpretation treats other texts as though they were allegories. Whereas the argument from prophecy or even typology is thought to discover the clear meaning of the texts cited, a meaning which at first was still hidden, or perhaps also a deeper meaning, allegorical interpretation starts from the supposition that the texts have two meanings or even more, and claims that the immediate sense is only the outward covering of the true meaning. Indeed, even individual words have a meaning other than the immediate one. Thus the sower who goes out to sow is in truth the one who proclaims the word of God, and so on (Mark 4.14 etc.).

This method is not Israelite or Jewish, and unlike typology it is not even Christian, but Hellenistic in origin. When myths, and especially stories about the gods from Homer (who nevertheless was always held in the highest esteem) became offensive or even incomprehensible in their original sense, allegorical interpretation represented an attempt to remove the offence and so rescue the 'true' meaning. This mode of exegesis also found a way into Hellenistic Judaism and even into the work of the scribes of Palestine. With the help of allegorical interpretation the Alexandrian Jewish philosopher Aristobulus – a contemporary of Jesus Sirach, about the middle of the second century BC – was able to interpret the religious tradition of the Old Testament as the true philosophy and to present the Jews to the learned world as a nation of philosophers. And Paul's contemporary, the Jewish philosopher Philo of Alexandria, wrote a commentary on Genesis and the giving of the law by Moses with the help of the allegorical method.

If this method made it possible to reconcile the ancient validity of a traditional heritage – for Philo scripture was divinely inspired – with new insights and needs by attempting to understand the new interpretation as in fact the true meaning of the old text, Christians would find it obvious that they should not apply this hermeneutical key to the Old Testament which they were to understand in a Christian way.

Paul is already doing this when in I Cor. 5.6–8 he understands leaven as an image of impurity, when in Gal. 3.6 he interprets the seed in the singular (Gen. 22.18) in terms of Christ, the rock from which water springs out (Ex. 17.6) as a spiritual rock which accompanies the Israelites (I Cor. 10.4), or infers from the prohibition against muzzling the ox which treads the threshing floor that the preacher may live on his activity (I Cor. 9.8–10). In Gal. 4.21–31 (cf. 4.24) the apostle even states explicitly that the Old Testament text which he quotes (Gen. 16) must be understood allegorically: the sons of Sarah and the maid Hagar, Isaac and Ishmael, represent the believers in Christ who inherit salvation and those who do not believe and are cast out.

Whereas with Paul allegorical interpretation is only applied to particular points, and with the exception of Gal. 4.21–31 is only connected with individual features, in Hebrews this method is developed more fully. In the view of the author of the Letter to the Hebrews the Israelite–Jewish law has been done away with because it was weak and useless (Heb. 7.18). Now it no longer applies in a literal understanding but in a new allegorical sense which is first to be discovered in the light of Christ. Hitherto it had concealed this true sense as a 'shadow of good things to come' (Heb. 10.1). This gives the author the right to interpret it allegorically, especially when it deals with Old Testament worship. The worship of Israel was meant to bring about expiation and healing, but it could never fully achieve its aim. So it acquires its real sense only in the light of the true fulfilment in Christ, the true high priest (Heb. 4.14–16; 7–10), who has shed not the blood of animals but his own blood once for all (Heb. 9.1–15). Here typological contrasts (Heb. 7.9f.: Melchizedek – Christ; 8.2–5: tabernacle – heavenly tent; 9.23–28: the earthly – the heavenly) and allegorical interpretation (Heb. 3.6; 7.2f.; 10.20; 11.13–16; 12.22; 13.11–13) go hand in hand. At this point typological and allegorical interpretation have long since ceased simply to serve in discussion with Jewish or Judaizing opponents; they are now involved in the theological appropriation of the Old Testament as the book of the church, the correct interpretation of which is equivalent to the theological development of the Christian faith.

The Letter of Barnabas then goes on to appropriate and take up the Israelite and Jewish heritage almost by force. This letter, which is probably to be dated around AD 100, already presupposes the separation of the Christian community from the synagogue and with sharp polemic warns against a regression into Judaism. Whereas the Letter to the Hebrews allowed the validity of the original literal sense for the pre-Christian era, the Letter of Barnabas denies any such meaning altogether; on the contrary, the Jews have always misunderstood their own scripture. The scriptures are a Christian and not a Jewish book. Interpreted allegorically, they bear witness only to Christian faith and Christian morals. Thus circumcision means the circumcision of the heart (Barn. 9), unclean animals are bad men with whom people are not to come in contact (Barn. 10). All the chief Christian truths are already prophesied here: the pre-existence of Christ, his suffering, his cross and his return (Barn. 5–8; cf. 9.8; 8.3; 7.9).

Alongside such a take-over by Christian theology we have the more naive appropriation to be found in I Clement, which was written at the end of the first century from Rome to the community in Corinth. Here the Pauline problem of the Israelite and Jewish law as a legacy and a theological stumbling-block of the first order has been settled: of course the ceremonial law is no longer valid, the ordinances of the Old Testament are an analogy to the new ordinances of the Christian community, and faith is regarded as a virtue of which the Old Testament can offer many fine examples. Here the Old Testament has become so Christian that allegorical interpretation is no longer necessary except perhaps to give some details an edifying Christian sense, as for example the scarlet thread of Rahab the harlot (Josh. 2.18), which is meant to represent the blood of Christ.

Skilful and artificial interpretation with their typology and allegory on the one side, and naïve Christian acceptance on the other, increasingly smooth out the problem; the Israelite and Jewish legacy becomes a 'Christian' Old Testament. Where faith becomes a virtue, the conflict between righteousness by faith through Christ and the works of the law no longer sharpens men's eyesight for the contradiction between the old that is past and the new that has finally dawned. The law, interpreted as an eternally valid moral law – as it is by Justin (about 150) – is not done away with by Christ, the new lawgiver, but confirmed; on the other hand the ceremonial law applies only to the Jews; otherwise scripture, which is to be interpreted allegorically, is a prophecy of Christ. This as it were unproblematical understanding which is already presented by Justin largely shaped the normal view held by the church and has continued to do so down to the present.

7. The 'Old Testament'

The understanding of the Old Testament and its relationship to the New had inevitably to be expressed also in the final establishment of the Christian canon of scripture and its parts. Whereas first of all the inherited scripture had been the only holy book, a new series of scriptures of genuinely Christian origin now came into being alongside the old scriptures. We cannot describe this process in detail (cf. W. G. Kümmel, *Introduction*, IIA, 475–501; H. von Campenhausen, *Formation*, IIA, 262–268). Even before the final completion of this collection of writings as a Christian canon of twenty-seven works – in the West by the Synods of Hippo Regius (393) and of Carthage (397) – the question of the name of the collection must have arisen. This terminological question is eminently theological, since the designation expresses the understanding of the new collection of writings in its relationship to the old book, 'the law and the prophets', as it was once termed.

Paul had already described the eschatological salvation that had appeared in Christ as 'new' in its relationship to everything previous (II Cor. 3.6, 14; 5.17; Gal. 6.15). In so doing he could take up the specific use of the adjective 'new' in apocalyptic and indeed already in later prophecy. Here the word already denotes something utterly different, the great and absolute renewal in the last days, the new heaven and the new earth (Isa. 65.17; Rev. 21.1; II Peter 3.13) and especially also the 'new covenant' (Jer. 31.31–34). The eucharistic tradition is also familiar with the idea of a covenant (Mark 14.24; Matt. 26.28) or a new covenant (I Cor. 11.25; Luke 22.20), and in so doing refers back to the promise in Jer. 31. If the Hebrew and Greek terms are translated 'disposition' or 'foundation' instead of 'covenant' or 'testament' it becomes clearer that the reference is never, say, to a one-sided treaty but to *an order of salvation* founded by God. If the old and the new have this relationship to the eschatological ordering of salvation, then it is the obvious thing to transfer this conception to the *documents* which bear witness to these two orders. Paul already does this when in II Cor. 3.14 he writes about the *reading* of the old covenant. Here we find for the first time the term from which the designation 'Old Testament', which was applied to the collection originally called the law and the prophets (and the writings), was ultimately derived. Of course at this stage there was still no New Testament to form a collection of writings over against the Old Testament. The term also continued to describe the new order of salvation. Irenaeus (about 180) stressed the unity of the Creator and the Redeemer and the difference between old and new in his fight against Gnosticism and its rejection both of the 'God of the Jews' and of his scripture; he thought that he could recognize a pedagogical course of God's saving dealings with man which progress from covenant to covenant: Adam, Noah, Moses, Christ. From such an arrangement of the old and new covenants in the history of salvation it is not a long step, though a decisive one, to apply the same terms to the documents which are constitutive of the two divine foundations of salvation and thus to classify them theologically and to relate them to each other. Melito of Sardis, a contemporary of Irenaeus who like him comes from Asia Minor, uses both the traditional 'law and prophets' for the books of the Old Testament and also the term 'books of the old covenant' (*tes palaias diathekes biblia*, cf. Eusebius, *Church History* IV 26.13f., and H. von Campenhausen, IIA, 264f.). There is still no mention here of the books of the new covenant, but Melito's terminology in fact seems to presuppose this. Clement of Alexandria (about 200) is the first to use the word *diatheke* not only for the old and new covenants, the old and new orders of salvation, but also for the two parts of a canon of scripture. The term means both the covenant, the establishment of divine salvation, and also the documents which belong to it and bear witness to it. This is still the case with Origen (died 254). The translation *testamentum* (= testament) at last became exclusively a technical term for the parts of the canon. Here the word loses its original specific meaning as a testamentary disposition, a will, and says nothing specific about the content of the collections of which it is a description; only the 'old' and 'new', *vetus* and *novum*, indicate a fixed theological relationship. The Old Testament is old only in its relationship to the New, the New Testament is new only in its relationship to the Old. Unlike *diatheke* (= divine ordering of salvation), the designation 'Old' and 'New Testament' leaves open the question of the significance of and the justification for this arrangement. The old heritage is firmly bound up with the new and the new can no longer be separated from the old, but the hermeneutical problem of this connection, which has been concealed rather than solved by typology, salvation history and most of all by allegorical interpretation, remains to be solved.

8. *The unity of Old and New*

Of course to begin with, the early church did not find its legacy a theological and existential problem. Right from the beginning the scripture which had come down to it bore unmistakable witness that the one God who in the last days had come to bring salvation in Christ, had created the world and mankind and as Creator remains the Lord of men and of the world; that even though he had come near in Jesus Christ he was still the unapproachable, the wholly other, whose otherness cannot be done away with by mystical absorption and beatification; and that he is wholly other in person, in will, and contingently even in comparison with all the logic and Logos-thinking of the philosophers and of popular philosophy. In its abiding relationship to the Old Testament, the New Testament is not the communication of a newly discovered or newly revealed universal truth. Nor is it the foundation document of a new religion. It is the testimony to the new and eschatological action of the one God who has always been at work through law and prophets, judges, kings and men of God in a history which ends in the eschatological community of Jesus Christ. As the true people of God, this community knows itself to be totally different in quality from all the old and indeed the newly-founded religious communities. The legacy of the Old Testament prevented early Christianity from being submerged as a mystery religion in ahistorical mysticism and myth, or from hardening into a timeless philosophy, the 'eternal' truth of Christ. The community kept alive – as a legacy of the prophets – the awareness that love of God is not realized in absorption into God but in keeping the commandments, in love for one's neighbour and above all in the everydayness of earthly life; that man has been told by God 'what is good and what the

Lord requires of you' (Micah 6.8). Thus the freedom of the Christian man does not mean unbridled arbitrariness, but involvement in the service of God.

However, the function of the Old Testament was not just to preserve and to limit. From the very beginning, in a positive sense, it interpreted the Christ event and faith in Christ. When the earliest community was already preaching that the decisive event of the death and resurrection of Jesus Christ had taken place 'according to the scriptures', it meant something more, something different, from a scriptural proof in a superficial and primitive sense. Moreover, the shaping of, say, the passion narrative with the help of quotations from the Old Testament did not just serve the ends of polemic and mere proof, as a defence against anyone in particular. Rather, the language of the Old Testament, its ready-minted images and symbols, its laments and its jubilation, its honorific titles, were filled with new eschatological content and were thus 'fulfilled'. These became the language of a preaching in which the new gospel could be presented as the message of the one God, the Creator and Redeemer. The preaching of the earliest community was largely preaching with the help of Old Testament texts, yet it was something more, something different from the interpretation of texts as this was practised by the Jewish scribes: this was the Word which comes from Christ, even if it took its words from the text. And as surely as words and language are more than a mere garment or an empty vessel, more than neutral and interchangeable designations for any content whatsoever, so from the beginning the connection between the Old and New Testaments – understood both as old and new ordinances of salvation and in the sense of the two parts of the canon – was clearly recognized, in a more substantial way than might be suggested by the argument from prophecy, typology and allegorical interpretation. The Word of the cross and the resurrection cannot be detached from the words in which it is given, but those words had their own prehistory in Israel's experience of God's dealings and the effect of those experiences – their significance for the present – in the Christian church. We must go into the significance of this aspect at a later stage, in more detail (see below ch. VII, 2 and 3, 223ff.).

The substantive mutual interrelationship of old and new, and then also of old and new writings, this unity of scripture in its two distinct parts, prevented a radical solution to the theological and hermeneutical problem of the Old Testament in the form of simply doing away with it. Gnosticism, with its dualism and its contrast between the creator god and the redeemer god, between the evil world of matter and the spiritual self which is held captive in the world of darkness as though in a prison, identified the god of the Jews with the creator god, from whom the redeemer god who had revealed himself in Christ was strictly to be distinguished. Even in its more moderate forms (say in the letter of Ptolemy to Flora written about 150, a discussion of the significance of the Old Testament law which accepts that the moral law of the ten commandments was not done away with by Jesus and allows its validity), Gnosticism derives the law from a god of a lower order, who has a position somewhere between the redeemer God and the devil. But despite the varied influences of Gnosticism on Christianity, Gnosticism never managed to gain a footing in the church. It already found a clear-sighted opponent in Paul.

Marcion (about 150) then drew a sharp contrast between the god of the Old Testament, the creator god (demiurge) and 'god of the Jews', who is strictly righteous and given to revenge, but lacking in all goodness and as imperfect as his creation, and the god of mercy who reveals himself in Christ. Accordingly he rejected the Old Testament, refusing to interpret it in allegorical terms. It is, however, significant that Marcion's so to speak consistent Paulinism inevitably led to an attack on genuine Christian tradition. Marcion wanted to recognize only the gospel of Luke, which he thought to be Pauline, and ten letters of Paul for use in his church. Even these writings, which were canonized as the exclusively true evidence for the message of Jesus and of the apostle Paul, had to be edited in order to purify them from what were supposed to be Jewish falsifications. Thus Marcion's canon was an antithetical counterpart to the collection of Israelite and Jewish writings which had hitherto been regarded as the only sacred book of the church. However, the Israelite and Jewish legacy had already become too 'Christian' for the alien nature of a Christianity purified along Marcion's line to escape notice. Marcion was 'the founder of a new religion; his contemporary and first literary opponent, the apologist Justin, already recognized this'. So wrote Adolf von Harnack in the first sentence of his book on Marcion (*Marcion: Das Evangelium vom fremden Gott*, IIA, 1). And Marcion's God was alien not only in relationship to the evil world but also in relationship to the God of Jesus, Paul and the church in general. Thus Marcion's canon of scripture was unable to win the day.

Instead, it raised within the church, which hitherto had not had a canon of its own apart from the holy scripture which it had inherited from the Jews, the question of the authentic and true canon. After much toing and froing and discussion of details, this question was eventually answered unanimously in practice: the answer given was that the church's canon consisted of both Old and New Testaments.

9. *The dogmatic suppression of the problem*

Allegorical interpretation largely became normative as a method of exegesis. Origen (died 254), probably the most significant exegete of this period, carried on this exegesis with due regard to philology by means of careful textual criticism and with the help of reference books. What he tried to discover was not, however, the literal sense – which Marcion had required – but the higher spiritual sense. Only allegorical interpretation brought this to light. The argument that he used against opponents who regarded this kind of interpretation as utterly arbitrary is striking: without allegorical interpretation the Old Testament requires the sacrifice of calves and lambs! Of course the correctness of the method and the validity of its results is not based on cheap slogans; it has an ontological and philosophical foundation. The multiple sense of the divinely inspired scriptures (literal, moral and spiritual) corresponds to the trichotomy of reality (body, soul and spirit), which in turn is matched by a threefold interpretation (historico-grammatical, physical, allegorical). Thus Origen's hermeneutic claims to have an ontological basis.

In the struggle against Gnosticism and other heresies the justification and necessity of the allegorical interpretation of scripture in accordance with the Alexandrine pattern almost became a dogma.

So-called Antiochene theology, represented especially by Diodore of Tarsus (died 392). Theodore of Mopsuestia (died 428) and the brilliant preacher John Chrysostom (died 407) had another hermeneutical concern which had already been indicated by Paul: the text was to be deciphered and made topical in terms of typology and salvation history on the basis of its literal meaning as ascertained by philology. However, the subsequent condemnation of the doctrine of the heads of the Antiochene school prevented their hermeneutics from having success in the East. From now on scriptural interpretation increasingly declined in importance here; it became the interpretation of a tradition, the interpretation of interpretation.

To begin with, the West was more interested in practical theology and the church than in hermeneutics and theory. Thus Tertullian (about 200) stresses the significance of the literal meaning and establishes practical rules for exegesis: it is important to note grammatical and historical connections; obscure passages are to be illuminated from clear ones. He also requires and encourages the regulation of interpretation by the rule of faith, the *regula fidei*, or the 'canon of truth'. The trinitarian baptismal creed is elevated to the status of a normative norm, as part of incontrovertible 'apostolic' truth which is beyond discussion. A fixed canon of scriptures recognized by the church is matched by a clear rule of faith and the 'apostolic' ministry of bishops and teachers which hands down, guarantees and supervises true doctrine. The gift of the spirit authenticates with its truth (*charisma veritatis*). Here we have the beginnings of the church's elevation of dogma – dogmatic control over the interpretation of scripture and its decline into a mere auxiliary discipline. This brings with it a decline in the status of scripture itself. Allegorical interpretation, which began to find a footing in the West under the influence of Philo and Origen, also contributed to this process by its stress on the 'other' sense. The real exegetical and hermeneutical problems were increasingly concealed by the church's dogma.

In the West the Alexandrine tradition of the allegorical interpretation of scripture is chiefly continued by Ambrose, archbishop of Milan (died 397), with his doctrine of the threefold meaning of scripture (historical-literal, mystic and moral). Jerome (died 420), the great translator of the Bible into Latin and the creator of the Vulgate (what is 'in general circulation') – since the Council of Trent in 1546 the Bible of the Roman Catholic church – is more a representative of the Antiochene line of grammatical exegesis, observing the historical differences and thus also the differences between the Old and the New Testament. However, even he is ultimately also convinced that to keep to the literal meaning produces heresy, and that it is therefore important to grasp the deeper meaning of the text.

Augustine also takes over the allegorical method from Ambrose, despite his 'Antiochene' observance of the literal sense. Both the literal and the spiritual sense are valid for him, and as in Origen this hermeneutics has a philological and ontological foundation: the manifold sense is matched by the distinction between the *signum* and the *res*, the symbol and the substance. The facts themselves are signs of, transparent to, the 'true' facts; accordingly the words too have a literal and a figurative sense. The rule of faith (*regula fidei*) determines whether they should be understood literally or figuratively in a specific instance. Thus this conception, too, excludes an independent hermeneutic. The doctrine of the fourfold sense of scripture which was first formulated by John Cassian (about 400) is simply the scholastic elaboration of the old allegorical distinction between the literal and the 'other', spiritual sense. The spiritual sense, the *sensus spiritualis*, is now developed into the allegorical (what is to be believed), tropological or moral (how to behave), and anagogical (what to strive for), depending on the particular sphere of application. Two hexameters help to teach this basic exegetical rule and to impress it on the memory:

Littera gesta docet, quod credas Allegoria;
Moralis quid agas, quo tendas Anagogia.

The real emphasis was thus placed on the threefold spiritual or mystical sense, which was also understood as an expression of the trinity of faith, hope and love, or as a representation of the divine Trinity. However, the literal sense, which was still retained, and the exegetical rule which allowed spiritual interpretations only when they confirm passages understood in a literal sense, prevented total arbitrariness and with it the total loss of the actual Old and New Testaments and the message of the Bible which is independent even of the church's ministry, the rule of faith and tradition. Of course the hermeneutical problem of the relationship between the two parts of the canon and of the Christian validity of the Old Testament remained even further from a solution, indeed it was a task that was hardly recognized. We can understand L. Diestel's comment (Ic, 188), 'Thus the inner harmony of scripture was determined by the ever rising dominance of dogma and allegory.' And this statement can be further expanded: as Paul says with reference to Jewish interpretation, dogma and allegory are like a veil which conceals the true meaning of scripture; they stimulate a harmony in the church and theology where in reality theological and existential questions of the utmost importance are awaiting an answer.

IIII

THE OLD TESTAMENT IN THE LIGHT OF THE REFORMATION AND UNDER FIRE FROM HISTORICAL CRITICISM

1. *Present realization in the sacraments*

From its earliest beginnings Christianity has been a historical entity in a particularly distinctive sense. It is not just a historical entity in respect of the fact that it is historically conditioned, has emerged and grown up out of a historical beginning, and cannot be detached from its origins. The same claims can be made for other phenomena. Nor is it a peculiarity of Christianity that it has its own history and that it has made an impact on history; its nature cannot be understood solely in terms of the history of Christendom. Rather, the nature of Christianity consists in the fundamental link with its historical origin which is proclaimed and believed in as *the eschatological and ultimately valid saving event in history*. Christian proclamation preaches the Christ event, the cross and resurrection of Christ under Pontius Pilate, as a saving event which, although datable and in the past, is nevertheless present. It has a meaning for the present day and brings about salvation now. Thus as the lapse of time has carried the period of the saving event further and further into the past, the question of the present realization of salvation has become increasingly urgent, even if it might not always be put in so many words.

The theology of Luke already offered an early answer with its division of time into periods of a salvation history directed by God. Another answer is contained in the rule of faith and the confession of faith, the more-than-historical, trinitarian pattern of which nevertheless also reflects history: from the Father, the Creator, via the history of the Son under Pontius Pilate, to the Holy Spirit, who had already spoken by the prophets, to the apostolic church and finally to the last things and eternal life. Yet another attempt to maintain the paradox of history and the eschatological and ultimately valid saving event, and to put it into words, is the christological dogma of the two natures, the divine and the human natures of Jesus Christ. These interpretations, despite their concern to maintain the paradox of the historical and at the same time ultimate, eschatological origin of Christianity nevertheless tend to separate the ultimate, eschatological saving event from history and thus abandon the paradox.

The doctrine of the twofold meaning of scripture – its literal and spiritual senses – corresponds to the doctrine of the two natures of Christ, while the other doctrine of the verbal inspiration of scripture, originally a feature of Hellenistic Judaism, which states that the scripture is literally inspired by God or the Holy Spirit, similarly takes the canon out of the sphere of ordinary reality and with it the saving event to which it bears witness. Now if interpretation of scripture, understood in this way to be holy, is regulated by the rule of faith and by dogma, and if, conversely, the Bible has developed finally and authoritatively into the rule of faith and dogma, then to interpret it further, making it relevant and giving it practical application, is not the first task of theology. In that case the church is no longer constantly directed towards the business of interpreting scripture, to the words which are preached anew in each particular situation and in which Christ and his salvation are made present. On the contrary, since the church as a body of people in the present cannot live from past salvation and on the basis of reminiscence alone, other ways of making salvation present take the place of interpretation and proclamation. One can follow Gerhard Ebeling ('The Significance of the Critical Historical Method', IB, pp. 33ff.) in speaking of an 'imitative historizing' realization in the present, when in sects and then in the mainstream church and especially in monasticism artificial situations are created and ways of living organized which are meant to be similar to the biblical ideal. The imitation of Christ and his first disciples takes the place of discipleship. Or salvation is realized in the present by means of contemplation or meditation or mystical absorption. The cult of relics similarly has a hermeneutical function: salvation remains visibly and tangibly present in the relics. Pilgrimages to holy places and of course especially visits to the Holy Land can also be understood in this sense. However, since monastic contemplation and mysticism cannot be for everyone, for the great mass of believers worship, the sacraments and church buildings become increasingly significant.

Salvation is made present in worship, performed in accordance with the rhythm of the church's year, and in a church which with its statues of the saints, altars and transubstantiated hosts is a heaven on earth. The making-present of the Christ event in the sacrament, and the sacrament itself, become the nucleus of Christian life, and the church becomes an institution for salvation which continues the saving event into the present through the uninterrupted succession of bishops.

This solution to the hermeneutical problem had far-reaching consequences for the understanding of scripture. Its validity and its divine character were not put in question, but *it* was not the first vehicle for the communication of salvation by interpretation and preaching. Salvation is present only in the sacrament and is communicated only by the sacrament. By contrast, the scripture serves merely as an introduction, by teaching about revealed truths. It becomes the divine textbook of the saving truths and facts of the church and of dogma. Measured by salvation given through the sacraments, it too only serves as law, to the degree that Christian life and the organization of the church are subject to the divine laws which have been manifested in scripture. Thus scripture becomes a divine lawbook (see ch. IV, 2, 105ff.). In principle, both parts of scripture are assigned this quality as teaching and law in equal measure. The sacramental solution to the problem of realizing salvation in the present forces the hermeneutical question of scripture, the relationship of its two parts and the significance of the Old Testament, to one side and silences it, as though it had in fact been solved.

2. *The rediscovery of scripture*

As we must now demonstrate, the rise of a historical consciousness and with it the awareness of the difference between particular periods, the historical differentiation and the historicity of all human existence, was the great turning-point in the understanding of scripture. The reason why this turning point also had exceptional *theological* significance, shook theology to its foundations and raised basic questions which have still not been solved, is that at an early stage *the Reformation had brought back scripture from the periphery to the centre of the church and theology.* The Reformers themselves were no historians, nor – despite some beginnings in this direction by Luther – did they as biblical scholars make use of historical criticism. However, the rediscovery of scripture in the Reformation brought to light again the long hidden questions of proper interpretation and the hermeneutical problem of the relationship between the testaments. If scripture came to occupy a central point, then the hermeneutical problem inevitably acquired fundamental significance. If exegesis was understood as an essential theological discipline, then in the end the results of exegesis had to be of more than merely historical significance. The shift of emphasis from the sacrament and a sacramental approach to scripture and scriptural preaching was more than just a shift of accent. Furthermore, the Reformers' appeal to scripture and scripture alone (*sola scriptura*) was more than a polemical doctrine, the significance of which disappears when peace has been concluded. And although the Reformation took up the academic, philological achievements of humanism – one need think only of the Greek text in the New Testament which was edited by Erasmus of Rotterdam or the *Rudimenta linguae Hebraicae* by the Hebraist Johannes Reuchlin – and put them at the service of biblical interpretation, they were not concerned with a return to the sources as such, out of humanist, historical and academic interest. Rather, in the controversy with the traditional theological system of thought, with the church organization which carried it on and guaranteed it, and with the hermeneutical presuppositions on which it was based, there developed increasingly clearly the revolutionary Reformation insight that finally threatened to bring down the whole structure of church and doctrine in its existing form. This consisted in the discovery – or as the Reformers understood it, in the rediscovery – of the earliest Christian truth that faith comes from preaching and listening to preaching, and that such preaching takes place in the power of Christ (Rom. 10.17).

Now faith is the acceptance of the message which brings Christ's salvation, and therefore the acceptance of salvation itself. Salvation, the eschatological, ultimate, final salvation which Christ brought and still brings, is recognized as being inseparable from the proclamation of this salvation. In view of the essential link between salvation and the message of salvation, all other ways of making salvation present and bestowing grace which have hitherto been regarded as valid are forced into the background, subordinated to preaching or even rejected utterly as false ways and false doctrines. That Christ alone brings salvation through grace (*solus Christus, sola gratia*), and that faith alone receives salvation and is itself purely the act of accepting (*sola fide*), are merely different aspects of the same insight, which correspond to one another as correlates.

The radical exclusiveness which is expressed in this often repeated 'alone' must necessarily also affect the understanding of scripture. The word of Christ may not be identical with scripture, but it cannot be heard without scripture. The aim of interpretation is to put it into words again and to allow it to express its own message alone. Here 'alone' means without an alien authority which has already decided on the matter in advance: this matter, namely the message of Christ and his salvation – and thus *salvation itself* – is not communicated and presented outside it or even without it in the tradition of the church, in sacrament and ministry: it lies in *scripture itself*.

Just as salvation cannot be separated from the word that proclaims it, so the word cannot be separated from scripture. Nevertheless, for Luther the Word of God and scripture are certainly not identical. *Sola scriptura* does not have the same meaning as the similar formula to be found in earlier reform movements which were critical of the Pope (including John Wycliffe, born about 1328; the so-called Waldensians, so named after Petrus Waldes, about 1200; Johannes Hus, executed in 1415, and the Hussites), i.e. that scripture is the only valid divine law (*lex divina; lex Christi*), nor is it a biblicism which no longer draws a distinction between the essentials and the inessentials, slavishly revering the literal sense and claiming the immediate validity of scripture as a whole. *Sola scriptura* points rather to the place and time of the historical origin of the testimony to Christ, to the sole source from which this testimony is made. As testimony to this origin scripture is its 'own interpreter' (*sui ipsius interpres*); it is clear in its own message (*claritas*), though some individual passages may remain obscure; it alone is the judge, the norm and the rule (*iudex, norma et regula* – thus the Formula of Concord of 1577).

Now this Reformation principle of scripture, which declares scripture to be the normative norm (*norma normans*), concerns not only the New Testament but the whole canon of the Old and New Testaments, as the Formula of Concord expressly states: there is a distinction between the holy scriptures of the Old and New Testaments on the one hand and all scriptures of a different origin on the other (*discrimen inter Sacra Veteris et Novi Testamenti litteras et omnia aliorum scripta*). Thus the Old Testament, too, of course along with the New Testament, becomes the norm and rule of the Christian church. This inevitably raises once again the old question of the possibility and the limitations of such a validity.

3. Luther and the Old Testament

To begin with, Luther too accepted the position of the traditional church doctrine of the fourfold sense of scripture and was convinced of the justification for and necessity of allegorical interpretation. His immediate rejection of scholastic methods and his totally new understanding of the task of theology and the nature of the church as the community which lives from the proclaimed word did not lead to an increasing attention to the literal sense. Even at a later stage, Luther made lavish use of the allegorical method. But his Reformation brought about more than a change in exegetical method. It introduced the liberation of scripture from its Babylonian captivity under the sway of the church's doctrine and teaching ministry, from tradition and allegorical harmonization. Even the reaction of later orthodoxy – including neo-orthodoxy – has only been able to slow down and conceal this development, not to bring it to a halt. If scripture is the normative norm, then interpretation is the principal task of theology. However, interpretation expounds and brings to light what had earlier been either not understood, misunderstood or hidden. This is true of both testaments to the same degree. Now if such principles are in fact observed in the course of interpretation, the differences between the two testaments and indeed within them cannot remain hidden. The argument of the opponents of the Reformation that by no means everything in scripture, which is claimed – *sola scriptura* – to be the rule for true belief, corresponds with Luther's Paulinism, drew attention to these differences and made it necessary to differentiate between passages with greater and lesser authority, between the Word of God which was only authoritative earlier for other men, and the Word of God which speaks to man's existence today.

The most important distinction is that between the gospel as an oral message and scripture, which only has an attendant function and is not itself the word of salvation, the gospel that brings salvation. Despite and because of the principle of *sola scriptura* as the decisive hermeneutical principle of scripture which is its own interpreter, the word of Christ, the word about Christ, that presents Christ, is the norm of scripture, the criterion of the 'canon in the canon' and the hermeneutical key for the right understanding of scripture.

Luther is able to make the venture of measuring the New Testament by this standard and criticizing the Letter of Jude, II Peter, Hebrews, Revelation and especially James (his judgment on this as a 'straw epistle' is famous). It was even less possible to take an uncritical and undifferentiated view of the Old Testament as holy, divine and valid. Of course Luther was convinced that Christians have the right to refer to the Old Testament as the first part of their scripture and that the Jews do not. Indeed the Old Testament law was first given to the Jews (the people of Israel) and the promises of God indeed applied first to his chosen people. But since the Jews have rejected and crucified Christ and even dared to apply the prophecies of the suffering servant of God in Isaiah 53 to themselves as a nation suffering among the Gentiles, they have been rejected by God and do not even have a claim to be living according to their own law, which has lost its validity outside the promised land. They are to obey the laws of the peoples among whom they are scattered as a punishment just as they themselves recognized Pilate as the ruler of the Jews. Before the Jewish 'Crucify him!', which was the great turning point, of course Israel was the people of God who had been chosen out of the world of the Gentile nations and had experienced a unique history under God's word and through God's guidance. If God has also now made the Jews witnesses to his anger, the Old Testament still attests, as before, God's promises and his gracious guidance of the course of history. This is the reason why it can still be called sacred history – not, to be sure, because anything sacred has been accomplished in it. And the Old Testament still continues to speak of this history. In addition it is an inexhaustible collection of examples of the way in which men live, love, hate, suffer, fight, sin and find mercy under God. The fact that the world-view of the Bible – heaven, earth and underworld – still corresponded largely to their own and that the political, social and economic conditions at the end of the Middle Ages in Europe were not too different from those presupposed in scripture made it easier for the Reformers to make this rediscovery and to have this apparently direct access to the literal sense of scripture. Furthermore, the conviction that human nature remains essentially the same down the centuries, and that although times and circumstances change man still finds himself in similar situations and confronted with comparable questions, concerns and needs, made it possible to understand Old Testament texts in an analogous way and to apply them to the present as being still valid, instructive and redemptive. Thus Luther's theology of the existential encounter brought about by the Word which arouses faith could embrace the existential significance and the contemporaneity of the old texts without reflection on hermeneutical theory and without the application of a carefully thought out hermeneutical and exegetical tool.

This new exegesis which sought out the literal sense of the text and understood it as a statement about man for man did not, as we have seen, understand the history reported in the Old Testament as a history of saints. It also succeeded in making comprehensible in human terms the many scandals and acts of cruelty of which the people of the Old Testament were guilty, instead of explaining them away or offering moral excuses, though Luther at times could put forward the view that God had allowed evil or had even instigated it through the Holy Spirit in order to achieve his higher, good ends. We should stress the point that such an interpretation which dares to talk about evil can be fully in accord with the intention of the text. There can, for example, be no doubt that in the Yahwistic source of Genesis, Abraham, Jacob and other figures in their group are in no way meant to be moral examples and yet are presented as instances of faith and figures in a divine history.

Luther's existential approach also – and especially – gives him access to the Psalter and makes it possible for him to appropriate the lamentation and joy, the temptation and the consolation expressed in the Psalms, to make himself at home in these prayers and to allow them to speak to his own Christian existence. The later recognition of modern scholarship on the Psalms that the 'I' in the Psalms does not refer to historical individuals but is concerned with a religious type, and that the Psalms presuppose typical rather than uniquely historical situations, confirms the fundamental appropriateness of this kind of approach to the Psalter.

Of course for Luther the Old Testament is not just a collection of examples or a prayer book for Christians. Luther the exegete can differentiate. Thus in arguments with his opponents who try to play off against him the scripture to which he himself refers (*sola scriptura*), he can stress that not all passages of scripture have the same authority and that there is a difference between the Word of God which was once given to others and the Word of God which applies today. These distinctions are necessary in the New Testament and even more within the Old Testament. At this point it should be noted first that the law of Moses was given to the Jews (Israel) and only to them. It is a national law and one which is confined to the Jews; it does not concern Christians, even though it may have been promulgated by God on Sinai through the mediation of Moses. This judgment concerns not only the ceremonial law in the narrower sense but the whole of the law as it is contained in the five books of Moses, the Pentateuch. Observation of the literal sense also shows that many regulations were simply popular customs which Moses later elevated to the status of a law. Of course his legislation also contains passages which are not confined to one particular nation. These are the parts which correspond to the divine law which holds for all men, and which is written on their hearts. So these passages also hold for Christians. They find their clearest expression within the Old Testament in the ten command-ments, the Decalogue. But this also includes regulations which belong to the Jewish ceremonial law, namely the commandments against images and the sabbath commandment: these ordinances are no longer valid for Christians.

Luther's theological understanding of the law in general and his judgment on the Old Testament exercise an influence on one another. If only the law written on man's conscience is in force as God's own will, it is nevertheless the case – precisely here – that Christ is the end of the law. Luther quite rightly referred Paul's statement (Rom. 10.4) not only to the law of Israel and the Jewish people and not only to the ceremonial law – in any case, these no longer have any significance for Christians since they are only meant for Israel – but to law generally, and he understood the abolition of the law in good Pauline dialectical terms. Just as Paul can write, 'Do we then over-throw the law by this faith? By no means! On the contrary, we uphold the law' (Rom. 3.31), so Luther also teaches that the law is no possible way for man towards life, salvation and justification and that man can-not justify himself by the works of the law; on the contrary, such self-justification with the help of the law is his besetting sin. True, the law of God written in our hearts, as contained in the ten commandments and as expressed most fully in the twofold commandment to love God and our neighbour, is still God's holy will and demand. Christ is the end of the law because he alone has fulfilled the law. Those who believe in him take part in this fulfilment.

A contrast is drawn between the law understood in this way, which proclaims the demands of God's will and, because it is not fulfilled, shows man what he must do and yet does not do, what he must be and yet is not, and thus reveals God's wrath and leads to death, and the gospel, which brings a promise and assurance of life. The distinction between law and gospel becomes the most important hermeneutical key for scripture – *sola scriptura* – which is its own interpreter, and for the definition of the relationship between the two testaments. With Luther it works almost like a divining rod for tracing the correct meaning of individual statements in scripture.

The distinction between law and gospel is matched by the distinction between the Old Testament and the New. At this point we should note that 'testament' is still (or again) used here in its original sense of a divine ordinance of salvation and a decree of God (cf. above, ch. II, 35ff.). The two testaments or covenants understood in this way are not, however, identical with the parts of the canon which are called the Old and the New Testaments. Just as the old covenant does not coincide with the writings collected in the Old Testament, so the gospel is not identical with the New Testament.

In any case, the gospel is not primarily a writing, but an oral word, an oral promise, a message, a living voice (*viva vox evangelii*). This stress on the essentially oral nature of the gospel is doubtless meant to guard against the misconception that the gospel is a doctrine – fixed once and for all in writing – instead of a message of an action of God in Christ in the unrepeatable sphere of history, or that the gospel itself is a – written – law, a new, Christian law. The law is put into writing as both a ceremonial and a national law, and also as the ten commandments, which are written on tablets. The Old Testament – now understood as the first part of the canon – is a writing which prophesies Christ. Here its written character serves to keep and to secure the earlier testimony.

For Luther, then, the word of the gospel and scripture, the gospel and the New Testament, the law and the Old Testament, are not identical. The Old Testament comprises both law *and* gospel. But by this criterion the New Testament, too, must be read as law and gospel, and not everything written in it is pure gospel. Because of this Luther felt justified in occasionally passing critical judgment on the Letter of Jude, II Peter, Hebrews and Revelation and indeed on the synoptic gospels. The dialectical distinction between the law and the gospels is fundamental, and a matter of principle; that between the Old and New Testaments as parts of the canon is not. The distinction between the testaments is only a matter of degree: the Old Testament has more law, the New Testament has more gospel. The distinction is also of a temporal character: in Luther's view the gospel can be found in the Old Testament as promise and prediction, whereas the New Testament proclaims its fulfilment.

By making this fundamental distinction between the law and the gospel, Luther did more than give fruitful expression to the heart of Paul's message in a changed situation. At the same time he pointed back to the way in which Paul deals with the Old Testament: in so far as the law of the old covenant contained in the Old Testament is more than a mere code for Jewish social life, it is both done away with and given a radical form. In the same way, however, the promises, demonstrations of grace, assurances and predictions which are also attested in the Old Testament are shown to be fulfilled in a new way in Christ. However, now that the theological distinction between the law and the gospel corresponds in anthropological and existential terms to the two fundamentally opposed possibilities of human existence – salvation through one's own efforts or divine redemption, realization of one's self or life as a gift, man as the supreme being or man as truly himself only under God – this distinction also provides the hermeneutical key for both New Testament and Old Testament texts. For Luther, the hermeneutical key – what is the understanding of man in this particular text? – and the theological criterion – the law and the gospel – coincide.

This hermeneutical and theological approach made it possible to form a new view of the unity of scripture and the differences between its various levels, which do not necessarily coincide with the division of the canon. It also made possible an exegetical approach which took account of differences and which remained oriented to the most fundamental anthropological and theological distinctions without splitting hairs. Luther's hermeneutical and theological key – law and gospel – made it possible for him to find the gospel in the Old Testament as well; here he could discover examples of faith, of existence based on God which could at the same time be apart from or even against God, and which could help in providing a basis for Christian life in the present day. And he could achieve this without having to do violence to the literal sense of the text. There can be no doubt that here we find the beginnings of a solution to the problem of hermeneutics which is not out of date even today, although historical-critical scholarship and the general discussion of hermeneutics have gone some way beyond Luther's own position.

Of course, Luther's existential approach to the Old Testament texts and the use of the hermeneutical key provided by the dialectical opposition of law and gospel are based on the conviction that the Old Testament – with the exception of social code of the Jews – is of direct importance to Christians as both law and gospel. Indeed, only the Christians, as opposed to the Jews with their sinful misunderstanding and lies, can understand the Old Testament properly as a Christian book. Judged by the original meaning of the texts, this conviction is a prejudice which can only be justified by a persistent refusal to accept the literal sense. The *sensus litteralis* consequently becomes the *sensus litteralis propheticus*, and no progress has really been made beyond allegorical interpretation.

In other respects, too, this fruitful hermeneutical approach is not maintained consistently and is not carried on without the accessories of tradition. It is combined with the historical and theological judgment that the gospel before Christ can only be the promise and the prediction of Christ. For Luther, the connection between the proclamation of salvation, the gospel, and Christ implied a linear extension of the gospel over the time since Christ, in contrast to which its earlier history could only be a time of prophecy and promise. The existential and theological criterion of law and gospel was combined with the temporal and linear scheme of prophecy and fulfilment. This made it possible for Luther to read the Old Testament not only christocentrically – i.e. in the light of a belief which is primarily belief in Christ and which keeps to the word of Christ communicated essentially through the New Testament, elevating the hermeneutical and theological criterion of law and gospel to be the supreme standard – but also christologically. In other words, that means that he seeks the deepest meaning to be found not only in the messianic predictions in the narrower sense which are to be found in the prophets, but in Moses and his books, and in the Psalms. These are not only a prediction of the gospel and therefore themselves gospel, but also a foretelling of Christ and his life and death. Luther did not differ in this respect from the ancient church ever since New Testament times: it was already the view of Justin that Isaiah and the Psalms had predicted the details of Jesus' destiny, and that all the divine epiphanies recorded in the Old Testament were manifestations of the Logos Christ.

Luther's dialectical distinction between law and gospel was, however, of permanent significance and lasting force. Freed from the traditional dogma of the character of the Old Testament as promise and prediction, this distinction can be used as a clear hermeneutical principle and criterion without the need to establish a new dogma or a new rule of faith concerned with correct interpretation which stands above scripture. The dialectic of law and gospel is in fact taken from scripture itself, so that a mode of interpretation which derives its bearings from this dialectic is simply taking seriously the Reformation principle that scripture is its own interpreter. As the fundamental theological distinction is matched by the equally fundamental polarity of two possibilities of understanding human existence, its use as a hermeneutical principle makes possible a scholarly method of interpretation freed from the demands of dogma, which approaches the text as a web of human words and expressions of human life, without feeling that it must inevitably fail to do justice to theology by such an anthropological orientation. It was left to those who succeeded Luther to draw these consequences. They would have been inconceivable without the impulse to which he gave rise, and without the priority which the Reformation accorded to scripture and exegesis they would hardly have attained the theological and intellectual significance which they in fact acquired.

It is in fact possible to regard the 'free investigation of the canon' which was proclaimed by Johann Salomo Semler about two hundred and fifty years after Luther's Reformation as a legitimate legacy of the first beginnings and promptings of thought which are to be found in the Reformation. There is good reason for calling Semler the Luther of the eighteenth century. Granted, no direct line can be drawn from Luther to Semler and the later scholars who applied historical criticism to the Old and New Testaments. Too many influences from elsewhere played a part here: the Enlightenment, philosophical idealism, romanticism, secular history and archaeological discoveries, and even analytical literary criticism. However, historical criticism as applied to the biblical writings took up and continues to take up a basic concern of the Reformation in changed circumstances and with different means. It did this and continues to do it by seeking to lay open the way to an encounter with scripture by questioning and demolishing supposed certainties and assurances, and thus in its own way asserting the *sola scriptura* even in the face of Protestant authorities and traditions in dogma and ministry. The analogy to the Reformation doctrine of justification: only through faith in Christ, only in the light of his Word, is in fact unmistakable (cf. Gerhard Ebeling, 'The Significance of the Critical Historical Method', IB, 55ff.).

4. *Dogmatic system and church restoration*

To begin with, of course, historical criticism and its findings had a negative effect and seemed to take the ground from under church doctrine and the life of faith. This was the way in which it first attracted the attention of a wide public, largely presenting a negative aspect, so that right down to the present it is suspected of mounting an attack on Christianity. However, this should not tell against its legitimacy in the tradition of the Reformation; there are other reasons for such a reception. These lie in a retrograde movement of which there was already evidence in the time of Luther. This is not the place to investigate whether this reaction and the conservative attitude of the church was historically inevitable and whether it was really necessary. Be that as it may, the fact is that the churches which came into being as a result of the Reformation developed their own dogmatics and a new scholastic system. Dogmatics tended to become a system, and in a system it was difficult to accommodate the distinction between law and gospel, which was related to human existence. Moreover, it was difficult within a clear dogmatic system to give expression to the peculiar overlap between the old covenant and law and the new covenant and gospel on the one hand, and the two parts of the canon on the other, as opposed to an identification of the Old Testament, the old covenant and the law, and the New Testament, the new covenant and the gospel. Moreover, it was easier to understand the principle of *sola scriptura* in a different way. Instead of being seen, as it was originally, in terms of a hermeneutical principle stating that scripture was its own interpreter, it was more easily understood as an assertion of the identity of scripture and the Word of God. Thus the clarity of the subject-matter of scripture, i.e. the gospel in its polarity to the law, became what was supposed to be the clarity of the inspired literal sense of scripture. This dogma of verbal inspiration – which is what it amounted to – smoothed out all distinctions and nuances which had either already appeared or were just beginning to appear. For if holy scripture is verbally inspired, the distinction between the Old and New Testaments is concealed.

Thus in the last edition of 1561, Melanchthon's *Loci communes* of 1521, the first systematization of the Reformation approach, teach that the same voice of the prophets and apostles can be heard teaching all the essential truths of salvation: sin, redemption through Christ, eternal life and the true worship of God. The assertion of an identity between the two testaments which speak with one and the same voice (*eadem vox*) is then largely qualified by the claim that the promise of the gospel was only begun in the old covenant. So here too the polarity of law and gospel which embraces the two testaments is combined with the other theme of a salvation history which runs from promise to fulfilment.

To begin with, *Calvin*'s understanding of scripture was of more importance for later theological developments, especially in Switzerland and the non-German-speaking churches of the Reformation. It was hardly different from that of Luther and his followers except in its emphasis. A man of the second generation, an outstandingly learned interpreter, a dogmatic theologian, a churchman concerned for church order because of its importance for salvation and a preacher all in one, Calvin was more than a 'church father' of the Reformed church (renewed on the basis of the Word of God and the ordinance of the gospel). Taking up dogmatic thinking from before the Reformation, especially Anselm of Canterbury's theology of satisfaction (that Christ had vicariously acquired the merits which man had failed to achieve), Calvin became the great systematic theologian of the Reformation. Although he did not particularly stress the fact, for Calvin, scripture as a whole is inspired. It is inspired in that it is the instrument of the Holy Spirit, but not in the way that was claimed by the later orthodox doctrine of inspiration, namely that the Word of God and the word of scripture are identical. Its inspired quality, understood in this way, presupposes its unity in principle. For Calvin, this does not of course mean that salvation can as it were be read directly from the inspired words. Inspiration of scripture is no guarantee of salvation. Salvation is received only through faith, which perceives the truth and the significance of scripture through the testimony of the Holy Spirit (*testimonium Spiritus Sancti internum*), and that is completely outside man's disposal. Nor does the pre-eminence of scripture exclude historical and philological criticism. Whereas Calvin the dogmatic theologian requires the unity of the inspired scriptures, which are the written testimony to the one Word of God that bears the name of Jesus Christ, Calvin the exegete is well aware of the distinctions and nuances within scripture. For him they arise from the fact that the one Word of God is expressed in different ways, but is aimed at one and the same salvation. If with Luther law and gospel are seen in a polar relationship, which seems to pull God's will in two directions and even to express it in two different sets of words, Calvin's understanding tends rather to preserve the unity of the two as two aspects of the same word of God: even the law is aimed at man's salvation, in that it wards off the disaster of sin and convinces man of his sinfulness.

This view is not fundamentally different from that of Luther, but it puts the stress in a different place: the pure *dialectic* of law and gospel here becomes an ordinance of salvation leading from the law, which wards off corruption and convicts the evil one, via the gospel to sanctification under the law. The law only leads to death if Christ is ignored, and freedom from the law is based on and consists in the fact that Christ has vicariously fulfilled the law. Thus the law has lost its death-dealing power, but not its force as law.

The unity of law and gospel understood in this way finds its expression in the term 'covenant'. This word is a translation of the Latin *foedus* = treaty, which again is a not wholly adequate translation of the Hebrew *berit*. Since the Old Testament *berit* as applied to God never signifies a two-sided treaty, but a union with mutual obligations, covenant in this new dogmatic usage means both the promise and the approach of God, and his claims and his law. At the same time, covenant understood in this way became an important doctrinal principle, a theologoumenon, in Reformed dogmatics, with the help of which it was possible in particular to define the relationship between the testaments as a history of covenants – Adam, Noah, Abraham, Christ.

Here, too, Reformed dogmatics was able to take up the thought of the early church: in his polemic against Gnosticism Irenaeus had already stressed the unity of the testaments and had rooted this unity in God's own self, the one God who acts in several covenants. As early as 1534 a monograph appeared from the pen of Heinrich Bullinger, Zwingli's successor in Zurich, with the title, *De testamento seu foedere Dei unico et aeterno* (On the testament or the only and eternal covenant with God), which made the concept of the covenant the corner-stone of biblical theology. From then on covenant, which was fully developed as a theologoumenon especially by Caspar Olevian and then by Cocceius (see 63ff below), remained the biblical clamp which held Old and New Testaments together in Reformed dogmatics and was to guarantee the biblical character of such dogmatics.

The interrelation between law and gospel expressed in the concept of the covenant corresponds to the essential unity of scripture in the two Testaments, and the unity of the scriptures as a witness to the one saving will of God attests and describes *the inner unity of the law and the gospel.*

The juxtaposition of the testaments also calls attention to their temporal sequence and thus to the uniqueness and historicity of the Christ event. But both are testimony to Christ, the Old in a shadowy way, in expectation and promise, the New as a document of fulfilment. Now this distinction too is one of degree only, because Christians after Christ, like the faithful men of the Old Testament before him, live only by faith and not by sight, and in the expectation of his return. So although the faithful men of the old covenant, Adam, Noah, Abraham, Isaac, Jacob and the prophets and men of God, lived before Christ, they were illuminated by the one Son of God so that they could recognize the truth and the salvation of God. Once the unity of the Bible was stressed in this way, it was no longer possible to make parts of it of relative importance, as a Jewish social code, in the way that

Luther once did, or even to repudiate it. Even the ceremonial law is rooted in the covenant of grace; it was the basis and form of religion in the old covenant and its worship, which pointed forward in a shadowy way to Christ. The sacrificial law, too, is fulfilled by Christ's sacrifice, in relation to which it already has its true meaning. This christocentric approach – which is doubtless correct in the context of Christian theology – is taken much further and much deeper than it is in Luther: God has finally and definitively revealed himself once for all in Jesus Christ and has brought salvation, so Old Testament texts are interpreted in a directly christological way. Inferences are drawn from the texts to support what the dogmatic approach has already decided to be there. This means that on the one hand the richness of the Old Testament is at least partly suppressed: if the Old Testament texts themselves have no christological message, or do not prophesy Christ, and yet are reshaped and interpreted or transformed in this direction, they can no longer have their own content. On the other hand, the weight of the Old Testament interpreted directly in a Christian way can also make itself felt to a considerable degree in another direction. What we have here is more than the interpretation of the Christ event with the help of Old Testament conceptions and terms. This was already done by the earliest community when it called Jesus the Messiah, the Christ, the Son of God, the Son of David, the Son of man. The interpretations taken from the Old Testament now begin, rather, to assimilate the New to the Old, and the danger arises that the eschatological, final and ultimate newness of the Christ event and its power to bring liberation from all the old circumstances, which are now said to be past and gone, can no longer be given full expression. In such apparent equalization the Old Testament begins to dominate the New, and the new covenant becomes the restoration of the old which had been broken by the sin of Israel. The recognition, already expressed in the Old Testament, that the new covenant will not be like the old one (Jer. 31.32), seems to be forgotten. We may not wish to accuse the Reformer Calvin of a new legalism, but he certainly seems to have laid the foundations for this and to have prompted a development towards a legalistic pattern of Christian life in the communities which appealed to his authority. This can only be denied by those who have no eyes for what actually happened afterwards.

5. The dogma of inspiration and the predominance of dogmatic theology

It is clear that the new dogmatic theology also concealed the hermeneutical problem of the Old Testament by swallowing it up, instead of demonstrating it or even solving it. Because of this failure, and because of the course of doctrinal history after the Reformation, it was inevitable that when the problems were raised again they were now put forward with greater force. The new (or renewed) questioning, which began to topple the dogmatic constructions which had been erected, seemed to put in question the church and Christian belief as a whole.

In a way which was probably historically inevitable, early Protestant orthodoxy was concerned to safeguard the legacy of the Reformation. But if the Reformation brought with it a questioning of man's security and an exposure of the falseness of the assurances that were thought to be provided by dogma, sacraments and ministry, this attempt at a safeguard must inevitably have been problematical from the start. The dogma of the inspiration of the Bible, carried to extremes, is one of the most important principles of orthodoxy. Of course, the view that scripture is inspired had a long history.

Within the books of the Bible, II Tim. 3.16 speaks of the Old Testament as a writing which is '*theopneustos*', which in the Latin translation is rendered by the concept of 'inspiration' (*scriptura divinitus inspirata*). In view of the context, the thought here is probably of the particular, exalted significance of scripture, which is permeated by the Spirit of God and given by God himself. This distinguishes the Bible from purely human writings. The supposition is certainly not that by virtue of this quality the scriptures are superhuman, divine and inspired down to the last syllable. In any case, the Old Testament is familiar with the conception that God himself dictates his commandments or has even written them on the tablets of the law (Ex. 34.27f.; 24.12; 31.18; 32.16). Jewish doctrine could argue from this that God had dictated the law directly to Moses word for word, and that the prophets and the writings, the two other parts of the canon, were similarly inspired. Hellenistic Judaism then developed a theory according to which the individual books of the Bible go back to inspired prophets who wrote down the revelations of God in a state of inspired ecstasy. Human authors in this way become mere instruments, without wills or characteristics of their own. Despite the influence of Hellenism and Hellenistic Judaism, this strict version of the theory of inspiration failed to maintain a footing in the early church. It is indeed the case that from the time of Irenaeus (*c.* 180), Origen (died 254) and Augustine (died 430), among others, scripture was thought to be inspired, but it was not thought that the biblical writers had been used as pliant implements in some ecstatic frenzy, with no individual awareness of God. On the contrary, inspiration was thought of as an illumination and an intensification of human intellectual capabilities.

It was only after the Reformation, when the authority of scripture – *sola scriptura* – had been produced as a weapon against tradition, the teaching ministry and sacramentalism, in an utterly consistent way, that this development of the scriptural principle could be used in controversies with the church of Rome, with enthusiasts who claimed to possess the Spirit, and also as a defensive measure to protect and reinforce the Reformation understanding of the scriptures. This development was the work of Protestant orthodoxy. For all their stress on the priority of the writings of the Old and New Testaments and the inseparable connection between the scriptures and the Word of God, the Reformers had never identified Word and scripture, and even Luther had used the Word which proceeds from both law and gospel as a criterion for criticizing scripture itself, which even allowed him to dare to speak of a strawy epistle. Now, however – and this was an essential characteristic of the orthodox doctrine of scripture – the dialectic of the Word of God and scripture was surrendered in favour of an identification which had the merit of didactic usefulness.

This led, as it were, to the duplication of the process of revelation: revelation, to which the scriptures bear witness, is accompanied by the supernatural event of the formation of an inspired scripture. Inspiration is understood as a divine impulse to write and as a communication of the precise wording. The supernatural origin of scripture is the basis for its truth and clarity down to the last syllable. The Reformers might originally have thought of clarity in terms of uniformity of subject-matter, i.e. the gospel, but now this became clarity in the grammatical sense, though of course this did not exclude the mystery of what was meant by the words. This shift from the subject-matter to the way in which it is expressed and to the words in which it is framed is matched by a change in the understanding of the subject-matter itself: the gospel, which derives its existential force from the words of scripture, becomes a doctrine, a way of teaching and providing instruction in the truths and the mysteries of salvation, which the believer has to accept. In its most extreme form this doctrine claims that all the letters of the canonical scripture and even the

Hebrew vocalizations are inspired in this sense (this is the case with the Lutheran superintendent Johann Gerhard in Coburg or with the two Reformed theologians, Johann Buxtorf senior and junior, in Basle). The Reformation concern for the doctrine of inspiration may have been to preserve the *sola scriptura* in the controversy with the teaching authority of the Roman Catholic church, but in fact it gave a very inadequate formulation to the legacy of the Reformation, systematizing it and certainly falsifying it (however unintentionally). The medium and the instrument of the gospel become the letter which is revealed by a miracle and set down on paper, a kind of 'paper Pope'. The truth of the gospel becomes the clarity of scripture and what it contains. The hermeneutical principle that the gospel contained in scripture and attested by it is its own interpreter – *sola scriptura* – becomes a doctrine of scripture which defines – and in a rational way domesticates – the miracle of its derivation and origin. This is now set above scripture as a new doctrinal tradition explaining the content of scripture as doctrine – *doctrina*, as already in Calvin – about the truths and mysteries of salvation. The doctrine of scripture, which is set above scripture itself, now has a formal and material function as a new rule of faith and imposes new restrictions on exegesis. As the subject matter of scripture is a mystery, the doctrinal tradition of the Reformation – in a different way from, and yet similarly to, the Roman Catholic church – decides what is the true understanding, and exegesis is limited to an auxiliary function which does not fit with the supposed status of holy scripture as a normative norm.

In the end, the identification of gospel, inspired scripture and infallible doctrine finally levels out all differences, nuances, climaxes and nadirs and with them the distinction between the Old Testament and the New. Thus everything written in scripture and presupposed by it appears as divine doctrine: the Aristotelian and Ptolemaic view of the world with the earth at the centre (according to Josh. 10.12 the sun stands still!); angels, devils, demons, miracles; the creation of the world in six days; the biblical framework for world history with the enumeration of years, and so on. The integration of the orthodox system of doctrine is imposing, but it inevitably condemns anyone who has doubts about a single 'biblical truth' as an utter heretic, because such doubts put in question the doctrinal truth of the Bible as a whole and thus undermine the foundation of the doctrinal system. The sharpness and cruelty with which even the church, reformed in accordance with the word of God, could react to such questioning is shown by the struggle against the so-called Socinians and the execution of

Michael Servetus (1553, cf. below, 149). However, fundamental questioning inevitably provoked a revolution.

6. *The beginnings of a theology of history*

Even negative ideals are seldom realized. There can be no doubt that during the period of orthodoxy, as in the pre-Reformation church, the gospel was still proclaimed and believed, and the writings of the Old and New Testaments were not encased in the hard rationalistic shell of their supposedly verbal inspiration, but also found notable interpreters in theology and the church, not least in church music – we might think of the cantatas and oratorios of Johann Sebastian Bach which are based on biblical texts.

Elsewhere too, however, the independent validity of scripture, which had been rediscovered by the Reformation and had not been denied by Protestant orthodoxy, battered against and broke through the encrustation of dogma. This did not only happen because it was recognized that the dogmatic system needed a biblical basis and biblical proof. The Bible was used as a collection of didactic statements that proved dogma (*dicta probantia*), and there arose a new theological discipline which took upon itself the task of collecting the *dicta probantia* and making them the standard for dogmatic theology.

Thus as early as 1560–1565 there appeared two collections of biblical proofs by Johann Wigand and Matthaeus Richter, the Old Testament part of which bears the name *Syntagma seu corpus doctrinae veri et omnipotentis Dei ex veteri Testamento tantum, methodica ratione ... dispositum* ('A complete collection [of passages] on the doctrine of the true and almighty God taken only from the Old Testament and arranged in a methodical fashion) (Diestel, Ic, 290). In accordance with orthodox doctrine and its understanding of the Old Testament, all the truths of the Christian faith are already 'proved' from the Old Testament. Nevertheless, here too we can still see the Reformation primacy of holy scripture.

However, the primacy of the Bible and the independent force of the biblical writings began to put pressure on the structure of Christian doctrine elsewhere than in such sets of biblical proofs.

The most significant pioneer in this respect was Johannes Cocceius (1603–1689, born in Bremen and later active in Leiden). His approach was meant to be not only a biblical basis for existing dogmatics, the correctness of which was to be proved subsequently, but a theology that was directly oriented on the Bible. A historical development was set over against the static system of doctrine. Although Cocceius himself went on to understand this development as a doctrinal system, his work (IIIB) in fact amounted to a rediscovery of the historical references of both Old and New Testaments. Continuing specifically Reformation approaches as represented by Zwingli, Calvin, Bullinger, Olevian and others (see 58 above), and taking up genuinely biblical categories, Cocceius uses the concept of the covenant as a clamp and a principle for organizing the sequence of salvation history into a number of periods. It progresses from covenant to covenant. This defines the relationship between Old and New Testaments in terms of the theology of history. This exercised a powerful effect against the dogmatic tendency to fuse them together, though Cocceius, like the theology of his time, was convinced that there was also direct testimony to Christ in the Old Testament.

This conviction was also the basis for his view which does not teach a simple temporal sequence of law in the Old Testament and gospel in the New, but, starting from other presuppositions and using other means, re-expresses their dialectical relationship. The first covenant was the covenant of works and the natural covenant which is written in men's hearts, and this was codified by Moses. However, even the *protevangelium* in Gen. 3.15, with its promise of eternal redemption, is a dialectical counterpart which announces the continuing course of God's history. It leads from the covenant of works, which is done away with by the sin of Adam, via the establishment of a covenant of grace, to the appearance of Jesus Christ in whose blood the new covenant is founded, and then at last, by way of the time of the church and sanctification, to the resurrection of the dead. This history – which is at the same time both a heavenly/divine and an earthly/ human process – is a history of the progressive abrogation of the fatal consequences which follow for men from the breaking of the covenant of works; that these consequences are effective down to the present day is indicated by the fact that while the covenant of works is invalid, it is still not without its aftermath. Law and gospel, works and the righteousness of grace, and thus Old Testament and New Testament, do not follow one another in a straight line, but have a dialectical relationship in the course of time, despite the increasing clarity of revelation.

It is, of course, no surprise that even this biblically oriented theology does not work out without typological exegesis which reads the system into the text. In this respect Cocceius is no different from his contemporaries. But his recognition of the dialectical and temporal-historical distinction between the two testaments and thus of the historicity of revelation, which broke through static dogma and was criticized by orthodoxy as innovation, was indeed pioneering.

Johann Albrecht Bengel (1687–1752) presented similar ideas in a German context. As for Cocceius, for Bengel the Bible of Old and New Testaments is an interconnected whole which was willed to have this form by God. Christ is its goal and its content first and last. For Bengel, too, revelation is not static and doctrinal; it is to be understood historically in accordance with a history directed by God – the *ordo temporum* (IIIB). Here, too, the return to the Bible and to biblical history gives a powerful impulse to philological and historical exegesis, even if this is crossed with the prior assumption that the whole of the Bible makes up a harmony. In Bengel, we also find the effect of another powerful influence, that of *pietism*, which can no longer be content with mere correctness and cold doctrine, and seeks from the Bible not only true teaching, but edification. Edification should not be misunderstood here in terms of superficial piety; it means the foundation of Christian existence and the Christian community on faith in Christ, which is directed towards the Word communicated through scripture. To hear this Word is the goal of exegesis, hence the hermeneutical instruction with its almost existentialist ring, which has been the motto of the Nestlé text of the Greek New Testament down to the present day: '*Te totum applica ad textum: rem totam applica ad te*' (Apply yourself wholly to the text; apply its whole content to yourself).

7. Philology and history

Despite his biblically oriented theology, Cocceius had been primarily a dogmatic theologian. He cannot therefore be called the father of biblical theology as a special discipline. His federal (covenant) theology on historical lines was itself a closed dogmatic system. But it did claim to be based directly on the Bible itself. However, the Bible does not disclose itself without being interpreted, and exegesis in turn is impossible without linguistic, philological, text-critical and historical knowledge. Cocceius had a good deal of this, but above all, his kind of theologizing is an incentive to acquire even more historical and philological insights.

Some of Cocceius' contemporaries also had insights of this kind. However, philology and history, applied to the biblical texts, could in the long run undermine the dogmatic system and bring down the whole edifice of doctrine like a pack of cards, even if there was no intention to produce a theological system or to criticize the church's dogma.

Not only outright attacks – like that from Socinianism (see 148f. below) and then the general onslaught of rationalism (see 148ff) – were to prove dangerous to church doctrine and the significance of the Old Testament. If sober textual criticism like that of the Roman Catholic Jean Morin (1591–1651) – which was only carried on in order to avoid having to recognize the 'Protestant' Hebrew text – showed up differences in the textual tradition of holy scripture, discrepancies between various manuscripts of the original text and even in translation, what was the relationship between the dogma of the verbal inspiration of scripture and the reality that could be ascertained? To put this question was to answer it, even if the answer was slow in coming and caused great confusion, serious doubts, or was even suppressed. Philological and historical learning were still not the perquisites of a wide public. But such illuminating insights as could be communicated before any kind of exegesis, simply by comparing different forms of the text, could not in the long run remain secret knowledge.

It is to the credit of Reformation theology that despite all the resistance from the church and from within theology, it never suppressed this critical knowledge, but developed it as far as possible. It made critical biblical scholarship its own concern instead of leaving it to philologists, historians and archaeologists.

Philology, historical criticism, archaeology, the general study of religion, and even philosophy and reflections on hermeneutics which were developed and applied by theologians within theology, spurred on by the new enlightened spirit of a new time with its new picture of man and – thanks to Copernicus – of the world, rased to the foundations the dogmatic construction which once supported the church. The history of this destruction as a rediscovery of scripture which was only possible in this way, cannot and need not be described in full detail here; readers must be referred to H.-J. Kraus, *Geschichte der historisch-kritischen Erforschung des Alten Testaments* (Ic), and, for the parallel New Testament area, W. G. Kümmel, *The New Testament. The History of the Investigation of its Problems* (IIIb). Here we can draw only the main outlines and the most important contours of these developments within scholarship, since they are necessary for a proper understanding of the hermeneutical problem of the Old Testament as it presents itself today.

In its most extreme form, the dogma of verbal inspiration also taught the inspired nature of the consonants and vowels of the Hebrew text. So it is understandable that a vigorous debate would ensue when Louis Cappel (Ludovicus Capellus, 1585–1658), French professor of Hebrew, demonstrated that the vocalization had only been added to the text in the post-Christian period by Jewish scholars. It was not therefore of Christian origin. Now products of Jewish learning after Christ could not have been inspired by the Holy Spirit. This was the only possible conclusion. The mere fact of the anonymous publication of Capellus' book, entitled *Arcanum punctationis revelatum* (The mystery of vocalization revealed), in which he demonstrated the real derivation of the vocalization, is evidence enough that what seemed to be simply a philological question was explosive because it attacked the dogma of inspiration. His conclusions are no longer doubted today, and those who challenged them – including the Hebrew scholar Buxtorf (see 62 above) – finally had to return their blunt swords to their sheaths if they were not to perish by the sword themselves.

However, works without immediate explosive force also began to exercise their influence. In the years after 1641 the Dutchman Hugo de Groot (Hugo Grotius, 1583–1645), jurist, philologist, theologian, diplomat and statesman, had written his *Annotationes ad vetus et novum testamentum* (Notes on the Old and New Testament). The work was intended to help personal reading of the biblical texts by providing explanatory notes, and not to lay the foundation of a biblical theology in the style of Cocceius or Bengel. The historical value of these notes lies in their freedom from dogmatic and other preconceptions and in the way in which they make the text the object of a cool scientific approach. Even the authority of the New Testament, which was postulated unconditionally by dogmatic theology, and with it the authority of Old Testament quotations in the New Testament, could be put in doubt if a clear historical and philological approach gave good reason. The only true and tenable sense is what is meant by the text itself. The fact that Grotius did not play off this approach in polemical fashion against the traditional ecclesiastical, dogmatic and christological interpretation was either a matter of inconsistency, or more probably a wise concession on the part of a man who was more concerned with peace than with polemical destruction.

The critical work by the Roman Catholic priest Richard Simon (1638–1712), *Histoire critique du Vieux Testament*, 1678, extends further and penetrates even deeper. It led to his expulsion from his order. Here we find not only textual criticism, but the foundation for the literary criticism and analysis of the five books of Moses, the Pentateuch. Simon develops a theory (a 'critical history') about the origin of the Old Testament which is a long way removed from traditional and orthodox views. He explains that Moses cannot himself be the author of the so-called books of Moses; he evidently entrusted the composition and editing of annals and laws to public scribes. Later writers will have drawn on these, and the present form of the Pentateuch will only have been reached after the confusion of the exilic period. In essentials, this is an anticipation of the later documentary hypothesis, which suggests that the Pentateuch arrived at its final form as a result of the interweaving of several continuous narrative threads (documents), or the fragmentary hypothesis, according to which the Pentateuch is a combination of early independent traditions (fragments) which were not interconnected. Simon's method and results are no longer tenable from a present-day perspective, but he too did important pioneer work in a sphere into which few at that time were prepared to venture.

Persecuted as a heretic and imprisoned in Brussels, and then set free again after a recantation, the French Protestant theologian Isaac de la Peyrère discovered that the rule of dogma extended beyond the realm of the intellect. He put forward a theory about the origin of the Pentateuch which differed from that of Simon, but which was none the less a departure from traditional teaching. He used arguments old and new to deny the Mosaic authorship of the Pentateuch, thinking rather of writers whose work must have predated Moses and have been used by him. His theory that there must have been men before Adam also roused attention. (These he called 'pre-Adamites' in his work *Praeadamitae sive exercitatio super versibus duodecimo, decimotertio et decimoquarto capitis quinti epistolae D.Pauli ad Romanos. Quibus inducuntur Primi homines ante Adamum conditi* [The Pre-Adamites or a study of Romans 5.12–14 which introduces the first men created before Adam], 1655.) At almost the same time in England Thomas Hobbes wrote his *Leviathan* (1651), developing his political philosophy and at the same time touching on the foundations of biblical dogma with his view that at least a large part of the fifth book attributed to Moses, Deuteronomy, could not have been written by him, and that the books of Joshua and Daniel were not – or not wholly – written by the people whose names they bear.

Jean Le Clerc (Clericus, 1657–1736), a theologian who emigrated from Geneva to Holland and a supporter of the more liberal Reform movement of the Remonstrants (the Arminians), would accept the validity only of purely scientific methods in textual criticism and the reconstruction of original wording and meaning, without reference to traditional doctrine; this scientific approach often demonstrated contradictions, oversights and inadequacies in scripture which were clear evidence of its human origin, regardless of the theoretical possibility of divine revelation.

Another scholar to dispute the inspiration of scripture, also in Holland, was the Jewish philosopher Baruch Spinoza (1632–1697). In particular he questioned Moses' authorship of the Pentateuch, putting forward detailed arguments based on the text in his *Tractatus theologicopoliticus* (1670). Spinoza does not stop at literary and historical criticism; his *philosophical* criticism also bears on the content of Old Testament religion. This he interprets and decries as a nationalistic and egoistic faith in election, which is limited to earthly things. His book is important evidence for the dawn of a rationalistic and scientific way of thinking. Characteristically for the time, it could only be published anonymously, and was said to have been produced in Hamburg rather than in Amsterdam. This was the beginning of a development which was to lead to a new Babylonian captivity. The Old Testament, scarcely freed from the fetters of dogma, was now to be given over to those concerned with abstract reason and rationalistic morality.

The standards of rationalism were not just applied from outside theology; theologians also acknowledged them. Deistic ideas spread to the Continent from England. Deism was more an attitude of mind than a theological or philosophical system, and sought to hold together belief in God, freedom of thought, and ethics. In Germany, Hermann Samuel Reimarus (1694–1768) wrote his *Apologie oder Schutzschrift für die vernünftigen Verehrer Gottes* (Apologia or Defence for Rational Worshippers of God), which was made public by Gotthold Ephraim Lessing; in it the so-called religion of reason was elevated to be the basis and touchstone of all alleged revelation.

A few years later, Johann Salomo Semler wrote his famous 'Treatise on the Free Investigation of the Canon' (1771–1775, IIIb). He argued that the foundation of the Christian religion, the Bible, should be fully opened up to free investigation, not in order to destroy the Christian religion but rather to demonstrate that its essential content was in accord with reason. Such a critical investigation shows that the Bible is a human book which came into being in history, even though it seeks to give testimony to the revelation of God. In this way the old distinction between the Word of God and scripture, to be found in the Reformers, is expressed again on new presuppositions. Semler's clear insight into the number of historical periods involved and the differences between them was of particular importance for future developments: the biblical writers could only be understood in terms of the particular conditions which shaped them; in terms of culture, morality, nation and historical circumstances, these conditions differed from conditions today. This insight excludes the possibility of a *direct* understanding in our present and a *direct* application to another, new present. Here Semler gave clear expression to the hermeneutical problem not only of the Old Testament but of the Bible in general and indeed of all writings from the past: 'It is therefore false to assume that Holy Scripture always, and in the first instance, brings about men's edification and must also be directly employed to that end. It is absolutely necessary that the proper historical knowledge first be acquired, and only later the saving knowledge awaited' (cited in W. G. Kümmel, *The New Testament*, IIIB, 66). This is to say that a direct 'dogmatic' approach to scripture, which postulates its validity here and now, is ruled out because of the historical interval involved. Theology must adopt a historical approach because its object, scripture, is a document which must primarily be seen as direct historical evidence. It must also adopt a historical approach because the revelation to which the scripture bears witness is given to a historical figure and is therefore itself a historical process.

However, rationalistic criticism and a growing historical consciousness were not the only things to shake the traditional edifice of doctrine. As early as 1675, Philipp Jakob Spener (1635–1705), in his '*Pia Desideria*, or a Hearty Desire for a God-pleasing Improvement of the true Protestant Church', had expressed a 'hearty desire' that dogmatics and church doctrine and practice might be improved by correct and simple biblical theology. They had not, he thought, left the true faith, but had become encrusted with a great many trimmings and other useless things which were no help to the true religion. Spener was not suggesting a new theological discipline called 'biblical theology'. Rather, the whole of theology was to be freed from Protestant scholasticism and to be derived from the foundations and principles laid down in the Bible and the Reformation. By virtue of its recourse to scripture and the principle of *sola scriptura*, Luther's Reformation was itself more than just a reform. Although it only gradually became aware of the fact and never drew all the possible hermeneutical consequences, this reform represented the overthrow of the foundations of doctrine, sacrament and ministry which had grown up from the time of the early church. So, too, the 'hearty desire' for biblical theology gave no indication of the explosive force which would be released through the realization of such a programme. Only someone who naively supposed that the biblical theology looked for would correspond to the existing system of dogma could fail to recognize this. The period of the Enlightenment was against such naivety. 'Biblical theology', at one time the designation of a discipline auxiliary to dogmatics involving the collection and arranging of biblical proofs for the doctrinal system, and then a programmatic demand that the whole of theology should be reformed on the basis of the Bible according to the desires of the pietists, now became an independent science over against dogmatics.

This final consequence had yet to be drawn by Anton Friedrich Büsching, who published *Gedanken von der Beschaffenheit und dem Vorzug der biblisch-dogmatischen Theologie vor der alten und neuen scholastischen* (Thoughts on the nature and advantage of biblical dogmatic theology over scholasticism old and new, 1758). This is evident simply from the title. Rather, dogmatic 'scholastic' theology is to be replaced or superseded by a theology which draws on the Bible and nothing else. This new biblical theology is itself dogmatics. However, Büsching does recognize that in some respects the 'scholastic' doctrinal system and the Bible do not correspond, and that dogmatics has suppressed the truth of the Bible.

Only one conclusion could be drawn from such a recognition, as from the historical and hermeneutical principles formulated by Semler, which from now on ruled out the direct use of scripture in dogmatics through the collection of proof texts (*dicta probantia*). And it was indeed drawn by Johann Philipp Gabler (1757–1826) in his *Oratio de justo discrimine theologiae biblicae et dogmaticae regundisque recte utriusque finibus* (Discourse on the right differentiation between biblical and dogmatic theology and the proper definition of their spheres of competence), which appeared in 1787, not many years before the outbreak of the French Revolution. Though it was by no means revolutionary – in his 'History of Modern Protestant Theology' (IIIB, V, 57) Emanuel Hirsch regarded Gabler as a 'half-baked rationalist' – this work was an important step towards a new theological discipline and thus towards a new understanding of theology generally. The real progress made here was in defining biblical theology as a *historical discipline* Its task was to work out what the biblical writers had meant. This was to be done by an exact historical attempt to distinguish the times in which works were written – the *ordo temporum* – the individuality of the writers, and the stages of development in spiritual and religious life. Recognizing the individual personalities of the writers, the uniqueness of their historical situations and the stages of spiritual development within the biblical writings involved the acknowledgment of their historicity and human fallibility and represented a challenge to the dogma of verbal inspiration. Gabler was not launching a polemical attack to destroy the authority of the Bible (see the quotations collected by W. G. Kümmel, *The New Testament*, IIIB, 98ff.); he hoped that careful historical criticism and a comparison with the historical documents of other peoples would prove to be to the credit of scripture, rightly understood. In contrast to a historical kind of biblical theology defined in this way, dogmatic theology has the character of Christian philosophy (*philosophia Christiana*); it is not historical, but relates to the present and takes a distinctive form depending on the confession within which it is practised. A remarkably rationalistic feature of Gabler's view is that biblical theology can remain the same at all times and in all places because it is a historical discipline. This is because he believes that its task is to depict events in the past which are finished and therefore cannot be altered, and to deduce from what is historically conditioned, and therefore relative, notions and concepts which are generally valid for everyone everywhere. Once again, this is only a partial recognition of the historicity of the scriptures which are to be investigated by the historical method: one element is time-conditioned and transitory, but within this shell there is something else which is universally valid and always true. Since this latter element is all that matters, and dogmatic theology quarries it from scripture by means of historical theology, refining out for the present the universal truths which it contains, biblical theology once again simply remains the handmaid of dogmatic theology. Above all, however, the fault of such an approach is not just that it misunderstands the historicity of the whole of scripture. To suppose that historical research can describe, and therefore understand, history as past events which are finished once and for all and consequently cannot be changed is to fail completely to understand the nature of the historical dimension. This draws even the academic historian with his own perspective and his own historical conditioning into the field of force of the tradition on which he is working and which he is trying to interpret. For Gabler, too, rationalism was a limitation which he was unable to overcome. Thus the proper distinction between historical and dogmatic theology which he tried to draw – *de justo discrimine* – remained blurred, as unfortunately it still does for many theologians two centuries later ...

Nevertheless, Gabler's work represents a decisive step forward. This is not just a matter of method. His insight into the way in which the content of the Bible is historically conditioned, relative and varied was of particular relevance to the Old Testament. What was now being described was not primarily the *biblical* history as a history of salvation and a *divine* economy of ages and covenants (which had been the approach of federal theology), but a history of *human* development, divided into periods and affected by the passage of time. In each individual period it was possible to see a development from a lower to a higher level. Gabler shared with the Scottish philosopher David Hume, who wrote *The Natural History of Religion* (1757), the conviction that this whole development was a progression upwards – and this idea has been a continual motive force in biblical theology. The divine salvation history and the pattern of promise and fulfilment now becomes a *history of human progress*, however little this can dispense with divine guidance and instruction. Of course this development must not simply be seen as the repudiation and the rejection of earlier stages. Gabler's pupil Johann Gottfried Eichhorn (1752–1827) had already attempted to make the alien and the miraculous features of the Old Testament comprehensible by means of a new concept, that of myth – which was the way in which men expressed themselves in the earliest stages of their development. Gabler then went on to apply this method to the New Testament. The gradual development from childish, mythical thinking to the highest stages of the Christian religion was from this point of view more important than the distinction between the two testaments. The dividing line between them was only one moment in the whole of this progression. Finally, the only important things in both parts of the canon were the truths valid for all times. On the other hand, for such an approach the Mosaic laws about worship were as obsolete as Paul's obviously time-conditioned admonitions, as for instance that women had to veil their heads (I Cor. 11.22ff.). Thus the strange amalgamation of rationalism and historical insight which brought to light these historical differences also led to the two testaments being placed on different levels.

However, an important step forward had been taken towards historical differentiation, and Gabler's programme was soon incorporated in a biblical theology which was carried through by means of historical research. The work in which this was done was written by the Orientalist and theologian Georg Lorenz Bauer (1755–1806), who, like Gabler, worked in Altorf. It is significant that here biblical theology is already divided into a theology of the Old Testament and a theology of the New. 1796 saw the publication of Bauer's work, *Theologie des Alten Testaments oder Abriss der religiösen Begriffe der alten Hebräer. Von den ältesten Zeiten bis auf den Anfang der christlichen Epoche* (Theology of the Old Testament or an Outline of the Religious Concepts of the Ancient Hebrews. From the Earliest Times to the Beginning of the Christian Epoch). This was followed in 1800–1802 by a *Biblische Theologie des Neuen Testaments* (Biblical Theology of the New Testament). This separation and division was not simply caused by external considerations. A recognition of the various 'stages' of development, particularly a recognition of the passage of time, made such a division (with its consequent specialization) necessary. The reason for this distinction between disciplines was not so much academic specialization as the fact that once the historical differences had been recognized, specialization became unavoidable as a matter of method. Historical work could only progress if the instruments with which it was carried on were constantly refined. The title of the Old Testament part of Bauer's theology is well worth interpreting in historical terms! It is a theology *or* a chronological, historical account. This 'or' betrays the dilemma which had arisen. How could theology be *both historical and theological*? How could a chronological, historical account and a systematic presentation of theology be reconciled? The dilemma is one which has still not been resolved clearly and unanimously in discussions about the proper form and content of a biblical theology. It should also be noted that Bauer claims to provide an outline of 'religious concepts'. Even in the title of the work there is once again evidence of pressure from rationalism and the old dogmatic tradition on the new historic method, and this is clearly the case as the work itself proceeds. Elsewhere the relationship between Old and New Testaments is defined in terms of the history of development, and Christianity is seen as a religion which has grown out of Judaism. Of course there is more than continuity in this development: the higher stage represented by the Christian religion also displaces some Old Testament conceptions, like that of the political Messiah.

All this was already a token of the future. As a result of developments in the period after Semler and Gabler and the first attempts at realizing the new programme of historical theology, both biblical theology and historical work on the Old (and similarly on the New) Testament became increasingly specialized, and increasingly won independence from dogmatic theology. This new independence and freedom was still bound up with certain presuppositions of rationalist and Enlightenment philosophy, and to that degree was still constricted, but it did usher in a growing separation from traditional church doctrine. At the same time, because of what was thought to be the objective character of historical research, the new approach was necessarily different from all other previous and indeed contemporary approaches. Indeed, it left largely on one side the question of the theological, spiritual and existential significance of the biblical history and the results obtained by historical criticism for the present day. This developing autonomy of historical research over against dogmatics was certainly also a polemical matter, aimed at the tradition of the church and its predominance. Its impetus aided emancipation. Historical results which conflicted with traditional church doctrine were preferred; they proved especially welcome to those who produced them, occasionally causing a perverse delight at the difficulties that they would present to dogmatic theology.

If dogmas disappear as fixed points and eternal truths prove to be historically conditioned, what guide is there along the river of history? Now that dogma could no longer provide any map, it was supposed that a combination of understanding and a loving concern for individual peculiarities of history might prove to be the key. Church dogma was now replaced by idealist and romantic presuppositions, which were rarely thought through clearly or taken account of properly. Thus Johann Gottfried Herder (1744–1803) wrote under the significant title *Vom Geist der ebräischen Poesie* (The Spirit of Hebrew Poetry), and was pleased to steep himself in the language of the Psalter, leaving behind the limitations of rationalism. This approach prompted and in part anticipated the later research of Hermann Gunkel and others, the method of which was more exact, while at the same time introducing the thought and experience of Romanticism as hermeneutical presuppositions. Thus listening to the scriptures threatened to turn into being overwhelmed by the aesthetically pleasing melody of their background music. Stress on the historical, human, poetic, primitive character of the Old Testament tempered the independence and the alien character of the Old Testament *message* and forced it into the background, instead of prompting a real encounter with it.

Wilhelm Martin Leberecht de Wette (1780–1849), along with Schleiermacher one of the first professors of the new University of Berlin, who later worked in Basle, also understood feeling as a religious *a priori*. He was influenced by the romantic philosophy of religion put forward by Jakob Friedrich Fries. For all his historical criticism of the Bible he was very much a churchman, and attempted to liberate theology as a discipline and also Christian faith from the narrow-mindedness of rationalism. All the strange things in scripture, whatever seemed to be logically and historically impossible, miracles, myths understood as naively childish poems, were by no means obsolete simply because of their character; for religious sensibilities they could be images which reflected the divine nature itself. Aesthetic symbolism thus becomes the hermeneutical key which not only opens up dimensions hitherto unsuspected and calls attention to them, but also prevents access to an adequate understanding of what was originally meant and intended.

We shall have to discuss elsewhere (119, 153ff.) the fundamental rejection of the Old Testament by Friedrich Daniel Ernst Schleiermacher (1768–1834). This shows that the 'religious *a priori*' and 'religious sensibility' of the romantic and idealist movements could themselves prevent access to a genuinely historical understanding. Schleiermacher's christocentric theology, with its orientation on redemption, has a tendency to dissolve the historical Christ event (which includes the historical setting of Palestine, the particular period under Pontius Pilate and the history of Israel, along with the legacy which has come down in the Old Testament) in favour of an ahistorical christological and soteriological principle. The abandonment of the Old Testament is at the same time both the cause and the consequence of his approach.

As in the time of Marcion, this deliberate rejection of the Old Testament was not put into effect. In the long term the purely historical approach was a much more dangerous threat to the validity of the Old Testament; at one and the same time it both allowed its validity and showed it to be an alien work.

The designation which biblical theology was later to take as a mark of its new understanding of itself is significant in this respect. Biblical theology, at first the collection of biblical texts in the service of dogmatic theology, then a pietistic summons to the reform of theology which would show a way back to the simple truth of the Bible, now drew the outward – indeed extreme – consequence of its historical character and called itself the history of Israelite religion, as in the case of Rudolf Smend with his *Lehrbuch der alttestamentlichen Religionsgeschichte* (Textbook of the History of Old Testament Religion, 1893). This was to abandon the divisive 'or' in the title of G. Lorenz Bauer's theology. Without question the new name represented a new content. This content was history, understood as a process and a development moving from one stage to the next, one level to another. A division into theologies of the Old Testament and of the New was followed consistently by a division into a multiplicity of theologies, indeed religions, within the Old Testament and similarly within the New. There were religions of the patriarchs, of the time of Moses, the great prophets, post-exilic Judaism, wisdom and so on. Once the unity of the biblical canon had been broken, the parts of the canon also fell apart in the stream of history. Gabler's belief, that he could find some permanent foundation in conceptions and terms which would hold for all time, now proved to be a mirage. In history, everything is in flux. Hegel's philosophy and the idea of development served as landmarks in this flood, which threatened to overwhelm everything. Johann Karl Wilhelm Vatke (1806–1882) in particular sought to apply the philosophy of history put forward by Georg Friedrich Wilhelm Hegel (1770–1831), with its upward progression of thesis, antithesis and synthesis, to the Old Testament. His book, 'A Scientific Account of Biblical Theology. The Religion of the Old Testament developed according to the Canonical Books' (1835, IIIB), follows its philosophical model by dividing the religious development of Israel into three stages: pre-prophetic, prophetic and post-prophetic; these reflect a dialectical process with a logical progression, in which each unit has its rational significance. At the same time, starting from biblical theology, Vatke makes the attempt to bring history and a systematic approach to theology together in harmony: the historical process is a reflection of the absolute spirit in its movement; the outward course of history is the vehicle for the universal, by which the universal is made present and manifested. Vatke's conception is certainly imposing, but it stands and falls by factors other than the Hegelian philosophy on which it is based. Historical research, too, went beyond itself and soon showed that the manifold variety of the historical and the contingent could not be conceptualized and reduced to a logical system as easily as that. *This meant that history itself became a problem.*

8. The questioning of the 'biblical history'

The New Testament, too, raises the question of the correct interpretation of its historically conditioned message and especially of the mythology which is an integral part of its view of the world. Another question in the Old Testament sphere, however, is that of the theological significance of the course of history. When the New Testament is taken by itself, this either does not arise at all or is only a matter of marginal concern; in any case it does not appear in a central place. By contrast, the Old Testament relates a course of history which runs from Adam to the restoration after the exile. The problem is complicated by the fact that over large areas the historical picture sketched out by the Old Testament itself does not correspond to the real course of history worked out by historical criticism. The agreement between the history narrated in the Bible and the history of Israel was shattered by a number of blows which followed one after another in quite rapid succession. We have already mentioned doubts about the tradition that Moses was the author of the Pentateuch. Doubts and attempts in some way to retain the traditional picture of the rise of the first part of the Old Testament canon had occasionally come together. But the traditional picture could not be saved. De Wette had written a critical dissertation on the theme that Deuteronomy, the fifth book of Moses, was to be distinguished from the four preceding books of the Pentateuch and was the work of another author (*Dissertatio critica-exegetica, qua Deutero-nomium a prioribus Pentateuchi libris diversum, alius cuiusdam recentioris auctoris opus esse monstratur,* 1805). He sought to demonstrate, in terms which many people still accept today, that Deuteronomy in no way came from Moses, but was identical with the law which was dis-covered and introduced in the time of King Josiah of Judah (*c.* 620). This provided a fixed point, which could be dated almost exactly, for establishing the periods to which the various strata of the Pentateuch belonged. Eissfeldt has rightly pointed out that this produced the Archimedean point of pentateuchal criticism, 'to which it could attach itself in order to take the tradition of church and synagogue off its hinges, and put in its place an alternative dating of the Pentateuch and its parts' (*Introduction*, IIA, 171).

So much can be shifted around this Archimedean point, however, that one can consider putting it rather later, and a later date is often argued for with good reason. However, the point still remains 'Archimedean'. For if Deuteronomy is put late, this not only puts in question the Mosaic authorship of this part of the Pentateuch – that, and other things, had already happened in an earlier period of scholar-ship – but means that all the parts or strata of the Pentateuch which are later than Deuteronomy must be put in the period after 620. In fact de Wette's *Dissertatio critica* provided the impulse for a formal revolution in views and conceptions not only of the origin of the Pentateuch (the Torah!), but of the whole course of Israel's history and religion.

In a brilliant and indeed historically unique interplay and exchange of opinions going beyond national and confessional boundaries, the Old Testament scholars Eduard Reuss (1804–1891) in Strasbourg, Karl Heinrich Graf (1815–1869), Reuss's pupil from Mulhouse in Alsace (he did not have a chair), Abraham Kuenen (1828–1891), professor in Leiden, and finally Julius Wellhausen (1844–1918), professor in several German universities (Göttingen, Greifswald, Halle, Marburg), developed the Graf-Kuenen-Wellhausen theory which has been named after them.

According to this theory, which even now is still generally accepted in principle and is well founded in fact, the Pentateuch is composed of a number of different ancient documents, namely the Yahwist (J), the Elohist (E) – these sigla or designations are taken from the different names for God, Yahweh and Elohim, which are used in these documents – and the Priestly Writing (P). Whereas J and E are usually put in the early monarchy (tenth to ninth century), D is to be dated at the end of the seventh century, following de Wette's argument. As the Priestly Writing already presupposes Deuteronomy, and thus must come after de Wette's fixed point of 620, P must be dated even later, evidently in the exilic or post-exilic period. To P must be assigned above all the 'Mosaic' ritual legislation of the central books of the Pentateuch.

This hypothesis revolutionized all previous views and especially the general understanding of the Old Testament: the *law* and legalism, the worshipping community and its rites, come at the *end* and not at the beginning of the history of Israel and Judah. This history was then written by Abraham Kuenen (*De godsdienst van Israel*, 'The Religion of Israel', 1869–1870) and Julius Wellhausen (his *Sketch of the History of Israel and Judah*, which first appeared in 1881 as an article in the *Encyclopaedia Britannica*, was reissued separately in 1891; the *Prolegomena to the History of Ancient Israel*, ET 1885, was a revision of his *Geschichte Israels* of 1878). This was an enormous synthesis of the results of literary-critical analysis, which is still impressive even today. The new historical picture affected not least the understanding of Old Testament *law* (see ch. IV, 4, 124f.).

The new insights of the time proved as striking as real discoveries, but the new scientific account of history still recognized a course of history which began with Abraham and his descendants and extended via Moses, the exodus, the wanderings in the wilderness and the conquest down to the foundation of the state under Saul and David. The historical and critical view of history was a reduction of the biblical picture which had been purged of legends, miracles and oriental exaggerations and largely corrected so that the lawgiving by Moses in the central books of the Pentateuch could now be understood as a product of a later period and as an example of Jewish formalization. Even the recognition of the secondary literary character of the Sinai pericope left the wider framework of the course of history untouched. Wellhausen may have thought that his analysis and the overall picture of Israel's history and religion which resulted from it solved the main problems of Old Testament study, but it soon emerged that the new questions which were asked and the new methods to which they gave rise also threw up new problems and produced new solutions – which could often amount to a further disintegration of the historical picture which had been accepted hitherto. These new insights were not in fact brought in by literary criticism, which after the time of Wellhausen was increasingly refined and became ever more subtle, attempting to divide the sources further and to distinguish sub-sources and so on. The attention of a new generation of scholars, members of the so-called history of religions school (Albert Eichhorn, 1856–1926; Hermann Gunkel, 1862–1932; Hugo Gressmann, 1877–1927; Wilhelm Bousset, 1865–1920; Ernst Troeltsch, 1865–1923, and others), was directed more towards the elements of tradition contained in the written documents. The new question was that of the origin, history and function – *Sitz im Leben* – of these traditions before they were included in literary documents. Were they – like the psalms – part of a collection, the Psalter? Were they fixed in writing – as in the case of the prophetic books – and compiled as a literary whole? This new method of form criticism and traditio-historical criticism was not meant to replace the earlier criticism; it built on it, presupposing its results but going on beyond them. Whereas the sources identified by literary criticism could be dated and given a geographical context – at least hypothetically – and were undoubtedly of Israelite origin, the traditions which had been given fixed form within them showed many similarities with extra-biblical traditions and a number of borrowings from non-Israelite models. Many parts of the Old Testament did not seem to be original any longer: its view of the world, its myths – the creation, the flood and so on – and its prayer literature seemed to be common to the whole of the Near East and to be an expression of the general religious attitudes and world-view of that area in ancient times. It was easy to arrive at exaggerated conclusions in the ecstasy of new discoveries: everything in the Old Testament was thought to have been shaped by

Babylonian culture and to be dependent on it. Hugo Winckler, Alfred Jeremias and Peter Jensen, the 'Pan-Babylonians', thought that the Old Testament was no more than a late and unoriginal expression of a single, all-embracing Babylonian view of the world, and Friedrich Delitzsch sought to present this approach as a piece of popular polemic (cf. 153f. below).

However, it was not the polemic associated with the so-called 'Bible-Babylon' dispute, and the exaggerations that went with it, which took scientific discoveries one stage further and made the hermeneutical and theological problem of the Old Testament more acute. The extensive and serious research carried on by the history of religions school gave biblical religion a place in the wider history of religion, even if its individual peculiarities and specific features were not overlooked. Moreover, the traditions fixed in the written sources, documents, books of the Old Testament, were detached from this context and proved to be subject to historical change and constant development before they were given their final and ultimate literary form. Genre criticism and traditio-historical criticism were the tools by which this development could be documented and described. But what was the significance of *this history of constant change*? Did the history itself have any theological relevance? This question now became acute. The pressure became even greater when the consistent application of the traditio-historical method to the Pentateuch demonstrated that the picture of the early history of Israel, the canonical salvation history, which still corresponded largely to the canonical presentation, was not supported by historical research, even after it had been purged and reduced by literary criticism. The works of Gerhard von Rad (*The Problem of the Hexateuch*, 1938, ET 1966, IIIв), and Martin Noth (*The History of Pentateuchal Traditions*, 1948, ET 1972, IIIв), caused a revolution in this respect. According to the investigations of Martin Noth, which went even further than those of von Rad, the Pentateuch proved to be made up of formerly independent and original complexes of tradition.

The patriarchal narratives, the theme of the exodus, the wanderings in the wilderness, the conquest in Canaan and the revelation on Sinai were all regarded as particular themes, each with its own special origin. The theme of the wandering in the wilderness in turn proved to be made up of formerly independent traditions about particular places and characteristic features of the wilderness (sagas about springs of water, about manna, and so on). These themes were once the traditions of particular groups or clans who were the ancestors of what was later to become Israel, and were only later brought together and incorporated into Israelite tradition.

The result of this was to shatter the framework of the Pentateuchal narrative, since the sequence of themes was secondary to the independent individual traditions and the various sources which were originally the bearers of this tradition. The Pentateuch could not be used directly as history. In other words: the conquest might have taken place before the exodus from Egypt or the exodus before the events on Sinai. Indeed, it is no longer possible to answer the question about the sequence of events, as the contents of the Pentateuch consist of reflections, in the form of sagas, on experiences and even confessions of different groups. Even a somewhat more conservative view which would regard the theme of the exodus and the Sinai tradition as an original unity cannot make good the fundamental destruction of the framework of the Pentateuch and thus the course of the canonical history.

Just as Julius Wellhausen once summed up the analytical results of literary criticism in a great synthesis, so too Martin Noth wrote his *History of Israel* (1950, ET[2], 1960, IIIB) in which the themes of the Pentateuch were discussed as the 'traditions of the sacral alliance of the twelve tribes'. The history of Israel itself took place in Canaan, and only after the conquest.

Noth's book is a classic, and well reflects the state of scholarship at the time when it was written; it has also had its reputation enhanced because it exercises extreme restraint over the question of the theological significance of the traditio-historical approach and the way in which it is used to provide an account of the early history of Israel. However, this question cannot be suppressed permanently. If the history of Israel, however it may be understood, has a theological significance, however that may be expressed, the question must now be whether the relevant picture is that provided by the Old Testament history, or the real course of history reconstructed by research, or the tradition as such, or indeed all the aspects of this history.

9. *Attempts at a new 'theology' of the Old Testament*

Wilhelm Vatke attempted once again to reconcile historical theology and dogmatics and thus to solve the hermeneutical problem which lies in the relationship between history and its present validity. In terms of the standpoint and the presuppositions which he shared with

Hegel, this attempt was successful. However, even this artistic harmonization of historical research and Christian philosophy shattered when the progress of historical research brought increasingly to light an abundance of phenomena, events, interconnections and chance elements which could no longer be brought together in any philosophical or theological system. Thus historical theology, and especially Old Testament theology, which long before the history of religions school had increasingly been turning into the history of religions, kept moving further and further away from dogmatics, so that its very theological quality was becoming questionable. Interest in the history of religions brought to light not only those features which formed a connecting link across the ages, despite the interval of time, but also features that were wholly other, original, primitive, natural, primal and naive. Phenomena were discovered and investigated which seemed to have hardly any relevance to the life of the present-day church, or indeed to anything in the present. As a result the Old Testament, which was (and indeed could be) understood only in historical terms, seemed to have lost its significance for theology and the church unless it was interpreted along the lines of old-fashioned dogma. At one time historical theology had seemed to criticize and ultimately to put in question the dogmatic system of the church, with the help of the authority of scripture. But as historical work progressed, it now seemed to have denied even the authority of scripture. And whereas at one time historical research had emancipated itself from dogmatics, dogmatics seemed to have the right and indeed the duty to emancipate itself from history, the 'historical' Bible and with it the previous foundations of the church – that is, unless it maintained the traditional relationship between dogmatics and scripture. Here we find the beginnings of an ominous development which seems to have had an effect right down to the present time: large areas of theological theory and practice have been characterized by an emancipation first from the Old Testament and then from the New Testament message of Christ. From now on the authority of the Bible was succeeded by an approach the content and method of which were both oriented on contemporary popular philosophy, the arts and Marxism.

The full significance of this dilemma and its practical effects have only begun to emerge in the present situation of theology and the church after the counter-movement represented by the theology of the Word of God. However, it is much older and has deeper roots. They lie hidden in the hermeneutical problem, which itself began to emerge in the course of historical research. This is the problem of the relationship between history and theology, historical-critical method and dogmatics, historical distance and the validity of history for the present, and finally the dialectical unity of history and the eschatological event of salvation which has taken place and continues to take place, in other words the relationship of history and eschatology. The static quality of dogma has largely concealed this dialectic, while historical investigation tends primarily to stress the gulf between past and present, banishing the Old Testament in particular to a remote distance. Only hermeneutical reflection on the phenomenon of history, which has arisen anew in the wake of historical research, and consideration of the process of interpretation and the conditions which make understanding possible, can put us in the position of being able to understand again and express in a way which will be fruitful for the church the dialectic of history and the present which is of the essence of Christianity.

It is against this background that we should consider the more recent efforts which have been made to return once again from mere historical investigation to theology. They have been closely connected with the dialectical theology of Karl Barth, Rudolf Bultmann and others with their 'back to the content', the proclamation of Christ in accordance with the scriptures.

Hence the remark by Carl Steuernagel, who at one time himself turned a theology of the Old Testament into a history of Israelite-Jewish religion, in the Festschrift for Karl Marti (IIIc, 266): 'If at that time it was necessary to liberate biblical theology from the fetters of dogmatics, today ... it is necessary to free Old Testament theology from the fetters of the history of Old Testament religion in which it threatens to waste away.'

However, it was easier to announce dissatisfaction with the situation and to formulate a programme than to put it into effect. This is clear from the discussions in the 1920s and 1930s and the unsatisfactory result of efforts to produce a more than merely historical theology of the Old Testament, over which there is a dispute even today. The difficulty was – and still is – that in dogmatic theology the hermeneutical problem of the Old Testament and its relationship to the New Testament was usually discussed in dogmatic terms in connection with the doctrine of scripture, whereas within Old Testament scholarship itself there was hardly any fundamental hermeneutical reflection which took account of the wider discussion over hermeneutics and the problem of understanding generally, and utilized the results which had been arrived at there. This has to be said despite attempts to tackle 'Problems of Old Testament Hermeneutics' (the original title of a collection of articles edited by C. Westermann, and published in English as *Essays on Old Testament Interpretation*, 1963, IIIc). Here the situation was very different from that of the New Testament. However, the problem also lay within the Old Testament itself. The Old Testament is a collection of very different religious, national and wisdom traditions spanning a whole millennium, with many parallels and cross-connections with and borrowings from religious and other traditions outside the Bible. Its character as demonstrated by historical research into the Old Testament cannot be expressed in one formula without restricting it or doing it violence, or without taking as a basis for an approach one central point which then comes to dominate the whole interpretation.

Theologies of the Old Testament which have been written so far, and which again deliberately call themselves 'theologies', are almost all attempts to provide a theological evaluation of the Old Testament without losing sight of history. They follow the same pattern as Vatke, but without his philosophical presuppositions, in trying to relate historicity and validity, past time and the present day. One important step forward was that this problem was in fact brought to light again, having been kept in the background for a long time as a result of the voluminous and successful efforts of historical study.

In a much-discussed article written in 1926, Otto Eissfeldt attempted to conceptualize the problem ('The History of Israelite and Jewish Religion and Old Testament Theology', IIIb, 105–114). According to Eissfeldt the problem is in the last resort that of the tension between the absolute and the relative. Historical and theological approaches lie on two different levels. In the one a man is actively and methodically concerned to understand, while in the other, in theology, he is passive and is taken hold of by a higher power. 'Thus the very nature of our minds makes these two approaches necessary, and we simply have to choose either to arrive at a compromise between them, or to recognize the characteristics and the rights of each and to do them justice' (109). Quite apart from the question whether – after and despite Semler – theology and religion are not improperly identified here, this article is typical of the problematical situation. The gulf between history and normative theology which is to be validly binding is clearly recognized; the difficulty caused by this gulf is traced; the concern for intellectual integrity remains; and responsibility for the relevance of theology to historical understanding and the church, and therefore the need for a theology which uses historical methods, is not surrendered. Each of the two sides of the problem is uncompromisingly allowed its validity, but this does not produce any answer to the question how mediation between them is possible. The argument ends as it were still in the pre-hermeneutical stage, and the question of the possibility of historical work without presuppositions and a really detached and objective exegesis is never even raised. Conversely, faith and the theology (perhaps in embryo form) which stems from the believer appears to be an arbitrary action quite independent of scholarship and its results. It belongs in a different sphere of human existence, as though there were no connection between faith and understanding, and as though faith, to be real faith, ought to be a matter of believing the incomprehensible.

Eissfeldt himself did not draw this consequence, and certainly did not intend to; it can, however, be drawn, as is shown for example by the 'Theology of the Old Testament' written by the conservative Otto Procksch and published posthumously (1949/50, IIIc). For Procksch, faith is the instrument which opens up to us the world of the Bible, the wonder of God and his revelation. Here too, then, the hermeneutical problem, the problem of understanding, is passed over and in fact the significance of historical-critical exegesis is put in question, since *a priori* it cannot have a right knowledge of the subject-matter to which scripture bears witness.

After this general discussion about the nature of a theology of the Old Testament which was to be more than a mere history of religion, and whether it was possible at all (cf. C. Westermann, ed., *Essays on Old Testament Interpretation*, IIIc), a number of theologies of the Old Testament appeared, written since the 1930s. They cannot all be discussed and reviewed here; for that the reader is referred to the surveys by E. Würthwein and W. H. Schmidt (both IIIc). At this point we are only concerned with the way in which the hermeneutical problem of a general understanding of the Old Testament is reflected in the methods used in these theologies, and in the way in which they are organized.

The very title of Ernst Sellin's book is instructive: 'Old Testament Theology on a History-of-Religions Basis: Part I, The History of Israelite-Jewish Religion: Part II, Theology of the Old Testament' (1933, IIIc). Part I describes the history of Israel's religion down to the time of Jesus Christ, Part II is meant to contain theology as Christian theology and to present the faith and teaching of the Old Testament canon in so far as (!) the New Testament presupposes it to be valid. While the qualification expressed in the 'in so far as' is correct for a theology which claims to be Christian, it is again striking here that the work is divided into a *historical* part and a *systematic* part. This corresponds to the 'or' which we already find in the work by G. Lorenz Bauer (see 73ff. above). It is also worth noting that the part which seeks to be *theological* in the real sense is constructed in a systematic way and follows the traditional doctrinal framework of theology, anthropology and soteriology, or the doctrine of God, the doctrine of man and sin and the doctrine of judgment and salvation. We have to ask not only whether such a scheme is not too rigorous and lop-sided for the Old Testament, but also whether it does not raise even more fundamental doubts. Is not history forgotten too much in such a static system, which is thought to be necessary for the sake of 'theology'? Sellin's recognition that Old Testament theology can only be Christian theology, in an embryo sense, if it starts from criteria to be found in the New Testament and is measured against them, shows real progress on which we cannot go back; but it fails to grasp fully, much less solve, the problem of history and the normative validity of the Old Testament which is expressed in the duality of the history of religion and theology and the distinction between them.

Taking up the Reformed tradition and the beginnings made by the earlier federal theology (see above, 57f., 64f.), in the years after 1973 Walther Eichrodt developed a *Theology of the Old Testament* (IIIc) along different lines. It appeared in Germany in three volumes (in England and America in two), and has been reprinted many times. Here history and systematic theology no longer stand side by side. Rather, Eichrodt believes that he can present the world of Israelite belief as a structural unity and demonstrate its links with the New Testament by taking up a theme which is central to the whole of the Old Testament. For him this central concept is that of the 'covenant', which is developed as the covenant-relationship between God and people, God and the world and God and man. No attempt can be made here to review Eichrodt's theology as such; all that we can do is to demonstrate his hermeneutical position. Eichrodt does not attempt to resolve the dilemma of history and theology either by a 'both-and' or, in the style of G. Lorenz Bauer, with an 'or': he is in favour of a systematic approach. To avoid an alien dogmatics which does violence to the subject-matter, Eichrodt chooses a category from within the Old Testament — that of the covenant — and uses it to systematize the wealth of historical material. We cannot at this point discuss the question whether the notion of the covenant really has such central significance within the Old Testament; there are a number of good reasons to doubt this (cf. e.g. L. Perlitt, *Bundestheologie im Alten Testament*, 1969; IIIc, and below, 125ff.). That is not, however, the decisive point here. Another question is much more important, namely whether the Old Testament has a centre at all from which it is possible to organize the great wealth of tradition. Anyone who takes seriously the simple historical and exegetical recognition that the Old Testament contains heterogeneous collections of literature extending over a millennium will not be able to suppress considerable doubt. This doubt will be confirmed when he discovers that even Eichrodt, with his concept of the covenant, does not succeed in taking account of everything. A further question is by far the most important for theology, i.e. whether the *Old* Testament *can* have any centre at all for *Christian* theology, since in *Christian* theology Christ is the centre and the foundation, apart from which no one can lay any other (I Cor. 3.11). Now Christ is named only in the New Testament, and here for the first time his death and resurrection are proclaimed as an eschatological saving event. Finally, from a hermeneutical and theological perspective, we must ask once again why a systematic account of the collection of historical documents which is called the Old Testament should have any more *theological* significance than that of a chronological classification. If the Old Testament is to be thought to have any dominant central feature, of whatever kind, or any basic structures which extend throughout it, despite the inequality of the traditions, then it should be possible to demonstrate the fact with some skill through a historical approach, without resorting to systematics. Evidently the concern for theology leads to a departure from the historical approach and a move towards a system; the author (for his part) feels that he has found a solution to the problem of history and present validity, which is rooted in the content, simply by changing the presentation. Finally, however, the decision whether and to what extent and why the statements of the Old Testament can claim to be valid for Christians is left to dogmatics. As a result the problem is so to speak handed on within the faculty and left with another department, as though despite its more inadequate historical information that department were better able to provide a solution – which must consist in a justification for the present-day validity of the statements of ancient texts as worked on by historians. At any rate, this expectation has regularly been disappointed.

The same may also be said of Ludwig Köhler's *Theology of the Old Testament* (1936, ET 1956, IIIc), which according to its introductory remarks sets out to demonstrate the ideas, notions and concepts which are or can be of theological significance. It is important to note that like Sellin, Köhler correctly seeks to derive the criterion for what can be 'significant' in the Old Testament from the New Testament. In other respects his systematic account again follows the pattern of dogmatics: theology, anthropology and soteriology (judgment and salvation).

Limiting ourselves to the most important works, we may note that the concern of T. C. Vriezen, *An Outline of Old Testament Theology* (1949, ET 1958, IIc) is also a systematic one, though he has also published *The Religion of Ancient Israel* (1963, ET 1967). In the systematic part, which is by far the larger, Vriezen (like Eichrodt) begins from the notion of the relationship between God and man, i.e. the covenant. He treats the Old Testament in principle as part of the Christian canon and as a text for Christian preaching. For Vriezen the right to and the duty of such an approach stems from the fact that from the very beginning *the church* has *recognized* and defended the character of the Old Testament *as revelation*. This reference to the church's tradition answers the hermeneutical and theological question of the validity of the Old Testament from the start, but does not solve it. Even so, it is left to historical criticism to determine what is important and what is peripheral, and thus to make the essential truth shine out all the more brightly.

The works mentioned so far understand theology of the Old Testament primarily or even exclusively as a system which is given systematic form, and almost all fasten on some central point as an organizing principle: for Eichrodt and Vriezen it is the covenant, the relationship between man and God; for Köhler it is the lordship of God; for Fohrer (*Theologische Grundstrukturen*, IIIc), it is lordship and community; for Zimmerli (*Grundriss der alttestamentlichen Theologie*, IIIc) it is the revelation of the name of Yahweh as God's communication of himself. The special significance of von Rad's *Old Testament Theology* (IIIc) is that he ventures to write history as theology and theology as history. His theological history, which at the same time is a historical theology, sets out to be a re-telling, not of course a re-telling of the facts as ascertained by historical criticism, but a re-telling of the Old Testament historical witnesses themselves. The problem mentioned above, of the discrepancy between real history, or the picture of history obtained by historical criticism, and biblical history, or the history offered by the Old Testament, is decided in favour of the latter. The traditio-historical method which von Rad himself used showed the way in which the pre-literary complexes of tradition had changed in the course of history; by conveying an understanding of the traditions as testimonies of faith and the content of faith (*credenda*), this method now turns into a theology of the traditions (thus in the sub-titles to von Rad's work). Theology is the re-telling of the traditions with special reference to their character as testimonies to Israel's faith, whereas the real course of history including the history of religion is restricted to the sphere of purely historical work. Thus various problems which have come up in the course of the history of research and theology are taken together, and different attempts to solve them are combined in an imposing new harmony: von Rad returns in the first place to a theology of the Old Testament as a *historical* discipline and thus to the original and necessary beginnings of this branch of scholarship. Here he once again takes seriously in historical terms the course of a history which is seen once and for all with its conditions and conditioning factors, its contingency and its context, protecting it against the pressures exercised by a hypothetical centre. Secondly, von Rad attempts to take this history seriously *in theological terms*, by stressing that the history of traditions is itself a history of testimonies of faith. Thirdly, he again makes use of the earlier patterns of prophecy and fulfilment and type and antitype, giving a pattern and purpose to the historical course of the testimonies. Finally, he explains that the testimonies from history understood in this way have a Christian quality, because the course of history which follows the pattern of promise and fulfilment, type and antitype, is a salvation history leading to its fulfilment in Christ, and is given its theological stamp in the light of Christ.

This whole conception is certainly very significant, and all its details are still far from being explored. Indeed to many people it has seemed like the discovery of the philosopher's stone. However, here we can only investigate its basic hermeneutical principles and ask how much they are capable of supporting. Such an investigation will prove extremely instructive in showing us the present state of the hermeneutical problem of the Old Testament.

First we must ask whether the selection and stress on the view of history presented by the Old Testament itself, along with the re-telling of this history, is not a matter of *theology* in the strict sense rather than any other methical approach. Simply to pose this question is to answer it: if the picture outlined in the Old Testament – which is also historical – has the character of an expression of faith and the purpose of proclamation, then working out this character and this intention is nothing more and nothing less than, say, textual criticism, historical work. Von Rad's attempts to turn the history of religion into theology by changing the history of tradition into a re-telling of the kerygmatic picture of history, and to break out of the totality of what can be achieved by historical research into a historical theology, ultimately end once again in historians' history. This means, secondly, that the attempt to argue for the Christian character or the Christian significance of the Old Testament witness by postulating the focus of Old Testament history on the coming of Jesus Christ remains problematical. Such an orientation cannot be verified or even be made probable in any way by historical research. All the arguments that could be advanced against the pattern of prophecy and fulfilment and against typological interpretation tell against this aspect of the conception (see below, 209ff.). Thirdly, a feature of the total approach of this theology, which harmonizes various individual approaches, is that despite all the stress on the character of the Old Testament view of history as proclamation, we are never told whether the view of history presented has its own kerygmatic force, as a message which of itself promises and brings salvation, and as a form of address and promise, or whether it is no more than the forecast of a divine *action* and a saving *event* which later confirms the forecast by filling with significance what in itself is no more than an empty word. In order that harmony shall be preserved, the relationship between event and word remains obscure, though the tendency towards a salvation history of saving events and saving ordinances predominates: the testimony becomes a matter of 're-telling'. Even here, a concern not to fail to do justice to the historical character of the relevation leads to the attribution of a theological quality to the course of history. That in turn can only be claimed when this course culminates in testimony to the Christ event, which is to be demonstrated typologically and in accordance with the pattern of prophecy and fulfilment. As a result, the newest and most integrated conception of a theology of the Old Testament returns to categories and patterns of interpretation the use of which might be thought to have long since been put in question by sober historical scholarship. The hermeneutical problem of the Old Testament can be seen again through the fair semblance of harmony. Both a futuristic apocalyptic theology of hope and a theology of history oriented on the course of history, as well as a theology beginning from the kerygmatic intention of the Old Testament texts and concerned with proclamation, might claim to have received important stimuli from von Rad.

10. *Summary and prospect*

In conclusion, the following summary might be sketched out from a survey of the historical and hermeneutical problem of the Old Testament and the various attempts at solving it which have been made since the rise of historical scholarship. Historical consciousness and historical scholarship have demonstrated the great gap not only between the Old Testament and the present, but also between the Old Testament and the New Testament. Whether evaluated in a positive or a negative way, the Old Testament became an alien book. And once it had become a historical document, it could only be investigated and understood in historical terms. Theology which concerned itself with this collection of writings had therefore to make use of historical procedures (Semler, Gabler). As Eichrodt pointed out, if the Old Testament were to have any significance for the present or for Christianity, and were not simply to be rejected in polemical terms or tacitly ignored as irrelevant to the Christian church, this could only be as a matter of belief and doctrinal teaching – of whatever kind. Uneasiness at the discrepancy between historical research and dogmatic theology, and still more at the effective loss of the Old Testament, for all its formal place in the canon, transforms the history of Israelite and Jewish religion once more into a theology of the Old Testament, as a counter-stroke against the predominance of the purely historical approach. This new development regards itself above all as a combination of historical and systematic approaches in the expectation that the latter will give it new theological value and will confer new Christian significance on the Old Testament. Or (as in the case of von Rad) the attempt is made to take the *historical* character of Old Testament study seriously as a matter of necessity on which there can be no going back, and to treat the *history* of the religion of Israel *as a theology* of the Old Testament. The difficulties of these attempts have been described above. Nevertheless, the justification of *this approach as such* cannot be doubted. However, it can only be carried through after *hermeneutical* reflection which demonstrates and avoids the dilemmas to which von Rad's theology succumbed.

In reflection of this kind there must *first of all* be an awareness of the difference between knowledge and faith, and therefore of the difference between historical and dogmatic theology as a discipline on the one hand, and faith on the other. This must never be forgotten – remember Semler! Eissfeldt's well-intended distinction (see 85f. above) between two levels of consideration must not become entangled again in the mistake of subordinating history to knowledge and theology to faith. No matter whether it adopts a historical or a dogmatic method (of whatever kind), theology cannot prove the truth of the writings of the Old Testament and the New Testament, any more than it can prove the existence of God himself. For the sake of both God and the world, including the world of the Old and New Testaments, theology must protect itself against this attempt and this temptation. At the same time, however, it needs to try to avoid the other mistake, and not to separate faith and knowledge, faith and understanding as opposites. Christian faith understands what it believes, and therefore can only give an account of itself with words which can also be understood by non-believers. Faith is not an instrument of knowledge (Procksch), but the acceptance and existential appropriation of what has been understood. The person who believes does not understand any *more*, even when it is a matter of scripture, and an exegete is not made by faith, but by understanding, skill, experience, method, and above all a great deal of hard work. Similarly, historical research can never be a substitute for the Holy Spirit or for belief; at best, as in many cases, it can be an aid to understanding, so that people know what they are doing when they believe or do not believe. These considerations in turn bring historical and dogmatic theology closer together once again: historical and systematic patterns for organizing theology, over which there has been a good deal of dispute in more recent attempts at Old Testament theology, are not mutually exclusive. One is not more or less theological than the other. It is, rather, the theological subject which gives theological quality to the investigation. This subject is scripture which is itself words about God (*theo*-logy), and the aim of historical interpretation is to understand correctly its significance for the present. Its subject is not God himself, but men and their experiences of God, their attitude to existence in the face of the question about God, their understanding of themselves, the world and God as this is expressed in the texts of scripture.

Secondly, hermeneutical reflection brings to light an awareness of one's own historicity in the present. It has been an old error and a failing in historical scholarship, even biblical study, since it began in the Enlightenment, to act as though one could be concerned with history quite apart from any question of values or presuppositions, and as though even the history of religion could be studied objectively. Bengel's *Te totum applica ad textum; rem totam applica ad te* (see 65 above) is not just a piece of pietistic admonition; it is a hermeneutical principle without which no true understanding in the present is possible. In the light of this principle, the history of religion and the theology of the Old Testament come together again: the difference is not determined by the alternatives of either a supposed absence of presuppositions or some kind of Christian presuppositions; rather, deliberate and purposeful assessment by the standards of Christianity contained in the New Testament is what makes the study of religion into theology.

Thirdly, hermeneutical reflection should put the problem of history and the possibility of historical understanding in a proper light. In historical terms we can understand why, once historical consciousness had been awakened, historical-critical scholarship first and foremost began to stress the distance of the past from the present, its otherness and its alien character, its individuality and its special nature. Above all, from the perspective of the ethos and the presuppositions of the Enlightenment, we can understand how people felt that they had discovered a well-founded bridge between past and present in the assumption of ideas which were valid everywhere and for all time. And when this bridge was torn down by the flood of history, there still seemed to be a historical *line*, a *linear course of history* to bind periods together – unless one wanted to continue the arrogance of the Enlightenment in rejecting the whole of the past as primitive and barbarian. With the aid of the line which joins one to the other, historical understanding becomes an *explanation of connections* and a reconstruction of sequences, for which such sequences and connections, as cause and effect, are more important than the event itself and its quality, the specific nature of experience, joy, lamentation – in short, historical existence. The construction of such a historical line virtually brings about the disappearance of historicity. It is a mere point which no longer has any value in itself, but only by virtue of its place in the sequence.

Theology, too, took up this approach at an early stage and changed it into salvation history. Its influence can still be seen in von Rad's theology. No wonder that in this view, particular events, people and institutions are inevitably reduced to foreshadowings in salvation history. Over against this must be asserted that another way of understanding is also possible, for which the Old Testament is not primarily or even exclusively the evidence for a historical line which is to be reconstructed from it, and which culminates either in Christ or in the rigidity of Jewish legalism. 'Truly historical interpretation' (thus Rudolf Bultmann, 'The Significance of the Old Testament for Christian Faith', V, 13) asks what basic possibilities for the understanding of human existence are expressed in the traditions in order to be able to enter into a sympathetic dialogue with them, prompted by questions about human existence in the present, which need not always be framed in individualistic terms.

There is no going back on the history of the hermeneutical problem presented by the Old Testament legacy, the history of historical studies and hermeneutics. This irreversibility also conditions the historicity of present-day understanding. Only on this basis is it possible to present and to examine the various possibilities of gaining an overall understanding of the Old Testament.

IV

THE OLD TESTAMENT AS LAW AND
AS A COVENANT DOCUMENT

1. *Canon and law*

It is almost universally accepted that around 300 BC the Samaritan community became independent of Judaism and its centre in Jerusalem. The Samaritan canon of scripture is limited to the Pentateuch, which will therefore have been completed round about that time. Apart from certain features peculiar to the Samaritan text, it must have assumed its present form then. This is confirmed by the apocryphal Wisdom of Jesus Sirach, which in connection with a celebration of ancestors from Enoch to Simon the High Priest (Sirach 44–50) presupposes the evaluations of individual kings in the canonical books of Kings and therefore is already clear confirmation of their existence and validity. As Sirach (48.22–49.12) also knows the prophetic books of Isaiah, Jeremiah and Ezekiel and the book of the Twelve Prophets, this part of the canon must also have been completed round about 200. Two generations later, in the prologue to his grandfather's wisdom book, Jesus Sirach's grandson already presupposes a canon with three divisions, which also includes 'the writings' as a third part. It is important in this connection that even in such an early testimony to the origin of the tripartite canon of scripture, its first part, the Pentateuch, is designated 'law'. This designation at the same time expresses the evaluation, understanding and pre-eminence of this section of the canon: the Pentateuch has the force of law, and so the first part of the canon is canonical in an emphatic sense.

'Law', in Hebrew *torah*, in Greek *nomos*, is originally a designation for priestly instruction and teaching about the correct way of distinguishing not only between clean and unclean, sacred and profane, but also between right and wrong (Hag. 2.10–14; Pss. 15; 24.3–6). 'Law' can also be used as a term for a corpus of law which has consecutive passages of legal material. Thus, for example, in Lev. 6.2 we find, 'This is the law of the burnt-offering' (similarly Lev. 6.7, 18; Num. 19.10 etc.). In the prologue to the Wisdom of Jesus Sirach, 'law' has become a comprehensive designation for the Pentateuch, which now classifies even the non-legal parts as law, or at least understands them as part of the law. The prologue does not give the impression that it is saying anything new; rather, it seems to be reproducing existing usage and an understanding which has already become established. Sirach himself affirms the pre-eminence of the Pentateuch as the law, identifying it with the supreme divine wisdom (Sirach 24); in so doing he is writing as a conservative theologian against all 'modern' innovations and changes, which were abundant in the Hellenistic period.

Sirach is not the originator of such an understanding. The Chronicler had already mentioned the written law of Moses or Yahweh, the existence of which he presupposes even during the monarchy (e.g. II Chron. 23.18; 30.16). Although the Chronicler's view of history may be anachronistic in this respect – as in others – it is evident that this terminology was already familiar to him (*c.* 250?).

Of course we do not know when the name 'the law' or 'the law of Moses' emerged and became a technical term, since the beginnings of the formation of the canon are shrouded in darkness and can only be reconstructed hypothetically. However, the origin of the understanding which is expressed in the designation 'law' enables us to draw some certain, or at least highly probable, conclusions. The Chronicler's history, which attempts once again in a late period to describe the history of Israel from the beginning, ends with an account of the reforms of Ezra and Nehemiah (Ezra 7 – Neh. 13). Whereas Nehemiah appears here as a political reformer and governor, in all probability Ezra's work consisted of enjoining the *law* of God on the post-exilic community (Ezra 7.14, 25f.). This law was at the same time the law of the Persian king (Ezra 7.26).

That means that the old, inherited Israelite law was now put into force by Ezra, the royal plenipotentiary, as an imperial law; Israelite law becomes binding on the Jews of the post-exilic period as a code which was not only recognized, but even introduced and sanctioned, by the state (Ezra 7.26). Thus it was a Persian measure, a reform undertaken by the state in line with Persian imperial policy elsewhere, which encouraged the 'legalism' of the post-exilic period. Legalism is not just a religious or spiritual phenomenon; it was a pattern for living introduced by the state authorities, intended to bring peace within the realm of the Persian empire. In this context it does not matter which law formed the basis of the new religious community with its state privileges. The Chronicler will have identified it with the Pentateuch; in so doing he simply anticipated later developments which can be said to have ended in the designation of the Pentateuch as 'law'. What is more important is that the reform, which preserved old traditional laws and to this degree was conservative, was at the same time a transformation and an innovation: the Jew was no longer the descendant of Abraham, but the man who observed the law; the law, an official state requirement for membership of the Jewish religious community, now also (and at the same time) seems to have become the condition, appointed by God himself, for righteousness before God. The law *can* now be understood and implemented in this way. No matter how one assesses the person and intention of Ezra (and historians argue over this), and no matter how much of the story of Ezra may be attributed to the Chronicler, we may be certain that the new official requirement of obedience to the law, which makes the law the legal basis for belonging to a religion, represents an important development. It provides the criterion for distinguishing between *Israel* and *Judaism*.

In this connection, de Wette wrote a *Biblische Dogmatik des Alten und Neuen Testaments. Oder kritische Darstellung der Religionslehre des Hebrais-mus, des Judenthums und des Urchristentums* (A Biblical Dogmatics of the Old and New Testament. Or a Critical Account of the Religious Teaching of Hebraism, Judaism and Early Christianity, 1813). In it, as the title indicates, he distinguished between ancient Israelite religion and Judaism. He regarded the latter as a subsequent religious aberration which began after Ezra. De Wette's views influenced many later writers. In this sense, Wellhausen too drew a distinction in the title of his book: *A Sketch of the History of Israel and Judah*. This distinction often implies a negative verdict on Judaism: the history of Israel ends with rigid legalism.

Although there are unmistakable differences between Israel and Judaism, and the significance of the law is a decisive feature of them, the two entities cannot be separated without strain. They are bound together by more than heredity. Whatever our judgment on the details of Ezra's work, it is impossible that membership of the Jewish religious community could be made dependent only and exclusively on obedience to the law and individual decision, quite apart from membership of the Jewish people. The whole later development tells against such an assumption.

However, the links between Israel and Judaism and the continuity of history are not just of an ethnic kind. The content of the law which the Persian authorities imposed on the post-exilic community was nothing new. There is not the slightest indication that a completely new law was introduced at the time of Ezra. This would go against the wording of Ezra 7.25, where knowledge of the law is presupposed, and against the Persian practice of authorizing as imperial law the best known and most traditional law within individual satrapies. The law of Judaism, which shaped the Jewish people and ordered their life, was the law of Israel.

The earlier law is also genuinely Israelite in the sense that it was understood as God's law and as such had put its stamp on Israel from ancient times. This does not mean that a divinely authorized law regulated Israel's life as a state at the time when it existed as one. In this respect, the states which grew up on the territory of the Israelite tribes will not have differed from other states. Rather, it is possible to detect a remarkable autonomy of ancient Israelite law, even over against the state. It is evident that in Israel there was a law which was older than the state; this asserted itself, sometimes with difficulty and often in conflict with the instruments of state. The well-known story of Naboth's vineyard in I Kings 21 is a reflection of one such conflict. It is also notable that the Israelite and Jewish kings were not depicted as lawgivers, Whereas in the world of nations outside Israel, the famous king Hammurabi of Babylon acquired a lasting reputation for his codified legislation, in Israel David was praised as the great psalmist and Solomon as the wisest of the wise. This is all the more striking, seeing that in Israel, too, and especially in Jerusalem, the preservation of law and justice was regarded as the specific task of the king (Isa. 9.6f.; Jer. 22.15f.). The expectation of a coming Messiah, who will bring peace, justice and righteousness, is the eschatological form of this conception. Despite this, and regardless of the recognition of an extensive royal involvement in law and salvation, in Israel the king does not enact law. It is not the king, but Yahweh, who is the foundation of law and justice.   This brings us to the complicated and disputed question of the origin and character of Israel before it became a state. Since Noth's work on the early history of Israel (*Das System der zwölf Stämme Israels*, 1930, IVb), this question has been unanimously answered in terms of the idea of the amphictyony. On the analogy of supposedly similar organizations existing before the foundation of a state, especially in ancient Greece, the amphictyony has been seen as a sacred alliance or confederation of twelve (or also six) tribes, bound together in the common worship of a covenant God at a central amphictyonic sanctuary which they looked after by rotation – hence the number twelve, after the number of months. The proclamation of the divine law was an essential feature of covenant worship. In this respect, therefore, *the proclamation of the divine law was constitutive of Israel.*

Since Alt's work on the subject, 'The Origins of Israelite Law' (1934, IVB), apodeictic law (as he called it) has been regarded as genuine Israelite law, in contrast to casuistic law with its conditional form, which can be found throughout the ancient Near East. Alt included prohibitions, commands, pronouncements of death penalties and curses in this genre; common to them all is the absence of any indication of circumstances, such as is to be found in casuistic law, or of any gradation in the indication of penalties. Divided into ten or twelve statements, which allow no ifs or buts and threaten anyone who contravenes them with a curse and therefore with exclusion from fellowship with God and man and from the sphere of life, this law reflects the will of the divine lawgiver, who by his will gives Israel its life.

However, more recently this integrated picture has been questioned from various sides and with a number of different arguments (for the most recent account of the discussion see J. Halbe, *Privilegrecht Jahwes*, 1975, IVB, 34ff., 471ff., 511ff.). On closer inspection it has become doubtful whether what Alt called apodeictic law is all of the same genre and whether it really is a distinctive Israelite form of law. Above all, there is some question whether apodeictic law had a specifically religious character as a divine law proclaimed in the cult. Instead, it has been suggested (by E. Gerstenberger, IVB) that by origin apodeictic law was clan law, which was reinterpreted only secondarily as Yahwistic cultic law. The hypothesis of the amphictyony in the form in which it was put forward by Noth also seems to have been shaken by important counter-arguments: in the Old Testament there is no term which is at all an adequate designation for the amphictyony; Joshua 24 already presupposes an Israel made up of twelve tribes and therefore cannot be considered as a foundation document of Israel, quite apart from the late date of its composition. No trace can be found of any central amphictyonic sanctuary (G. Fohrer, ' "Amphiktyonie" und "Bund" ', IVB). A distinction also

has to be made between Israel as a tribal alliance and the holy war of
Yahweh, which was not waged by all Israel, but by individual tribes
(R. Smend, IVв). The antiquity of covenant theology (L. Perlitt,
IVв) and the concept of the covenant generally (E. Kutsch, IVв)
have also been put in question.

At this point we can only mention the discussion, and report its
present results to the degree to which they are *important for the
significance of law and justice* in the Old Testament (cf. also A. Gunneweg, *Geschichte Israels bis Bar Kochba*, ThWiss 2, 1972, 40ff.). First
of all it should be noted that the question whether the term amphictyony should still be used as a designation for Israel before the
formation of the state, given the criticism made of it and the
recognition that early Israel cannot be compared directly with the
amphictyonies of ancient Greece and ancient Israel, is of secondary
importance. We shall retain the term here for practical reasons and
because it is so familiar. However, it should be said that the discussion of the amphictyony hypothesis has not really been able to put
in question the fact that when the name Israel first appears in a
context we can understand, it refers to a coalition of tribes and
alliances in Canaan before the formation of the state. Furthermore,
the theophorous name with its El-element points to the fact that this
alliance had some religious character. There must be some connection
between the name and the organization of this alliance and the
number of twelve tribes; the number twelve cannot be purely fictitious,
since there is no obvious reason for such an invention. And whereas
M. Noth (*Das System*; 'Laws in the Pentateuch'; 'Das Amt des
"Richters" Israels', all IVв), A. Weiser (in his commentary on
Psalms, 1962) and G. von Rad ('The Form-critical Problem of the
Hexateuch', IIIв) may be wrong in their certainty that we can
reconstruct a central cult and a covenant festival and a covenant
renewal festival, we cannot cast doubt on the *religious* and at the same
time *legal* character of this early institution which called itself after
El = God without doing violence to the tradition. It may not be
possible to combine Gen. 35.4; Deut. 27.11ff.; 31.10f.; Josh. 8.32, 34;
24.25, all of which mention some form of proclamation of the law and
chiefly locate this at Shechem, in order to produce a complete
description of a covenant festival with a reading of the law which will
regularly have taken place at Shechem as a central feast of the
amphictyony. However, like Ex. 15.25, which also speaks of lawgiving by Yahweh, all these passages stand out remarkably clearly
from their immediate and wider context and cannot be eliminated as

later fiction without quite forcible treatment. Whatever the form of Israel's earliest worship may have been, the passages mentioned are so many indications that divine law must have been of considerable significance in it. It is also striking in this connection that in the period before the formation of the Israelite state, the only office recognized throughout Israel is that of the 'judge' (Judg. 10.1–5; 12.7–15; cf. I Sam. 7.15ff.). The designation points to the sphere of law. Here, too, scholars have become more cautious and restrained when it comes to giving a detailed account of the functions of the 'judge' than Noth was ('Das Amt des "Richters" Israels'). However, once again the information given in these passages cannot be derivative; it represents further evidence of the close connection between religion and law in earliest Israel. The peculiar expression 'foolishness in Israel' or 'that was not done in Israel' (Gen. 34.7; Deut. 22.21; Judg. 20.6; II Sam. 13.12; Jer. 29.23) is quite obviously ancient, and clear evidence for a specifically Israelite law which applied to Israel as a tribal alliance. The expression makes it plain that certain kinds of sexual relationships were tabu in Israel and that the prohibitions applying to them (Lev. 18.3, 24–30; 20.10ff.) were not a matter of clan ethics – what one might expect for the purity of the family and the clan to be preserved – but a law which applied to Israel and defined what was impermissible for Israel because it was 'foolishness'.

Thus it is difficult to deny that religion and justice and law and a 'judging' in Israel were closely connected during the time before the formation of the state. This connection is clearly determinative for Israel. Whether we seek to understand early Israel as a sacral alliance analogous to the ancient amphictyonies, or sociologically, in the light of the relationships and circumstances of semi-nomads (as, for example, R. Numelin, IVB), or as a symbolically real reality (Gunneweg, *Geschichte*, 41), Israel is given its constitution by a divine law; it is not defined by territorial boundaries, but is a 'personal alliance' and a legal community (J. Halbe, *Privilegrecht*, IVB, 464ff.) which is distinguished from other communities by a divine law. From the very beginning, Israel had obligations to a law which, since Israel worshipped Yahweh, bound it to Yahweh as the God who gave the law.

This explains, first, how the formation of a state with laws and justice of its own, not to mention its constitutional independence, necessarily led to conflicts with the old 'amphictyonic' order, which was not simply done away with on the foundation of the state. Saul came to grief in this conflict, and David, who was more brutal

and more perspicacious, found himself in considerable difficulties
(A. Gunneweg, *Geschichte*, 74ff.; J. Halbe, *Privilegrecht*, 479ff.). Thus
the conflict was as much a matter of religion as a matter of law. The
schematized opposition of king and prophet in the Deuteronomistic
history work goes back to the contrast between the laws and customs
of the amphictyony (as a personal alliance) on the one hand and the
state on the other. The collapse of the state, in the north in 722 and
in Judah with the events between 600 and 586 (and probably even
earlier), when the fragility of the constitutions of Israel and Judah
became increasingly clear, also saw the beginning of the great
restoration movement, the literary legacy of which can be found in
Deuteronomy and the Deuteronomistic history work. The new
pattern of life which was looked for and propagated here was the old
amphictyonic order of an 'elect' (Deut. 7.6f.) personal fellowship with
a new basis in covenant theology, a fellowship that met at the place
which Yahweh chose for his name to dwell there (Deut. 12.5, 11,
26 etc.), and where he was present when people called upon his name.
The rule of life for this community is 'this law which I set before you
this day' (Deut. 4.8); the law is as it were the form of God's nearness
(Deut. 4.7f.). Life before God is realized in obedience to regulations
and laws which, like the promised land, are a God-given possibility.
Just as the land must be cultivated if it is to bring forth its fruit, so the
regulations must be observed if they are to lead to true life. The
difference between life in early Israel and life after the collapse of the
state is to be found in the conceptuality, the theological clarity and the
expression of the law in written form (e.g. Deut. 17.18f.; 28.61;
II Kings 22.8, 11: the law as a law book), as in the utopian character
of this programme of reform, but not in the significance of the law as
such.

If a 'privilege law of Yahweh' (F. Horst, J. Halbe, both IVB) was
characteristic of Israel from the start, we can *also* understand how in
Israel all law and justice was ultimately thought to be instituted and
given its force by Yahweh alone. Casuistic and secular law therefore
only achieved the status of divine law through its connection and
involvement with Yahweh's privilege law which was primarily manifested in the Book of the Covenant (Ex. 20.22–23.19), then in the
legal corpora within the Pentateuch, and especially clearly in Deuteronomy. Once the tradition that the relationship between Yahweh
and Israel had been established on Sinai had become more deeply
rooted, it was inevitable that the Sinai tradition should not only
become the central theme of the Pentateuch but also attract to itself

all aspects of Israelite law and justice: all law is God's law, promulgated on Sinai through the mediation of Moses. Even Deuteronomy, while it might not be set on Sinai-Horeb, was still the farewell speech of Moses to his people.

The consequence and final result of this development, which extended over many centuries, together with the fundamental involvement of Yahweh in all justice and all law, is to be found *par excellence* in the Pentateuch. Three-quarters of it is made up of legal material. Thus the later designation 'law' for the whole of this strange collection of traditions, from earliest times to a very late stage, seems justified on quantitative grounds alone; in view of the quality and derivation of the traditions to which the designation was applied and the impulse towards the collection and arrangement of them, the term 'law' was neither incorrect nor even an unprepared-for innovation. There were equally good reasons why the law should be placed *before the prophets and the writings* as the first and most important part of the canon. The prophets certainly spoke here and now in respect of specific situations, and proclaimed salvation and disaster for the future. But their time required attitudes towards the present and order for the present. So prophecy continued to be directed towards the 'law'. Indeed prophecy pointed towards the law by accusing Israel of breaking it. It makes no difference whether or not the wording of individual regulations is cited. *Sine lege nihil crimen* – the principle also applies here: there can be no prophetic accusations and threats without the law. And where prophecy of disaster changes back into an announcement of salvation, this new salvation is still proclaimed as a new law which is now written in the heart (Jer. 31.33), or held in prospect in the utopian vision of an outline constitution for a restoration of the old order that has been lost, now depicted in vivid eschatological colouring (Ezek. 40–48). Here prophecy, on its periphery, becomes prophetic lawgiving. We are not far from a view of prophecy as interpretation and application of the law, and of the law itself as being given by the prophets. This can in fact be found in the prayer of Ezra (Ezra 9.11) and the book of Daniel (9.10), a development for which there is some intrinsic justification. The boundary between Moses (or the law) and prophecy becomes blurred, but the primacy of the law is in no way weakened. In the last resort, the law determines what true prophecy is (Deut. 18.20–22).

A similar pattern can be seen in connection with the third part of the canon, the writings. Their subordinate status can already be seen from their place in the canon and from the time it took to finalize this section of the canonical collection. It is also significant that the wisdom literature, which in origin is the least Israelite part of the canon, and whose universalism, international character and anthropocentric focus are furthest removed from a particularist law, can in a later phase of reflective thinking teach that the law and wisdom are identical (Sirach 24; Baruch 3.37–4.1). The law of the God of Israel is identified with the ordering of the world as investigated and taught by wisdom, according to which things go well with the good and badly with the wicked. The teacher of the law becomes the wise man and the wise man the teacher of the law – according to the Jewish philosopher Aristobulus, the Jews are a nation of philosophers. Here, too, the boundaries of the law become blurred and yet the primacy of the law becomes even plainer: the law alone teaches what is true wisdom.

2. *The Old Testament as law and as a basic ordinance of the church*

The designation 'the law, the prophets and the writings' for the Old Testament, and the understanding which it expresses, therefore has a long history. The late name 'law' for the Pentateuch proves to be bound up with the earliest information about the origins of Israel in a continuous history. During the period of the monarchy, this history went on largely underground or was maintained by prophets and other opposition groups; but it was not really interrupted. The Israel of Yahweh's law of privilege and the Judaism of the law may be different, but they cannot be separated; nor should the difference be exaggerated and developed to the point of being an absolute opposition.

There are good historical and dogmatic reasons for calling the Old Testament the law, the prophets and the writings. The terminology used in the New Testament takes up this description. In Luke the Old Testament is called 'Moses and (all) the prophets' (Luke 16.29; 24.27) or 'the law, Moses, the prophets, the psalms' (Luke 24.44). The designation 'the law and the prophets' is more frequent (Matt. 5.17; 7.12; 11.13; 22.40; Luke 16.16; Rom. 3.21). John 10.34; 12.34; 15.25 evidently calls the whole of the Old Testament 'law'. Here, too, the terminology implies the evaluation and the understanding: the Old Testament is seen first of all as law, and the question of the validity of the Old Testament presents itself first as the question of the validity of the Old Testament law in the sphere of the Christian community. It could be given very different answers, ranging from the Jewish-Christian recognition of the letter of the law (Matt. 5.17f.), through the dialectic of Paul (Rom. 3.28–31), to the *de facto* repudiation in the gospel of John (see 28ff. above). In this respect, too, the canon of the New Testament is not a document of church unity but of theological plurality. It is not surprising, therefore, that different lines were also followed at a later stage. Since neither the Pauline nor the Johannine position could achieve widespread influence in the theology of the communities or the church, a *via media* began to emerge most clearly. Both testaments or (before the completion of a New Testament canon) the Old Testament and the genuinely Christian tradition were understood as a unity: they were testimony to the one God and the one truth. Irenaeus already teaches that the one Word of God, Jesus Christ, who has already spoken in the prophets, is the one origin of the two testaments. So the Old Testament law also remains valid, in so far as it is not a ceremonial law understood in the literal sense and applicable to the Jews, which is done away with by the appearance of Christ. The allegorical method, then, allows the interpreter to discover another, higher sense, hidden from the Jews, even in the ceremonial law and to understand it as a shadow of what is to come (thus especially Origen). We have already noted, however, how allegorical interpretation conceals the problem rather than solving it (see 31ff. above). Elsewhere, too, a development in the church forced the problem of the Old Testament, understood as the law and in the light of the law, into the background. This development was also furthered by the Old Testament heritage and the legalistic understanding of it in contemporary Judaism: the appearance of Jesus Christ can itself now be interpreted, by the standards of the law, as the revelation of a new law. The new is preeminently new in that it brings to light the truth of the old, and in that way fulfils it. Just as the literal sense is surpassed by the allegorical, so mere external obedience to the ceremonial law is deepened, and becomes practising the commandment to love as a fulfilment of the law. The recognition of the law is made even easier by the identification of the moral commandments in the law with the universal moral commandment which holds for all men as the natural law (this can already be found in Irenaeus).

The adoption and acknowledgment of the Old Testament as law, its allegorical reinterpretation and the use of parts of it along the lines of a natural moral law, not only furthered a legalistic and moralistic understanding of Christian *belief* – faith as a virtue (already in

I Clement) – but also influenced the understanding of *the church*. Its organization was thought to have been prefigured and given valid expression in the Old Testament and the constitution of the ancient people of God (also already in I Clement).

If the church is the true Israel and lays not only *a* claim, but *sole* claim to the Old Testament as its holy scripture; if the Old Testament is valid for the community of Jesus Christ, then the law of the Old Testament and indeed the Old Testament generally, understood as law, must apply to the church. Like the canon of holy scripture, the rule of faith as a guideline for correct interpretation, and the episcopate as a controlling authority, a theocratic constitution is intended to help to secure the outward and inward existence of the church. The 'new commandment' (John 13.34; 15.12) and the 'law of Christ' (Gal. 6.2) are no longer instructions for a spiritual life in faith, but ecclesiastical and theocratic ordinances following the pattern of the Old Testament and governed by the laws (now given a Christian interpretation) which regulate not only worship but also all other aspects of life. The Christian church is to imitate the pattern in ancient Israel before Christ, where priests and levites were ministers in worship, taught the people, offered prayers and made sacrifices (so already I Clement at the end of the first century, the *Didache* in the second century, and especially the so-called *Apostolic Constitutions* in the fourth). In this way a Christian clergy came into being, alongside which the universal priesthood of all believers was no more than a theoretical entity. According to the Old Testament model, sacrifice was the prerogative of the clergy. Accordingly, the eucharist was now understood as a sacrifice. And since the Old Testament law requires daily sacrifice, the Christian priest now offered the sacrifice of the mass every day. Sacrifice in turn needs an altar; church buildings were arranged liturgically and built accordingly. And just as at one time the tent of meeting was the place where Yahweh made himself present, so now Christ dwelt in the tabernacle which housed the transformed hosts. Since Israel had kept the sabbath, and the strict observance of feast days had been a confessional act, it was now important to hallow Christian festivals. The privileged and exclusive status of priests and levites in the Old Testament was transferred to priests and deacons, and the bishop now took the place of the high priest. Just as the eucharist was interpreted in terms of the Old Testament sacrifices, so baptism was interpreted as a rite of initiation after the model of circumcision. Nor were the financial aspects of these analogies ignored: tithes were given to Christian priests as they had once been given to the house of Aaron.

Thus a theocratic self-understanding, a particular form of organization and a way of worshipping are combined, especially in the Latin church, into an integrated and closed system. The impulse towards this development, which already began to emerge from the first century onwards, may not have come exclusively from the Old Testament, but the form of the church and the way in which it regarded itself are inconceivable without the acceptance of the Old Testament as a valid law. It provided not only the model, but even more the legitimation for the church's understanding of itself and the form of its organization: the Old Testament seemed to have found its true fulfilment in a church which had taken this form, and conversely, the church in this form found the justification and the legitimation for its form in the Old Testament. Once Christianity became a state religion in the time of the emperor Constantine, this inner legitimation from the Bible as a whole was supplemented with external legality and authority. At one time the Persian empire had confirmed and sanctioned the law of Israel as a valid imperial law; now it was once again the state which gave force to the law of the church.

It was here that the Reformation brought the first great turning-point, though only where the Reformation movement managed to make and sustain a breakthrough. It was inevitable that concentration on the saving event of Jesus Christ – *solus Christus, sola gratia* – as something to be proclaimed on the basis of scripture – *sola scriptura* – would bring the traditional structure crashing down because of the attack on its very centre. The church as the new and true Israel, as a theocracy and an institution which made salvation present in the sacrament through its organization (see 43ff. above), had itself been an attempt at a comprehensive solution to the *hermeneutical* problem, namely, *how the salvation which had appeared in history could be realized in the present*; and if the Old Testament, interpreted allegorically, and the Old Testament law, applied to this new situation, were not a condition for the possibility of such a self-understanding and such an organization, they were the foundation and framework of the church which had understood itself in that way and given itself that form. This wider framework seemed also to have provided the solution for the hermeneutical problem of the Old Testament: the Israelite theocracy finds its fulfilment in the theocracy of the church, which also brings about the fulfilment of the law.

The hermeneutical approach of the Reformation was quite

different, with its exclusive – *solus, sola* – stress on the *proclamation* of salvation. It now put the Old Testament, understood as law, in quite a different light. If the Christian church is not an institution with a theocratic structure, which brings salvation, but has its existence where the Word of Christ is truly proclaimed and truly believed, the Old Testament, understood as law, cannot find fulfilment in the church. Either it is the social code of the Jews, and therefore no longer a matter of concern for Christians, or it only applies in so far as it is a formulation of the natural moral law. With a few alterations, the ten commandments can be put in the latter category. Above all, however, the far-reaching identification of the Old Testament and the law is abandoned, and the law (in both Old *and* New Testaments) is rediscovered as having a dialectical relationship with the gospel – again in the Old *and* New Testaments (see 51f. above). However, we have already demonstrated (see 55ff. above) that this first beginning was no more successful in coming to fruition than had been Paul's theology in the early church. Along with a new scholasticism, a new evaluation of the Old Testament as law came about within Protestantism. Contributory factors were Calvin's understanding of scripture, Melanchthon's view that, in principle, for Christians the Old and New Testaments had equal status, and finally the orthodox doctrine of inspiration which was applied to Old and New Testaments alike. Of course, the law no longer found fulfilment in the church as an institution for salvation organized along the lines of the law – this was the understanding of the Roman Catholic church (and the Eastern church, while differing, nevertheless saw itself in much the same light). It was now fulfilled in daily life and in practical sanctification, works which were well-pleasing to God. Granted, these works did not make a man righteous before God; justification was the force which made sanctifying action possible for him. Just as the Roman church claimed to be the true Israel and a true theocracy by virtue of being a sacramental institution for salvation, so the community of the elect and the justified who could now do good works and be sanctified by good works brought into being the true Israel and the true theocracy on earth. Transferred from the sacramental to the moral sphere, the Old Testament still had force as law, albeit in a Christian reinterpretation, and also continued to have an immeasurable effect after the Reformation – indeed especially then.

The bloody revolution in which Thomas Müntzer was entangled was doubtless inspired by a legalistic and theocratic way of thinking based on the Old Testament; it justified itself by claiming that scripture was one and that the testaments had equal value (this was argued by others besides Müntzer). Müntzer's form of the Reformation – like the fantastic and gruesome realization of the 'kingdom of God' in Münster by the Anabaptists – may have remained an episode, but theocratic and legalistic ideas had a longer and more profound effect in the Reformed sphere.

It was not just individual regulations taken from the Old Testament which left a visible stamp on life – for example, strict emphasis on the hallowing of Sundays and festivals, which almost brought public life to a standstill, and even required the cock to be separated from the hens so that the animals, too, could keep the Lord's day holy by refraining from work and remaining continent. Even more important was the application of a legalistic model from the Old Testament to the realization of a theocracy on earth, which coloured social and private life and still continues to do so even today.

As the law and covenant document of a theocracy, the Old Testament put its stamp on the Netherlands, Switzerland, England and North America, and also influenced those elements in the population which were not Calvinist. We can only hint at the direct political and historical consequences of such an interpretation of the Old Testament, without going into any detail. The Dutch rebellion against Spain was spurred on by the thought that the true Israel was fighting for its existence, and therefore for God's honour, against the enemies of God. So in the true Israel, as in ancient Israel, religion and nation belonged together. The Calvinist Huguenots fought even more bloodily, but with little success, for their faith, and for a long time formed a state within the state, until Louis XIV put an end to it by revoking the Edict of Nantes in 1685. Reformed Christians in Scotland under John Knox (died 1572) were able to assert themselves more successfully, but no less militantly, against Mary Stuart. Oliver Cromwell and his followers acted even more radically than the Dutch had done a century earlier in attempting to set up a theocratic kingdom of the saints by waging civil war, executing Charles I and convoking a 'parliament of the saints'. However, this kingdom of God also came to a mortal end when Cromwell died in 1658 and his son was incapable of assuming his father's mantle. All in all, the spirit of Puritanism, moral earnestness in the fear of God, assiduous activity and worldwide commercial enterprises remain characteristic of Calvinism; they have moulded human nature and brought about a state of material prosperity which Old Testament man, who thought that he could see

God's blessing in the vine and the fig-tree, the gift of children and a home in the promised land flowing with milk and honey, would not have dared to hope for. Nor have a fighting spirit and a conviction of fighting, like ancient Israel, for God's honour, as yet been quenched.

As a typical example from the arts of the inner amalgamation of Christian faith, Old Testament theocracy and militant politics, mention might be made here of Handel's oratorio *Judas Maccabaeus*: the attempt in 1745 to restore the Roman Catholic dynasty of the Stuarts, which had initially caused a panic in England, was foiled by a victory over the Young Pretender, Charles Edward Stuart. This was the occasion for which Handel wrote his oratorio, which identified the fight of Judas Maccabaeus for freedom and for religion with the fight and victory of the English Protestants. The Israelite and Jewish theocracy and their victories are the model and the law in accordance with which the present-day church appears as a theocratic community on a national basis, to propagate true religion and bring about the kingdom of God on earth.

Furthermore, there can be no doubt that colonialism, which not only was motivated by economies and foreign policy, but from the beginning strove for the extension of Christianity understood in these terms as a religious and ethical goal, also has deep roots here. Ideas of the nature of a happiness that is worth striving for, a form of order which will be pleasing to God, real freedom and the true interests of mankind may change, because they are historically conditioned and differ in individual cases; consequently the specific political aims of a church which understands itself to be not only a community which lives under the word of the cross and on the basis of that word, but as a theocratic fellowship of the elect who have been visited by grace, must also change. Specific goals may differ, but the self-understanding based on the Old Testament and governed by law remains constant, as does the conviction of being entrusted and commissioned by God himself with the establishment of his kingdom on earth, like Israel and Judas Maccabaeus of old. Although they are not identical, or even on the same moral plane, the Old Testament as a law and theocratic ordinance, Judas Maccabaeus who hewed off the head and right hand of the enemy (I Macc. 7.47), Cromwell's revolution, a theology of revolution, and the biblicist defence of negro slavery and discrimination against people who are supposed to have inferior rights (because of Gen. 9. 20–27), all have in common a link with the Old Testament understood as law and as the basis of a theocracy.

This hermeneutical approach and the understanding of the Christian faith which goes with it has been expressed particularly clearly in the recent past in a much-quoted work by the Dutch theologian Arnold A. van Ruler, which has as its immediate theme the relationship of the church to the Old Testament (*Die christliche Kirche und das Alte Testament*, 1955, IVb). Van Ruler puts forward the view that scripture consists of the Old Testament and the New Testament, that they are to be considered as a whole and interpreted in the light of that whole, and in no way are concerned solely with Jesus Christ, although they 'turn' around him, because he has solved the riddle of guilt (cf. 65). The explanation is this:

> Sanctification is greater than reconciliation. One day the Son will hand back the kingdom to his Father. Everything is directed towards this from the beginning ... May I put it tersely and sharply? Jesus Christ is an emergency measure over which God delayed as long as possible. Therefore he must not be forcibly sought in the Old Testament, even by Christian theologians investigating the Old Testament in their search for God (65).

The work appeared at a time when the discussion of the hermeneutical problem of the Old Testament had just begun. The debate it caused served especially to provide preliminary theological clarification of the hermeneutical principles on which the newly planned Biblische Kommentar Altes Testament (BKAT) could and had to proceed. The journal *Evangelische Theologie* devoted several numbers in volume 12 to the question of the Old Testament during 1952/1953. It immediately transpired that the authors involved wanted to attempt to revive typological exegesis within the framework of the historical-critical method. The justification for the typological approach (see above 90f. and below 186ff.) lies in a comprehensive view of both testaments and the relationship between them: the Old and New Testaments bear witness to the actions of the one God who acts in accordance with his nature in history, indeed in a history which finds eschatological fulfilment in Christ. Typology or typological interpretation traces these correspondences as types and antitypes, and brings them out. This presupposes that as antitypes, Christ and the Christ event surpass all previous types and put them in the shade. It makes clear that they are, as the term goes, foreshadowings, but only mere transitory foreshadowings. With direct reference to the basic view which has begun to crystallize in this discussion, A. A. van Ruler objects: is Christ really the fulfilment of the whole of the Bible? He answers his question in the negative. Jesus Christ is only God's emergency measure. No wonder that this slogan has been repeated so often since then!

This approach does more than take the ground from under typology: Christ is no longer the antitype which puts all the types in the shade. In addition, the possibility has been presented of developing an understanding of Christianity which is oriented on the pre-eminence of the Old Testament. It is not primarily concerned with redemption, with an emergency measure, but with created reality in its earthly and physical nature, and not just with the spirit and the soul and man's inner nature.

> It is concerned in a much more positive way with the creation and the kingdom, with the first and last things, the image and the law, sanctification and humanity, ethics and culture, society and marriage, history and the state. These are the things with which the Old Testament is concerned. So it cannot and must not be interpreted only in terms of christology, which is as much as to say theocracy. There remains a deep trust in the material things of this world, in the usefulness of man and the possibility of hallowing the earth (A. A. van Ruler, 82f.).

There can be no doubt that here van Ruler gives an apt description of the Old Testament, and that if the Old Testament has any significance at all for the present, it should be expressed and understood along the lines which he lays down. This would, of course be the approach which has always preserved the church from lapsing into a purely spiritual gnosticism and an ahistorical, fleshless, bloodless Christ-myth, regarding monastic segregation from the evil world as the only possible ideal for Christian existence. Where it has gained a hearing in its own right, the Old Testament has protected the church down the ages from such an extreme. Here Reformed theology and its practical realization in the Reformed churches – and nations and states – has exercised an inestimable positive influence. At the same time, however, van Ruler makes particularly clear the terrifying dangers which lie in wait here. To say that Jesus Christ is only an emergency measure between creation (protology) and consummation (eschatology) is to misunderstand the depth of sin and guilt. Quite apart from the New Testament evidence, this is a far cry from the radical understanding of sin in the biblical primal history of the first eleven chapters of the book of Genesis. Redemption, which is a matter of faith and therefore invisible, but which is present, if only in hope (e.g. Rom. 8.24; II Cor. 5.17; 6.2; John 8.51; 11.25), is replaced by the necessity for a visible realization of the rule of God as a 'sanctification of the earth' (op. cit., 85); living by faith in the forgiveness of sins through grace, as a fundamental renewal of existence (rebirth), and as the possibility of a new way of acting in the world in accordance with the commandment to love (sanctification), is replaced by a belief in 'the usefulness of men' (op. cit., 83). This is tantamount to a belief in the possibility of the realization, in this world and within history, of that for which more vigorous movements within Christianity than a lazy and inward-looking quietism hope and pray for from God alone: the coming of his kingdom.

Van Ruler's whole approach is marked out by his positive assessment of the Jewish theology of Martin Buber, with its idealistic and optimistic faith in the possibility of a realization of the kingdom of God within this world and within history, and also by his unintentional nearness to Thomas Müntzer, who regarded all the rest of holy scripture as an interpretation of Moses. Van Ruler is certainly not an exponent of Reformed orthodoxy. For all its stress on the unity of the scriptures of Old and New Testaments from John Calvin *via* Cocceius to Karl Barth, Reformed dogmatics has thought to find this unity essentially in the testimony of both testaments to the Christ event. It has attempted to define the difference between the testaments in terms of chronological succession, as expectation, promise and fulfilment (Calvin); as the covenant of works and the righteousness of grace (Cocceius); or as the time of expectation, the preliminary period, and the time of fulfilment (Barth I, 2, VIA, 70ff.). In this context it is inconceivable to think of Christ as an emergency measure. Nevertheless, we have gone into rather more detail about van Ruler's views here because his extreme position is a good indication of the tendency of the Reformed approach to lead to a theocracy along Old Testament lines. The only new element is the consequence (which is explicitly stated) that the Christ event is demoted to being an emergency measure. We are already familiar with the approach which in principle attaches the same importance to each of the two testaments, and in which the Old Testament must inevitably come out on top because criticism no longer holds its dead weight in check and there is no longer any brake on its claim to authority. The results of this have put their stamp on the Reformed churches and still continue to do so in some places. Those members of the Reformed church who in the seventeenth century formally went over to the synagogue and even had themselves circumcised were as much the representatives of an extreme and exceptional position as van Ruler is, but extremes and exceptions can be significant. We have learnt from the most recent past that a desire to 'sanctify the earth' in the spheres of the state, society and politics (whatever the actual content of this desire might be) can be reviewed in the spirit of the Old Testament theocracy without in any way continuing to be an exception.

Once the Old Testament has been acknowledged in an undialectical fashion, along with its law and its theocratic conceptions and the conjunction of law and religion which is presupposed from the beginning, without being submitted to the critical test of the cross and resurrection of Jesus Christ, the problem of the law and Israelite-Jewish religion as posed within the Old Testament becomes a problem for the church. How can the eschatological people of God be given visible form within the world and within history, in other words, by human actions?

3. *The rejection of the 'law of the Jews'*

There have, of course, been those who have criticized the Old Testament and indeed repudiated it altogether precisely because it takes the form of law. Although the tendency to put the two testaments on the same level as Christian parts of the one Christian canon eventually prevailed, the difference between their contents never disappeared entirely from view. The question whether the gospel of Jesus Christ which is proclaimed to sinners and justifies them can be reconciled with the Old Testament law and law in general, and if so how, was never far away. Although on the one hand Jesus could be made to say that he had not come to destroy the law but to fulfil it (down to the last detail, Matt. 5.17f.), the church continued, on the other hand, to preserve the reliable tradition that Jesus regarded the law with considerable freedom. Moreover, while Paul's theology may never have come to influence the whole of the church, the very presence of his letters in the New Testament canon provided a counterbalance to legalism and a legalistic approach to the Christian church which it was hard to ignore. Whenever people took up Paul's thought, they also began to question the idea of the Old Testament as law (and ask how far it is law).

This is where Marcion started from in the early church. He represented a radical version of Paul's approach, repudiating the Old Testament as a law and the document of another deity (see above, 39). Certain Gnostic themes may have influenced Marcion's doctrine and there is good reason for describing the church which he founded as a Gnostic sect, but the real impulse behind his approach was the opposition of gospel to law and the impossibility of reconciling the righteousness given by the grace and goodness of God with a righteousness based on the fulfilling of the law. Here law and gospel, which Paul understands to be in a dialectical relationship, are so diametrically opposed that the dialectic threatens to become a diastasis. This division is so deep that according to Marcion, the God of the law must necessarily be a different god from the God of the gospel. In an utterly unselfish act of mercy towards a creation which he himself has not made, the God of the gospel, who is pure goodness and love, has brought redemption from the evil law and its works. It is easy to interpret Marcion's doctrine of the two gods and to demythologize it: the law and the gospel, which with the help of the Old Testament Paul sees in a dialectical relationship, lose this dialectical connection, and are forced apart in such a way that they can be seen only as expression of the opposition of two gods. Marcion thought that he was drawing the right conclusions and avoiding Paul's inconsistency (which prevents him from rejecting the Old Testament), by presenting a genuine, refined Paulinism instead of a falsified Jewish version of the truth of the Christian faith. In reality, however, he gave up the dialectic of law and gospel as that of two possibilities of understanding and realizing human existence. He failed to realize that while law and gospel are mutually exclusive, the one does not do away with the other: the two of them remain associated. The gospel must continually be preached afresh to man, who continually succumbs to the temptation of legalism. This is the only way in which the gospel is not just the unmasking of an evil God, an evil law and an evil creation, but the proclamation of salvation which is addressed to an evil humanity, which seeks its own justification and its own autonomy even in its best attempts to fulfil the law. We may well ask whether the Old Testament, understood as law, is the indispensable precondition for such an insight of faith. Nevertheless, Paul knew of a law which was valid and efficacious for the Gentiles outside the Old Testament and even without it (Rom. 2.14f.). Be this as it may, in Marcion the repudiation of the Old Testament as being the law of an evil god leads to the loss of the essential dialectic of law and gospel. Indeed in the last resort it also leads to the loss of the gospel, which can no longer be proclaimed as the word of the cross, seeing that the cross and suffering and all the evils of this world are simply sent by the evil creator god.

Luther may not have drawn such consequences, but there can be no doubt that Marcion's way of thinking comes alive again in him when he dismisses the Old Testament law (where it is not common to all men and of universal validity) as being merely the Jewish social code. He never tires of saying how this law is completely optional for Christians. More important than this enormous reduction of the Old Testament law, however, is his concentration on the gospel of grace which alone brings justification: over against this, even the *valid* law cannot be considered a way to life and blessedness. Like Marcion, Luther sees the gospel of God's love as the only God-given possibility for man, but he differs from the great heretic of the ancient church by preserving the dialectical relationship of law and gospel. Marcion became the founder of a new church, and his church was a sect; Luther remained a Reformer.

Unlike Luther (and Melanchthon), Johannes Agricola (1499–1566) thought that the Old Testament law was a failure on the part of God to give happiness to men. This brought him very close to Marcion, and his position was rejected as heresy by Luther and Melanchthon in the 'antinomian dispute'. This was not, as Harnack thought in his book on Marcion, a regrettable inconsistency on the part of the Reformers; it merely shows that although the law had been reduced to 'the social code of the Jews', its permanent theological and existential significance had clearly been recognized.

Philosophical reasons could also be advanced for the rejection of the Old Testament as a law which did not concern Christians. For example, in his *Religion within the Bounds of Reason Alone* (1793), Immanuel Kant had sought to understand religion as a recognition of duties in terms of divine commandments. This legalistic and moralistic understanding of religion – which was characteristic of the time – led to his devaluation of the Old Testament: it was the law of the Jews. The Old Testament laws really have no religious quality, because they derive from an originally political organization; like other comparable political laws, they are concerned only with outward obedience and hold out only the prospect of reward or punishment within this world. In particular, they know nothing of any form of eternal life, so that they cannot properly be called religious. They are part of the particular organization of the Jewish people, who are quite different from Christians, as is shown, for example, by the latter's abolition of circumcision as a necessary condition of salvation. Kant clearly recognized that the law of the Old Testament went with the Jewish community and was therefore the law of a particular nation – the Jewish social code; however, he failed to recognize the interrelationship of law and religion, of the legal community and the religious community, which was an essential characteristic of Israel. His argument was rather: since the nature of the law is Israelite and Jewish, it cannot be Christian, because that which is nationalistic and particularistic cannot be divine. Whereas for Luther the Jewish social code was done away with because for Jews and Gentiles Christ is the end of the law, for Kant the Old Testament law no longer has any religious value because the nationalistic and particularistic features of the Jewish law are inferior to the universal moral law which has been manifested in Christianity. Thus, as elsewhere, Kant collected together and arranged in a well-grounded system ideas which in accordance with the moralistic spirit of the Enlightenment tended to be raised as objections to the 'law of Moses': merely external legalism without an inner moral quality, merely statutory regulations without moral improvement, mere particularism without a universal human validity, mere eudaemonism without moral purity. This represented a combination of criticisms of the Old Testament as law and more general objections to the Old Testament and its religion which must be discussed at greater length elsewhere (see 142ff. below).

Where suspicions about the Old Testament law and what is supposed to be its concern for material welfare, divorced from any notion of eternal salvation, are conditioned by the presuppositions and the standards of the Enlightenment, or are based on an inadequate sense of history and a deficient knowledge of the subject-matter, they can be dismissed without comment. More important is the theological objection which, without wishing to ignore the fundamental relationship and dialectic of law and gospel, still sees Old Testament religion as being essentially moulded and characterized by law and legalism. Here the dialectic of law and gospel is not to be found throughout both parts of the canon; the Old Testament *is* law and legalism, whereas the New Testament (at least the essential elements in the New Testament, leaving aside any straw epistles) *is* gospel. This identification of the Old Testament with the law and the New Testament with the gospel was not intended by Luther, Melanchthon and their followers; indeed, Melanchthon had expressly guarded against it and regarded it as a mistaken view, however common it might be (as in the *Loci communes* of 1521, cf. Diestel, Ic, 238ff.). At least it can be said that it was easier to understand and promote such a division of law and gospel into the Old Testament (which in fact contained law and was described as law) and the New Testament (which bore witness to the gospel) than to distinguish two parts of the canon which did not coincide with the dialectical polarity of law and gospel. Outside Calvinism, then, wherever the Old Testament was not formally incorporated into Christianity and the two testaments were not put on the same level, it was likely that mere legalism, and with it the Old Testament, would be undervalued and even rejected.

Schleiermacher, for example, follows the Lutheran tradition rather than the Reformed when, after putting forward other objections, he feels that he should find fault in particular with the legalism of the Old Testament. It is dangerous for Christians, because it may seduce them into a legalistic way of thinking (see *The Christian Faith*, V, § 132). The same line of tradition is followed by Harnack, who in his generous praise of Marcion includes Schleiermacher among those who have retained 'a sense of the individuality and the value of the Christian religion', putting him alongside Hegel but after Luther (who is, unfortunately, inconsistent) and Agricola (*Marcion*, IIA, 253). Harnack himself joins these witnesses to the truth of the gospel with his famous and much-quoted words:

> My argument, for which the justification will be found in the following pages, takes this form: to reject the Old Testament in the second century was a mistake which the Church rightly repudiated; to retain it in the sixteenth century was a fate which the Reformation could not yet avoid; but to continue to keep it as a canonical document after the nineteenth century is the consequence of religious and ecclesiastical paralysis (*Marcion*, 248f.).

Another significant figure to be included among those who would reject the Old Testament is that of Emanuel Hirsch with 'The Old Testament and the Preaching of the Gospel', (IVB, 1936). Hirsch attempted to show that even those Old Testament sayings which seemed to bear witness to the gospel were really legalistic in their concern: Christians had given them a meaning which they did not have. However, his argument was essentially (and deliberately) a circular one: in his view, the Jewish standpoint was the only key to an understanding of the whole of the Old Testament and its details, because since the time of Ezra this alone had been the norm which had determined the canon. Because the Old Testament as a whole is termed law, its details, too, had to be understood in terms of the law. The Old Testament was significant only as a legalistic anti-thesis to the gospel.

It is remarkable that Hirsch, who in other respects was so manifestly concerned to strengthen and advance a modern awareness of the truth, rejected the possibility of utilizing the modern *historical* and *scientific* understanding of the Old Testament to shed light on *dogma*, keeping to a firmly dogmatic standpoint oriented on the Jewish canon. As a result, he failed to see that the historical-critical method not only shows the Old Testament to be an alien work but also demonstrates that other texts than those preferred by the church – Genesis, Isaiah and Psalms – were not originally legalistic in tone and can also, so to speak, be rescued. Or might that not be the case? We should also mention that Hirsch gave a very impressive warning against a direct and undialectical use of Old Testament legalistic and theocratic conceptions in the church and in church politics, though on the whole this was overlooked because of the political conditions of the 1930s. He thus spoke out, with some historical and theological justi-fication, against Karl Barth's assimilation of Old and New Testa-ments, with its cavalier treatment of historical insights, and W. Vischer's arbitrary christological interpretations (*The Witness of the Old Testament to Christ* I, 1934; II, 1942, ET 1949, IIIc). Anyone who does not recognize the problems that arise within the Old Testament – especially, for example, its this-worldly theocracy – gives himself away and puts the church in a problematical situation which is in fact pre-Christian, because it has been superseded by Christ. The church cannot address contemporary governments in the way that Isaiah spoke to King Ahaz, especially since Isaiah's own preaching was problematical enough for his own day, let alone for ours (see 135ff. below).

Herbert Braun takes the same line, though we cannot describe his work as fully or at such length, when he says: 'The characteristic of the Old Testament is that grace leads to the law as the way of salvation; the characteristic of the New Testament – to put it briefly – is that grace leads away from the law as the way of salvation.' At the same time, however, Braun can concede, 'but the Old Testament at its climaxes already has a breath of the freedom of the sons of God' ('Das AT im NT', IIA, 24 and 31).

4. *The 'prophetic' understanding of the canon and the relativizing of the law*

We have seen the Old Testament as the sacred scripture of Reformed, psalm-singing freedom-fighters and men of God; and we have seen it as a mere breath of Christian freedom, but also, try contrast, as an initiation into the law. These almost diametrically opposed assessments cannot simply be derived from the various premises of Marcion, Schleiermacher, Harnack and Braun on the one hand and the truly Reformed tradition on the other. We have to take such differences of opinion into account, but they are not enough to explain the discrepancies. The conflicting estimates point rather to the dilemma contained in the Old Testament itself, which presents itself at this point as a multi-faceted ambivalence allowing a variety of possible interpretations and practical consequences. The estimates are therefore conditioned by the different possibilities for interpreting the actual texts of the Old Testament.

This becomes clear as soon as we consider yet again the origin of the Old Testament canon with its threefold division into law, prophets and writings. As was pointed out above (6f.), the Hebrew canon is itself a value judgment which gives the law priority over prophecy and even more over the third part of the canon. This division of the canon of the Old Testament, like the formation of the canon itself, was very much influenced by Pharisaism. The Hebrew, Pharisaic canon was a dogmatic decision, made in favour of those Jews who faithfully observed the law and directed against apocalyptic literature, with its appeal to authorities who either preceded Moses or were independent of him (Adam, Enoch, Noah, etc.). It was also directed against sectarian groups and their special writings, like the Qumran community with its sacred scrolls, and against the Christian community with its Greek version of the Old Testament (the Septuagint). This legalistic understanding of the canon, which was also aimed at the church, was the one that gained official recognition. It had deep and age-old roots going back to the earliest days of Israel.

At the same time, however, from the very beginning, it was not the only possible understanding or the only legitimate one. Quite a different approach may also be regarded as legitimate, because it too had been put forward since the earliest days of Israelite religion and is by no means the result of later Christian interpretation. It finds expression in another understanding of the canon which was also put forward by Judaism, though it was forced into the background under the influence of the Pharisees. Just as the legalistic understanding of the canon is first attested clearly and in so many words in the Wisdom of Jesus Sirach, so too a view of the canon is expressed in the *arrangement* of the individual books of the Septuagint. This may be termed 'prophetic', as opposed to nomistic: *whatever has been written by prophets is canonical*. The Jewish historian Flavius Josephus (first century AD) writes in his apologia for Jewish religion, entitled *Contra Apionem* (I, 8), that the Jews did not have a varied and unlimited collection of holy writings, but five books of Moses with laws and narratives about events from the origin of mankind to the death of Moses. Other prophets had written the history of their time in thirteen further books, covering the period down to the reign of the Persian king Artaxerxes. Finally, there were four more books containing psalms and rules of life. (The thirteen prophetic books referred to by Josephus are Joshua, Judges [with Ruth], Samuel, Kings, Isaiah, Jeremiah [with Lamentations], Ezekiel, the Book of the Twelve Prophets, Job, Daniel, Esther, Ezra [with Nehemiah] and Chronicles; the further four are Psalms, Proverbs, Ecclesiastes and the Song of Songs.)

None of the other writings, which were composed after the time of Artaxerxes, merited the same respect, because since then the prophetic succession had come to an end. Thus the prophetic understanding of the canon envisaged the activity of the prophetic spirit from Moses to Ezra; this prophetic spirit which inspired the prophetic books in the canon guaranteed their canonical value. Whereas in the nomistic approach, the canon was based on the law (indeed, the law as such was the primary canon and everything else – the prophets and the writings – was merely the canonical interpretation and application of the law), according to the prophetic understanding of the canon, those books were canonical which had been inspired by the prophetic spirit of God, which was at work between Moses and Ezra.

Of course Josephus, who puts forward this understanding of the canon, nevertheless presupposes the division of the canon which at a later stage was the only one to be recognized, and this division into law, prophets and writings implies the legalistic understanding. However, the other, prophetic understanding is expressed in a pure form in the Greek arrangement of the canon. Here, too, the Pentateuch forms the first part. As in the Hebrew canon, it is followed by the historical books from Joshua to Kings, but after that come the rest of the historical books: Chronicles, Ezra-Nehemiah and Esther. Thus the Pentateuch and the rest of the historical books are put together. The second part of the canon contains the poetic and didactic books: Psalms, Proverbs, Ecclesiastes, the Song of Songs and Job. The prophetic books, including the book of Daniel, make up the third part. The principle behind this arrangement is clear: the historical books describe the past, the poetic and didactic writings are concerned with edification and instruction for the present, while the prophetic books look towards the future (thus, rightly, O. Eissfeldt, *The Old Testament*, IIA, 570; J. C. H. Lebram, 'Kanonbildung', IIA, 178). It is also clear that despite its pre-eminent position, the Pentateuch is not understood primarily as law here, but as a history book. While this does not rule out a special significance for the time of Moses and the Mosaic law, and does not represent a complete contrast to the Hebrew canon, it does put the accent in a different place: the law is not the hermeneutical key *par excellence*, which will open up the whole of the Old Testament, nor are the non-legal parts subordinated to the law of God's rule. Rather, the Old Testament is understood as a prophetic interpretation of history in general and life in all its aspects: in the past (the historical books), in the present (the didactic and poetic books) and in the future (the prophets) (cf. Lebram, 179). Another justification for calling this view of the canon 'prophetic' is that (as is well known) many of the prophetic books of the Old Testament are constructed on the basis of the same tripartite scheme: disaster in the past, the wickedness of foreign nations as a characteristic of the present, and the promise of new salvation for the future.

We need not discuss here whether it was the nomistic or the prophetic understanding which provided the older and more original impulse towards the formation of the canon. Another question is more important in this context. Does the prophetic understanding resemble the nomistic understanding by taking up earlier elements, so that in this respect it may be held to be legitimate, or is it rather the expression of a tendency which can be observed elsewhere, namely that oriental cultures and religion become introspective and assert themselves against the threat of assimilation posed by Hellenism? If the latter is the case, then the prophetic understanding must be regarded as a late phenomenon with no genuine roots. However, the former alternative is the one to be accepted. Although it is probable that Josephus, for instance, puts forward his particular view of history and his prophetic understanding of the canon for apologetic purposes, and it may well be the case that the Greek arrangement of the canon points in the same direction, it can easily be demonstrated that the concern expressed in a form which is determined by the Hellenistic world of the time is in fact older. The kingdom of God is not ushered in by obeying the law; God himself brings about his rule through historical saving events, by freeing his people from slavery, guiding them through the wilderness, giving them a land to live in and establishing an order which will make it possible for men to live before God and with each other through God's grace. It is not self-evident that this is the case and that God acts in this way, nor can it be clearly inferred from reality, the world and history. However, there must be prophetic testimony to the fact and a prophetic promise that this will indeed be the case, and scripture is the written form of such a testimony and such a plan.

This view of the canon, of scripture and of the Old Testament in general, which has found expression in a particular arrangement of the canon, is in turn simply an expression of an understanding of God and existence, also attested in the Old Testament, which is in no way determined by the law.

The rediscovery of the fact that the law became predominant at a relatively late stage and that it is therefore only of relative theological importance, is one of the many fruits of historical-critical study. One result of a methodical analysis and synthesis can be expressed by the dry sigla J E D P. However, these conceal a formal revolution in scholarly views about the course of Israel's history and religion (see 79f. above). They demonstrate that the law came at the end, rather than the beginning, of the history of Israel's religion. This was the finding of the Graf-Wellhausen hypothesis. But if we regard this end as 'Jewish rigidity' and degeneration, such a devaluation also amounts to a favourable reassessment of the earlier stages of pre-prophetic popular religion, and especially, of course, of prophecy. This seems to do justice to the legitimate theological criticism of the Old Testament as law, while at the same time recognizing the prophetic dimensions of the Old Testament and protecting it against attack. In particular, it is now possible to cope with the polemic of Paul: seen in this light, it is not directed against the Old Testament as such, but against a false, nomistic, Pharisaic understanding.

In the first chapter of his *Prolegomena to the History of Ancient Israel* (ET, 1885), Wellhausen formulated the problem in a classic way:

> We cannot, then, peremptorily refuse to regard it as possible that what was the law of Judaism may also have been its product; and there are urgent reasons for taking the suggestion into very careful consideration. It may not be out of place here to refer to personal experience. In my early student days I was attracted to the stories of Saul and David, Ahab and Elijah; the discourses of Amos and Isaiah laid strong hold on me, and I read myself well into the prophetic and historical books of the Old Testament. Thanks to such aids as were accessible to me, I even considered that I understood them tolerably, but at the same time was troubled with a bad conscience, as if I were beginning with the roof instead of the foundation; for I had no thorough acquaintance with the Law, of which I was accustomed to be told that it was the basis and postulate of the whole literature ... Yet so far from attaining clear conceptions, I only fell into

deeper confusion ... At last, in the summer of 1867, I learned that Karl Heinrich Graf placed the Law later than the Prophets, and, almost without knowing his reasons for the hypothesis, I was prepared to accept it; I readily acknowledged to myself the possibility of understanding Hebrew antiquity without the book of the Torah (3f.).

The picture thus achieved is the simplest imaginable, and the theological solution to the problem of the law arrived at by the new historical approach seemed to be equally simple and illuminating. Paul was right, and the Old Testament was again given its due. However, the situation later proved to be much more complicated than Wellhausen had thought.

It is true that we can no longer question the justification for the sigla JEDP, and that we can have a meaningful discussion about the absolute dating of the individual documents designated in this way. We can even consider the character of the E passages: are they documents, fragments, a revision of J? We can also question the unity of the documents and so on, though there is no shaking the recognition that D and P, which contain the great complexes of law in the Pentateuch, are late works. Nevertheless, this does not mean that the law as a whole is the product of Judaism. For example, the Book of the Covenant in Ex. 21–23 is much older, and may even go back to the time before the foundation of the state. It is true that in their present form the ten commandments are late, but there are reasons for assuming that their original form is deeply rooted in the early period. And although Deuteronomy and the Priestly Writing are much nearer to Judaism as literary works than to the time of Moses, they contain legal material the archaic character of which is unmistakable on closer inspection.

This once again raises the question of the law. The question can no longer be whether the law stands at the beginning or the end, since it is at both the beginning and the end: the question is, what theological significance does it have?

5. *Law and covenant*

The question of the relationship between law and covenant is especially important here. Wellhausen still thought that he could deal with the law and thus with the theological problem of Old Testament legalism by means of literary criticism, shifting it to the Jewish periphery of the canon. Between 1940 and 1944, however, two interesting attempts were made to tackle the problem, which had flared up again, by means of traditio-historical criticism. In 1940, M. Noth wrote his work 'The Laws in the Pentateuch' (IVB), in which he sought to show that the laws were originally connected, not with the state, but with the tribal alliance. It was only after the exile, when the amphictyonic order had been dissolved and the law had lost its real point of reference and basis in life, that the law was made absolute. As in Wellhausen's work, the law is again made a symptom of decline, which is typical of Judaism but not of earlier Israel. This time, however, the reasons are different. Earlier Israel was more concerned with the notion of the covenant, which does not necessarily involve a law or legal regulations; here, as in Ex. 24.1f., 9–11 J, the covenant is an act which provides the basis for a relationship between God and Israel as covenant partners. The act itself is quite separate from the law. J. Begrich put forward a similar view in his article of 1944 ('Berit. Ein Beitrag zur Erforschung einer alttestament-licher Denkform', IVB). In his view, the original form of the covenant was a 'relationship in which one party, which is powerful, associates with a less powerful party. This relationship is defined more closely by the obligations which are accepted by the stronger towards the weaker, and by the action of putting the covenant into force. The concept does not rule out the possibility that the weaker party also has some active obligations' (58). For Begrich, too, the covenant is a secondary feature, in so far as it is understood to be a treaty binding on both sides, and is not a genuinely Israelite development. Again the solution is simple, but the actual evidence is much more complicated.

With reference to Noth's work, we must enquire how the law lost its connection with the covenant after the exile, in other words after the collapse of Israel as a state. After all, according to Noth it had never been a state law, nor had it been connected with the state. Surely the disappearance of the state would have revived the old connection between law and covenant? And this was in fact the case, for there is no clearer expression of a formal theology than in Deuteronomy and the Deuteronomistic literature. So clear is this expression that there is even a temptation to regard the whole idea of the covenant as being late (see L. Perlitt, *Bundestheologie im Alten Testament*, IVB). True, there is also mention of the written law in the same sphere of tradition (Deut. 17.18f.; 28.61; II Kings 22.8, 11), but a feature of that sphere is that the people are urgently admonished that it was God who chose Israel in his spontaneous, incomprehensible love, quite apart from any merit on Israel's side (Deut. 7.7f.). That once again puts in question a history of development which traces a line from a covenant without a law to the Jewish aberration of legalism.

Nor is Begrich's conception of the covenant tenable any longer, despite its correct insight into the nature of the covenant as a gift. A covenant, even when the party which makes it seems only to be involving itself, obviously lays obligations on the party in whose favour the covenant is made, even if it is only a question of the latter party accepting the relationship offered and living by it. When the obligation which is already implied is made explicit and specific by means of individual regulations, this is not by any means a secondary distortion of the original character of the covenant as a gift. To this degree the translation 'covenant' is in fact better than others which have been recently proposed, like 'obligation', 'self-obligation', 'expression of the divine will' (Kutsch, IVb), so long as it remains clear that in theological terminology 'covenant' does not refer to a legal relationship made between two partners, to which either side can object. The primacy of Yahweh's involvement needs to be maintained, and once that is done it can be seen that the obligations which God takes on himself always at the same time imply a claim on Israel.

Just as Paul's polemic against legalism only seems to have a purely juristic and forensic character, so too the concepts of covenant and law are not defined one-sidedly in terms of legislation and treaties (cf., rightly, Halbe, 227ff., and also Zimmerli, 'Erwägungen zum "Bund"', 171ff., both IVb). The various possible ways of rendering the term *berit*, depending on the context and the historical stratum in which it appears, are not exclusive alternatives. It is, however, clear that in theological terminology covenant means *God's institution of salvation*, which also implies an obligation and a claim, no matter whether commandments and law are mentioned explicitly or not. After a long discussion, it has also become clear that whereas an explicit covenant theology may be a characteristic of Deuteronomy and the Deuteronomistic school, and therefore late, the concept and the content are earlier. In this respect too, indeed precisely here, the Deuteronomistic movement reintroduced theological reflection but did not initiate it. Archaic passages like Ex. 24.3–8, where law and covenant belong together, or even Ex. 34.10ff., can hardly be dated in such a way as to provide evidence for the beginning of Judaism. In that case, law and covenant both go back to the earliest period. And once it is conceded that 'law' is not an inept designation for the Old Testament, because it echoes the earliest tradition, the use of 'testament' as a rendering for covenant, which has become customary within Christianity, is also appropriate: this term, too, alludes to a basic datum of Israelite and Jewish religion.

6. *The ambivalence and pluriform meaning of the law*

The problem of the *theological* association of covenant and law clearly cannot be solved by literary criticism or the history of traditions. The question cannot be answered by a reference to a development which begins with the covenant of free grace and ends with the law. It is true that Pharisaism can only be understood in the light of some sort of development, but the divergent forms of the canon and the different possibilities for understanding scripture and the canon have shown that the development does not just end in Pharisaism and legalism. Moreover, where are we to put the figure of Jesus in any development? After all, he too is part of Judaism. Judaism is too variegated a phenomenon to be regarded as the final phase of a process of evolution.

However, the earlier Israelite understanding of covenant and law is just as varied. The Old Testament can be understood generally and as a whole to be law, and was in fact so understood; it was seen as a law, a course marked out and prescribed by God himself as a way of achieving righteousness and life and salvation by doing what was required. At the same time, while the law understood in this way can be recognized and adopted as the right course to follow, it can also be rejected and repudiated as a false approach towards a righteousness based on works. Moreover, even within the Old Testament itself, it is by no means clear what makes up the law and what the law is concerned with, i.e. whether the law itself implies legalism or not, and whether those who concern themselves with the law must necessarily fall victims to legalism.

We have already pointed out that within the Deuteronomistic books, God's free election by grace is proclaimed alongside the communication of the law. In the same way, the Priestly Writing contains a motley array of legal material. By and large it controls the organization of worship; however, worship is an unceasing act of expiation inaugurated and made possible by Yahweh, which takes away the sins of Israel and dispatches them into the wilderness along with the scapegoat. Israel has to follow the laws relating to worship, sacrifice, liturgy and pilgrimage in order to perform its acts of expiation, receive forgiveness and experience the divine indwelling. Is this legalism or the acceptance of God's grace in faith? The obligation to obey the ancestral law as a national law sanctioned by the Persian empire in the person of Ezra seems to force the Jews into holding the view that it is only possible to become a proper Jew by fulfilling the law – but is this requirement an irresistible temptation to legalism? Be this as it may, the favour bestowed by the Persian government can be seen as a demonstration of God's grace, as is shown by Ezra's great prayer (Ezra 9.9). Here, too, there is a lack of clarity.

It transpires from this that it is possible to have a meaningful discussion as to whether the commandments in the Old Testament must always have a legalistic character, despite their incorporation in the covenant, because they exclude those who transgress them from the covenant. Similarly, we can ask whether forgiveness is simply an occasional permission to depart from the basic principle of retribution, whereas in the New Testament it is ·proclaimed as a true ordinance (see e.g. F. Hesse, ' "Gebot und Gesetz" und das Alte Testament', IVв), or whether the keeping of the Old Testament commandments and obedience to the Old Testament law are to be understood as a confessional act on the part of those who have been chosen and endowed with God's grace (e.g. G. von Rad, *Old Testament Theology* I, IIIc), rather than as a burden only part of which can be borne. Here, too, it is impossible to come down firmly in favour of just one of the two competing positions. The Old Testament is certainly also familiar with the principle of retribution; this is just as much a mark of the Chronicler, who attempts to demonstrate the functioning of the principle down to the last detail, as it is of large parts of the wisdom literature, and it can also be found earlier, in a less one-sided form, in the Deuteronomistic history work. However, even the Chronicler is aware that God's grace and mercy led to quite an unmerited change of fortunes in the Persian period (Ezra 9.9, 13). And within the wisdom literature, the book of Job, which centres on a doctrine of retribution that bears the distinctive traits of wisdom, finally breaks out of the vicious circle in which Job's friends, with their notions of retribution, are trapped. It also leaves unanswered Job's appeal to his sense of innocence and the accusation which he makes against God on the basis of his experience, which is also an accusation against human justice. This is not to claim that the kind of theophany depicted at the conclusion of the book of Job is the gospel. However, is not the end of the human notion of retribution, whether it is that put forward by Job's friends or by Job himself, the darker side of the gospel? Here, too, we have no unmistakably clear answer; the discussion is broken off almost violently, as it is elsewhere in the Old Testament: see, for example, Abraham's conversation with Yahweh as to whether the godless world of Sodom may be spared for the sake of the few righteous people within it. This conversation stops short when it arrives at the figure of ten righteous men (Gen. 18.32f.). Is there anyone who would take this to mean that God would save Sodom if there were ten righteous men, but not if there were only eight or nine? And what does 'righteous' mean here anyway? The author was evidently convinced that there was not a single righteous man in Sodom. Here Sodom is the symbol of a world which has turned away from God and therefore cannot be saved by righteousness, however paltry, because that does not exist; it can be saved only by the free and gracious action of God (see M. Noth, *History of the Pentateuchal Traditions*, ET 1972, 239). Still, even this theme must first be developed by an *exegesis* of the text: the meaning must be *brought out*. The text breaks off before the end and before it has made any clear statement or indicated any gospel, so to this degree it remains ambiguous. Is it unable to proclaim the gospel, does it not dare to announce the incredible break-out from the disastrous sphere dominated by guilt and godlessness, a break-out which is perceptible only by faith, or does it simply not go on that far? Is the interpretation sketched out above in terms of the hint at a gospel without words no more than Christian eisegesis and interpretation?

Because clarity cannot be achieved, it is also possible to argue whether, say, Psalms 1; 19B; 37; 119 are evidence of Jewish legalism (see M. Noth, 'The Laws in the Pentateuch', IVb, 102f.) or of 'delight in the law' (thus H.-J. Kraus, 'Freude an Gottes Gesetz', IVb). It is possible to interpret them in either way. For example, Psalm 1 makes no direct statements about the nature of the evil done by the godless or the good done by the righteous. There is no form of moral judgment: there is no mention of a reward for good deeds or of righteousness as a recognition of good behaviour, any more than there is mention of a punishment for misdeeds. Delight in the Torah and concern for it are the only determining factors. To be concerned with it is the fullness of life, and life without it is transitory and meaningless, like chaff blown by the wind. But what does Torah mean here? Is it instruction on how to act so that the person concerned achieves righteousness? Is it initiation into a life centred on God? In other words, is it law or gospel? It is useful to argue over this question, because both sides could be right: the law might prove to be an equivocal, multi-faceted, ambivalent entity.

Psalm 1 has been cited simply as an example. Even if modern historical exegesis were to demonstrate that it was originally intended as a psalm concerned with the law and was therefore a testimony to legalism, there would still be numerous other pieces of evidence for the ambivalence of the Old Testament material. And even something that was originally legal in intention can also be understood in terms of the gospel: Torah as instruction need not necessarily be understood as an indication and a recommendation to perform an action or to acquire righteousness. And although in its original context Ps. 119.105, which is often quoted in Christian liturgy, and which says that God's word is a lamp to the feet and a light to the path, is praise of the law it does not necessarily follow that the psalmist thinks of progressing along the road to blessedness and righteousness by following precept after precept, like one signpost after another. Another meaning might be that strength and power will be received from the word which is proclaimed and encountered in constantly different ways in each new situation of life and each new point of decision. Who can rule out the possibility that Old Testament texts did have this meaning, or that, even if they did not, they were understood and lived out in this way? Here, too, it emerges that legalism need not be the only end of the development. The end resembles the beginning and, like everything that lies between, is by no means clear; it is open to various interpretations.

The same thing is also true of the sphere which is indicated by the term *berit* = covenant. Here, too, the barren and often hair-splitting controversy as to whether *berit* should be translated 'covenant' or 'obligation' is instructive to the extent that it shows that the term is equivocal and ambivalent. The covenant established one-sidedly by God, through which he binds himself and makes promises, establishes a relationship which in turn by its very nature imposes an obligation too. Once again, everything depends on where the emphasis is put: is the covenant primarily the gracious approach made by God, and does obeying the law simply mean accepting the gospel in everyday *life*, which is always a matter of doing and leaving undone, so that the law is simply one aspect of the gospel? This is the dogmatic understanding which Karl Barth wanted to put forward when he suggested that 'gospel and law' would be a better sequence than 'law and gospel' (*Evangelium und Gesetz*, 1935, IVB; and cf. the discussion on this article in *Gesetz und Evangelium, Beiträge zur gegenwärtigen theologischen Diskussion*, 1968). This is in fact a possible interpretation and understanding. If Ex. 34.10–26 really contains early tradition, this text alone shows that God announces and promises *his* powerful and glorious work *before* all that 'I command you this day'. Early amphictyonic Israel under Yahweh's law of privilege was not a community placed under the burden of the law and primarily bound to offer service, but a people who believed themselves to have been freed from slavery by God, given land and brought into being as the result of such a liberation and such a gift. The fact that it was possible to restore such an understanding at a much later period, in a developed covenant theology, shows that this understanding of Israel, and with it this understanding of covenant and obligation, was not completely lost even during the monarchy. Of course the other aspect and another possibility can also be seen in the same context: Yahweh has given the land, but his people have to liberate it as his vassals and to put the inhabitants under 'the ban', exterminating them and destroying their altars, their idols and their sacred groves (Ex. 23.32f.; 34.11–16). This view, too, is 'restored' in Deut. 7, and the book of Joshua contains narratives to show how Israel acted in accordance with the covenant. Here Israel uses fire and sword, albeit in God's name and with his help, to establish a divine rule which would become a bloody example for all later crusaders who drew their swords from their sheaths, or blessed weapons, or made financial contributions.

Historically speaking, less blood was shed than seems to have been the case from the account in the book of Joshua, which was written later and has a good deal of fictitious and saga-like material in it. The conquest seems predominantly to have been a peaceful process, and both the Deuteronomistic injunctions not to spare the inhabitants of Canaan (Deut. 7.2, 16–25) and the ancient parallels (Ex. 23.22–24, 31–33; 34.11–16; cf. Num. 21.2; Judg. 1.17; I Sam. 15.3) seem to have been given their form at a later stage. However, this does not affect the fact that this aspect of the covenant, the law and the rule of God, which is without doubt *also* present and was without doubt also put into effect, is extremely questionable. Man's concern for power or even for self-assertion takes on a religious colouring in the form of the holy war, in which every able-bodied member of the people of God rushes to the help of their God (Judg. 5.23 and the rest of chapter 5; Ex. 15.1–21 and here especially the oldest part, 15.21), and everything that stands in the way of the zeal of God and his representatives, man or beast (Deut. 13.16f.; Josh. 6.21ff.), is put to the 'ban', i.e. annihilated, while their homes are burnt to the ground.

It is extremely significant at this point that although the injunction not to spare the original inhabitants of Canaan appears in the context of the covenant and the law and in connection with Yahweh's privileged claim on Israel, the Israel which is singled out here is no different in principle from the nations round about. The Moabites were also familiar with the ban in the holy war, as is clear from the famous Mesha stele (*TGI*, 51ff.; *KAI*, 181, 17; *NERT*, 237ff.). So this is no peculiarity of Israel, nor is it a specific aspect of law and covenant. Here once again we can see the ambivalence of the people who called themselves Israel and understood themselves to be the people of God. There was a constant temptation and danger that the people of God who had been set apart, as they believed, in the service of their God and with his aid, would forfeit their character and become just like 'the nations round about'. The ambivalence of law and covenant is more than just a linguistic phenomenon; it is, rather, a reflection of the ambiguity and uncertainty as to precisely what it is that constitutes Israel and the people of God. The most serious problem here is not that of the definition of the relationship between covenant and law, whether the covenant or the law has priority. In no passage in the Old Testament where covenant refers to the relationship between God and Israel is there any thought of a mutual treaty which can be broken by either side: the covenant is always God's gracious ordinance. This is also the belief of the authors of Psalms 1; 19B and 119, even if these prayers are to be understood in legalistic terms. The question is, rather, whether the covenant is realized only when the law is obeyed, and is of no effect when man is disobedient, or whether the promise of God given in the covenant, and the obligations which he takes upon himself, are stronger than human failure. The author of the Song of Deborah (Judg. 5) believed that there was a curse on the inhabitants of Meroz, who kept their swords in their sheaths and stayed at home instead of standing by Yahweh in the holy war in the hour of danger, while Jael the Kenite is 'blessed among women' because she treacherously killed the enemy general. In this approach he gives one possible interpretation of law and covenant, from which a line can be sketched out right down to the present (see 109ff. above). We do not know what kept the people of Meroz and others from the war. Did they simply stay away out of cowardice? There is no answer to the question, but it is not a meaningless one for that reason. Here already in the earliest period we can see something of the ambivalence to which reference has been made so often, and which becomes even more marked at a much later time: the 'true believers' whose views can be read in the book of Daniel regarded the Maccabees, who fought their battles on the model and in the footsteps of Deborah, Barak and Jael the Kenite, as no more than 'a little help' (Dan. 11.34), looking for their true and 'great help' from beyond, from God, and not from human action and fighting. Here, albeit in later, apocalyptic form, we have the other possibility of understanding and practising the law and the covenant. It does not always include quietism, the action of those who stay at home in the hour of need, but it is aware that human action can offer only a little help and that the existence of the covenant and therefore of divine salvation does not depend on it.

By virtue of this recognition, apocalyptic is without doubt the successor of prophecy. Israel's greatest prophecy, from the time just before the catastrophe which befell the nation and the people, was bound to present in a particularly urgent form the question which had always been in the background in connection with the law and the covenant: 'Was God's love, promised here, so overwhelming that even Israel's failure to observe the divine law could not annul the covenant, or was the concern of the zealous God for justice so great that one day the covenant bestowed in grace would be annulled in view of the transgressions of the people?' (W. Zimmerli, 'Das Gesetz im Alten Testament', IVB, 270). The greatness of pre-exilic prophecy consists in the way in which it recognized the terrifying dimensions of this question. Now, in the political crisis of the nation, a further problem arose which is closely connected with the previous one: the individual and his failings did not put the covenant in question to the same degree; an individual sinner could be excluded from fellowship with God and man (from both the covenant and the life of the community). But was not Israel itself in breach of the covenant if as a state it lived an autonomous life? What was the relationship between Yahweh's law of privilege and the autonomous character of the state? Is not political action the embodiment of human self-assertion, independence and autocracy? Whereas in the early period before the rise of the monarchy there might perhaps have been a belief in a complete conformity between Yahweh's law of privilege, the rule of God, divine law, political action and the holy war under charismatic rulers, from the time of the formation of the monarchy onwards the problem of this conformity (in the form of continually new and specific points of conflict between political and military necessity on the one hand and Yahweh's own covenant ordinances with their justice, law and further demands on the other) became increasingly acute. As the very foundations of state and nation began to shake under the onslaught of first the Assyrian and then the

Babylonian empire, the state and thus the identity of its members with the people of God inevitably became problematical in a way which extended far beyond the limits of any single conflict. This profound problem, which has yet to be resolved in contemporary discussion of religion and politics, was recognized by the great prophets of Israel. But each of them offered different answers.

For Amos, Israel's guilt is so great that forgiveness is impossible. In theological terms, that clearly means that the *law* has the pre-eminence here: an Israel which does not obey Yahweh's will is on the road to ruin. Amos' preaching announces an end to Israel 'for three transgressions, and for four' (Amos 8.2; 2.6). We cannot tell here whether this radical 'no' was conceivable only because Yahweh's 'Yes' still applied to *Judah*. 'Amos's no' (Smend, IVB) is quite unequivocal, and for those to whom it refers it means the absolute end. The law kills and allows nothing to survive: 'The end has come upon my people Israel; I will never again pass by them' (Amos 8.2).

Isaiah gives a different answer: Israel is on the road to ruin, but a remnant will return and a new Israel will rise from it (Isaiah 6–8). This new, true Israel is not founded on its own achievements, nor can it rely on confederates and military force (Isa. 30.1–5; 31.1–3); it 'believes' and finds its strength in 'stillness' (Isa. 7.4, 9; 28.16; 30.15). This renunciation of political alliances and military power can be seen in the dawning recognition that the people of God and God's rule are not identical with the members of the state and the state itself. Theirs is not a status that can be achieved by human beings with human means; it can only be received as a gift, by keeping a firm hold on God's promises (faith). This distinction between Israel and the remnant, Israel and the true Israel, is also expressed in a new insight into the old ambivalence of the ethnic, social and religious groups which call themselves Israel and understand themselves to be the people of God on the basis of a divine covenant and a divine law of privilege. Since Israel, now divided as a state into north and south, is a political entity which enters into alliances, prepares for war and generally involves itself in political affairs and intrigues, and chooses to live by its own human strength rather than by faith and tranquillity before God (Isa. 30.15f.), it has broken the divine covenant and is therefore doomed to destruction, like Sodom (Isa. 1. 10). However, the fall of Israel also brings about a division within it: the true Israel, of which Isaiah and his followers are already representatives, is singled out from the mass of people who are on the way to ruin (Isa. 8.11–14). Faith is constitutive of this new Israel, but in so to speak a negative sense: 'If you do not believe, you will not be established' (Isa. 7.9). Those who do not believe are delivered up to annihilation.

Isaiah is therefore well aware of the dilemma produced by the association of covenant and law: how is the rule of God, established in the covenant and promised for the future, to be realized in the specific actions of the people of God? He also recognizes that the state with its weapons and alliances, an embodiment of human action, human self-assertion, wilfulness and autonomy, cannot be identical with the theocracy and the people of God. Finally, he sees that if God's rule is really his own, and is possible only from God's side, man can do no more than react passively, in faith, 'holding fast' and 'remembering promises'; he cannot reach for his own weapons. Amos's 'no' may be unequivocal, but it is not a solution; it is a sign of the ultimate end. By contrast, Isaiah's 'yes' to the remnant still requires further clarification. Is the 'remnant' not one more entity within the world and within history, a group in and around Jerusalem who are equally this-worldly in relying on tangible miracles from Yahweh rather than on their own weapons? Is not 'We will speed upon horses' (Isa. 30.16) now replaced by a God-with-us (Immanuel, Isa. 7.14), which has a far greater effect than the strongest war-horses, by virtue of its miraculous power? Is human action in politics and war, which has now been condemned, to give way to God's miraculous intervention on behalf of the remnant? Isaiah does not give a clear answer to these questions. In any case, the insight that the empirical state in Israel and Judah is not simply identical with Yahweh's covenant people, who are supported by his law of privilege, and that the rule of God is not established by human action, but is only turned into its opposite, can lead to a mixture of utopianism and quietism which represents the furthest extreme possible from those manifest warriors who came to the help of their God with weapons in their hands. The idea of the 'remnant which returns' and 'believes' may amount to a breakthrough beyond the constraints of self-assertion and the feeling that God's rule has to be established or secured by human means – and to this degree may be a posthumous vindication of the people of Meroz who stayed at home – but it is not a breakthrough beyond the limitations and restraints imposed by the world and history. Even the remnant, and the new Israel which arises from it, is firmly rooted in this sphere and subjected to the necessity of establishing itself under the conditions of this world. The only difference is that this new existence is now looked for as a result of a divine miracle, and not of human action.

A law which calls for action now becomes a law which requires belief in miracles. So it need not have been disbelief and hardness of heart that caused King Ahaz to refuse to tempt such a God (Isa. 7.12).

The preaching of other prophets about the same dilemma of covenant and law, the people of God and the existence of the state, shows that it is not only difficult but impossible to obtain a single answer from the Old Testament, or even just from the prophets; we cannot therefore regard any one answer as typical of the Old Testament. Hosea also makes Yahweh say 'no': Israel is no longer his people and Yahweh is no longer Israel's God (Hos. 1.9). For Hosea, the monarchy is the beginning of all wickedness (Hos. 9.15), indeed an expression of the divine wrath (Hos. 13.11). For Hosea, as for Amos, the law has the power to kill. But God's 'no' to Israel is nevertheless in a paradoxically dialectical relationship with a 'yes'. The 'yes' does not weaken the 'no', but it does create Israel anew in the wilderness and out of the wilderness of its rejection (Hos. 2.14f.). The law may kill, but Yahweh gives life, for his love is stronger than the death-dealing power of the law. This is the way in which God shows that he is God (Hos. 11.8f.). So here hope is not directed towards a remnant that will be saved because of its faith; all Israel is under judgment and the covenant will only be renewed in the wilderness, to which it is made to return as to the origin of its existence, the place where it was wholly dependent on the gracious support and guidance of God (Hos. 2.14–20). The newly betrothed bride, Israel, is given everything that is established by the new divine covenant as a dowry: righteousness and justice, grace and mercy, faithfulness. The new covenant is pure gift, beyond judgment and independent of the works of the law.

At a later date, Jeremiah once again resembles Hosea by expressing similar ideas. God will only have mercy on his people and renew them (Jer. 29.1–7; 24; 32.1–16), granting them *shalom*, after judgment and as a result of this judgment, in Babylon and despite the Babylonian captivity. And according to the vision of the dead and their resurrection in Ezek. 37, the new, true people of God are brought into being so to speak from dry and lifeless bones. Here too, God and God alone puts his new beginning at the absolute nadir, when the law has exhausted its fatal power. The same radical renewal is also held in prospect with yet other words and images in the secondary promise of Jeremiah (Jer. 31.31–34); at this point the concepts of covenant and law appear. The law is also part of the new covenant, but now it is a law written by God himself on the heart, and men will obey the law spontaneously by virtue of their knowledge of God.

We have seen how the theological association of law and covenant is generally left ambiguous in the Old Testament. The prophets also recognize the problem, or at least suspect it, but they are by no means unanimous in their answer and are seldom unequivocal. However, behind all the ambiguities here there is a yet more fundamental problem. The problem of the law and the covenant is closely bound up with another issue which has once again become topical: can the rule of God and the people of God be brought into being within the world and within history, and if so, how? People often content themselves with the view that the prophets reject the wrong kind of politics, autonomous politics. But how can politics be other than autonomous? In fact the prophets rejected *all* alliances and therefore, since politics largely consists of entering into and breaking alliances, rejected all politics as the autonomous action of the people of God. This rejection is at the same time both an answer to the dilemma and the cause of a further problem. The dilemma lies in the identification of the people of God with the members of the state. The rule of God is to be realized in the nation and in the state, and the nation and the state are to understand themselves as the kingdom of God. There is no way out of this dilemma. The solution put forward by Isaiah and other prophets, to renounce alliances and preparations for war, is no solution, since the state cannot 'be tranquil' and 'believe' by avoiding politics without giving up its very existence. The recognition that the kingdom of God is 'not of this world' (John 18.36) can only be arrived at when it proves possible to break out of the framework of 'this world' and the need is no longer felt to realize the kingdom within history. In this eschatological context, where a distinction is made between faith and sight (II Cor. 5.7; Rom. 8.24f.; John 20.29), it is clear that even if the kingdom of God is in the world its character is not of this world (Bultmann, *Gospel of John*, IIA, 654), so that it cannot be established, as Isa. 31.4f. expects, either by human arms or by the descent of heavenly warriors (John 18.36).

The Old Testament fails to achieve this final degree of (eschatological) clarity. It offers a great variety of answers, but even so, many questions are left unresolved. It is possible to work out the questions and answers, even the questions which are either left unanswered or answered in a way which gives rise to further questions. But what is the solution? Who is right? Deborah and Barak, or the people of Meroz? Jehu (II Kings 9) or Hosea (Hos. 1.4)? Isaiah or Ahaz? Isaiah or Jeremiah? The Maccabees or the quietists? The zealots or Flavius Josephus, who blames them for the fall of Jerusalem? Or, to put it in a different way and in more general terms: in the last resort, is the Old Testament covenant or law – a testament, or a divine promise and an ordinance of salvation? Which is the right description? If we keep within the bounds of the Old Testament, either description is possible, since both are given. There is no possibility of drawing a line from law to covenant or from covenant to law. And it is easy enough to demonstrate that the problem of this ambivalence and ambiguity, which is an existential problem rather than a matter of abstract theology, was already recognized within the Old Testament. It is also clear that no solution to the problem was arrived at here. That does not, of course, mean that not only individual texts of the Old Testament, but the whole collection of them and every phenomenon of ancient Israel, are sunk in a twilight which blots out any clear interpretation; nor is it the case that the Old Testament contains one or more incomplete lines of development which are open either towards the New Testament or towards Judaism and only reveal their final destination clearly in the final stages, when they arrive at Paul's freedom from the law or at Talmudic Judaism. On the contrary, crusaders and zealots for the law can be found in the earliest stages, and zealots can also be found at the end of the development. That all law is preceded by the covenant promise is an article of faith in the earliest period, and remains the conviction of those who praise the law as the gift of salvation and a way of life, delighting in the fact. The ambiguity which is never resolved within the Old Testament is rather, in the last resort, the question of the ultimate validity of the law and the gospel. Because of this all-pervading ambivalence, individual texts and individual phenomena have no overall significance, even though their actual, individual meaning may be clear. The theocratic crusaders of Judges 4f.; the bloody deeds of Jehu (II Kings 9f.), initiated by the prophets and given their blessing; the battles of the Maccabees and the zealots; or Isaiah, who seeks to encourage tranquillity and faith; or Jeremiah's proclamation of salvation in the midst of judgment – are these the rule or the exception? And how can we determine what is the rule and what the exception, what is the climax and what is the nadir, what is intended as law and what as 'gospel'? If the number of relevant passages cannot be the criterion, then what criterion can be applied from within the Old Testament? The discussion of law and covenant among scholars, together with the various possibilities of understanding the canon and the different ways in which the Old Testament has been accepted into the church, not to mention the arguments about the right way to understand covenant, law and God's rule in Israel itself (which can already be found within the Old Testament), have failed to lead to a clear conclusion here. On the contrary, they show that there is no such criterion.

This is merely to state the facts; it is not an attempt to envelop the Old Testament in a mysterious darkness which can only truly be illuminated by a Christian interpretation. Because it is a collection of religious and national literature spanning about a thousand years, the Old Testament no more has a clear central point than any other literature. This is not surprising – it would be surprising if things were otherwise. Attempts to establish a centre in spite of this are either a counsel of desperation or lead to empty formulae, as for instance that God is the centre of the Old Testament (see e.g. G. F. Hasel, 'The Problem of the Center', IIIc; see also 88ff. above). But if there is no centre, there can be no intrinsic criterion. Pharisaism used its own criterion for interpreting and using the Old Testament, though this was not completely consistent. Judaism understood it, as it does now, in a rather less consistent way, ranging from Jewish orthodoxy, which sees the law as being literally binding, to the approach which sees it as nationalistic literature, crucial for regaining and strengthening a sense of national identity. Christianity inherited it as the 'Old Testament' and either made it its law, saw it as the constant goad and scandal of legalism, or read it as a promise of the new covenant, the law of which is written in men's hearts. So can and should anyone believe himself to be on the road to salvation if he takes 'his' Old Testament in his hand and interprets it in his own way, whether as holy scripture or nationalistic literature? The question can be answered both positively and negatively. Positively, in that the designation 'law' is as apt an evaluation as an understanding of the Old Testament as the national literature of Israel and Judah or indeed as covenant, testament, Old Testament. Depending on the standpoint of the observer, each of these views offers a central point from which the whole of the Old Testament can be considered. Negatively, in that the standpoint of the observer is not a purely arbitrary matter, and the evaluations and negative criticisms, the acceptance and the rejection to which he finds himself led, should not do violence to the texts as they were originally understood. On the contrary, they are what they are, evaluations. And above all, the rejection of Christ, or the proclamation of the end of the law, or the belief grounded in the Christ event, that man can become righteous apart from the works of the law, are not subjective views which can be exchanged at will. The phrase 'à chacun son goût' is

far from being an adequate description of them; these are fundamental decisions which embrace one's whole understanding of God
and human existence. In particular, even thosè who read the Old
Testament from a Christian perspective cannot legitimately use
subjective standards to produce a Christian reinterpretation which
makes even the last detail of the sacrificial law into a gospel of grace.
At the same time, however, this last perspective is probably itself the
criterion by means of which the clearest distinction can be made
between law and gospel; the dilemma present within the Old
Testament and the bare law (death-dealing in the literal sense) are
recognized; and the gospel can be heard from the Old Testament in
one way or another, whether openly, in hidden form, or through mere
hints. These comments do not introduce a new hermeneutical
programme: in fact the church has always read selections from the
Old Testament according to this criterion and has seen both law and
gospel in the Old Testament by using the same standard. Faulty
dogmatic and hermeneutical theories may think that they can find
Christ and his gospel in the law or – much worse – interpret the
gospel as a law, but practice has often been better than theological
theories – one only has to think of Luther or even of Calvin!
It was the practice of believing Christians through which the power of
the Old and New Testaments could be felt.

V

THE OLD TESTAMENT AS THE
DOCUMENT OF AN ALIEN RELIGION

1. *The alien nature of the Old Testament discovered and emphasized*

The question whether the Old Testament as a whole and in the last resort is to be understood as law or not, and even an affirmative answer to this question, belong in a sphere which may be termed 'theological' in the narrower sense. In this context there is no questioning of the validity of the law: it demands obedience, it kills, it directs men towards Christ. Both the law and the gospel are seen as divine institutions. The God of the Old Testament and the law is the God of the New Testament and the gospel. Paul had no doubt about that, and for many theologians in the twentieth century it has been the fundamental principle of belief, the very foundation of all their reflections on the relationship between the testaments (cf. e.g. Franz Hesse, *Das Alte Testament als Buch der Kirche*, IIIc, 21; and see 220ff. below). However, the distinction between law and gospel can take on wider dimensions: it can be seen as the distinction between a purely human law and a divine gospel, between the law of an alien religion and the Christian gospel, or even as the distinction between different religions, i.e. between the religion of Israel and of Judaism and the Christian religion. Once it has been developed to this degree, the distinction is no longer concerned solely with the law and legalism as opposed to the gospel: it throws into relief the alien nature of the Old Testament in comparison with Christianity. The distinction is pointed up even further when the content of the New Testament proclamation is also considered as it were from outside and regarded as a religion. Now religion takes the place of revelation – which may be thought to be found in both the Old Testament *and* the New Testament, or in the

New but *not* in the Old. Only those who believe in a revelation and feel that they have received one can speak of revelation in the strict sense; religion, on the other hand, can be treated in a quite objective way. To look at something objectively is to put it at a distance, to remove it from the sphere of personal concern and to subject it to sober reconstruction. And in this light the Old Testament seems more alien than the New, because it is the earlier document and because the content of the New Testament is more familiar in the Christian West, where it has influenced tradition and had considerable influence on the church.

Although this objective consideration of the Old Testament has been fully developed only in modern times, it has roots which go back a long way into the past. They can even be found in the gospel of John.

The synoptic gospels seldom speak of 'the Jews', but in the Fourth Gospel the term appears seventy times, both in a neutral sense (which is a striking fact in itself) as a designation for the people with whom Jesus was involved, and to denote Jesus' opponents. In the latter case, the term 'Jew' can be used in such a way and can appear in such a context that it clearly refers to those who cannot understand the Christ and therefore reject him, to his opponents. They cannot understand him, and reject the Revealer *because* they are *Jews*. We can read this out of John 2.18–21. Because the Jews believe that God is present in a temple built with hands in Jerusalem, they rule out from the start the possibility that God reveals himself in the death and resurrection of Christ. According to 8.48–59, the attack on Christ is mounted by the Jews as Jews and with Jewish arguments. John 10.32–38 is particularly noteworthy, because in this passage the Old Testament is not only described as law, but even as 'your law'. Here and elsewhere there is a clear indication of the difference between Judaism and the Old Testament understood as the law and the document of another alien and even hostile religion (cf. also John 9.29; 11.8; 20.19).

The Johannine community had obviously parted company with the synagogue and no longer regarded the Old Testament as holy scripture.

At a later stage, the mainstream church did not follow either Pauline or Johannine theology, each of which had its own particular understanding of the Old Testament. It settled for a *via media*, a 'catholic' line, explaining the alien character of the Old Testament more and more by means of allegorical interpretation, which produced another, more congenial sense, and accusing the Jews of unbelief because they had proved quite incapable of understanding their own holy book. Where, however, the church's doctrinal approach was not accepted, and it proved impossible to conceal the alien character of the Old Testament by means of allegory, much greater stress was laid on the distinction between the Old and the New Testaments in polemic against such a 'false' canon. Marcion must be mentioned again at this point. He took the Pauline contrast between gospel and law to such lengths that he rejected the Old Testament completely, as being the document of an alien religion. The basis for his view was not, of course, detached and objective historical consideration: such an approach was inconceivable in Marcion's time. The way in which he thought and argued was influenced by myth and Gnosticism, in accord with contemporary trends. However, his mythical doctrine that the Old Testament creator god, the god of the law and of righteousness (who was called the 'demiurge'), was a different god from the one proclaimed by Luke and Paul in their gospels, could be demythologized in the following way. There is a sharp contrast between existence under the law and life in accordance with the grace of the gospel; each different understanding of existence has a god to match, which results in two different religions: that of the Jews and that of the Christians. In this way the Old Testament, which is to be understood literally and not allegorically, becomes the document of an alien religion. For Marcion, its god is not a theoretical, theological entity of merely historical significance, but a dangerous reality and power.

Even where there was not such a one-sided stress on the alien and alienating character of the Old Testament, and where such extreme consequences were not drawn, the very existence of Judaism was a constant goad. The Jews were independent of the church and existed alongside it and in conflict with it; they also laid claim to the Old Testament and were concerned to live in accordance with its law, and in so doing provided a constant reminder that the Old Testament had a different character from the New. The ceremonial law, the food laws, the regulations for the sabbath and the requirement of circumcision which had been abrogated and abandoned (with whatever justification), represented an alien element which could only be incorporated into Christianity with the subtlest allegorical skills. Alternatively, people resorted to the expedient of appealing to passages in scripture which suggested that God did not really want sacrifices and ceremonies or that they were enjoined on Israel only because of its sinfulness and hard-heartedness (e.g. Jer. 7.21–24; Ezek.

20.19–21; Amos 5.21–27; Ps. 50.7–15). Or, like Origen, they argued that allegorical interpretation was right and proper because the laws were meaningless if they were interpreted literally; they could not be carried out, and they were only imposed on the Jews as a punishment, so that one day they would recognize their true and higher meaning. This also provides an explanation for the difference between Christian and Jewish practice, between Christianity and Judaism, although the God in question is always the same. Not only Marcion, but also the Gnostics think in terms of different gods: the 'God of the Jews', who is not identical with the Father of Jesus Christ and cannot be compared with him, is the prince of angels, the creator of the lower, imperfect world and the giver of the tyrannical law; because the Old Testament often depicts him in visible form, he is not the true God, who is invisible and spiritual. Although in Gnosticism this is often grounded in and explained by means of abstruse speculations and pseudo-profound, arbitrary interpretations, as in Marcion there is an unmistakable attempt to lay more stress on the new, distinctive and different character of Christianity (albeit misconstrued in Gnostic terms), as opposed to Judaism and paganism, than was possible in the mediating theology of the mainstream church. Here, figurative and allegorical interpretation was a way of substantiating the church's exclusive claim to the Old Testament in the controversy with heretics and Jews. Indeed, just as Origen thought that he could produce a *reductio ad absurdum* of literal exegesis with his remark that without allegorical interpretation people would have to keep on slaughtering animals for sacrifice, so allegorical exegesis became virtually the hallmark of orthodox biblical interpretation, whereas an emphasis on the literal sense was thought to be Jewish, Judaizing or downright heretical. At the same time, however, because the church largely surrendered the literal sense to Jews and heretics, it unwittingly conceded both that the Old Testament was an alien document and that a Judaism which appealed to a literal understanding of the Old Testament was an independent phenomenon in its own right. The hermeneutical problem of the Old Testament was suppressed, and an open question was closed on the authority of the church. No one dared to ask why scripture inspired by the Holy Spirit of God should prove to be so obscure and enigmatic as to require the art of allegorical interpretation for its decipherment. Anyone who, like Jerome, was concerned about the literal sense and realized the necessity of philological study, could easily fall under the suspicion of being a crypto-heretic, despite his faithfulness to the party line, his piety and his emphatic assertions that scripture was to be interpreted spiritually, and not according to the letter. We can understand this reserve, in view of a developing polarization of viewpoints: a concern for the literal sense was associated with an increasingly abrupt repudiation of the Old Testament, and the church had to guard against this surrender of its heritage, comprising the greater part of holy scripture, even if the weapons which it chose were unsuitable. The church could not accept Marcion's claim that the God of the Old Testament was a different God from the God of Jesus Christ, indeed a creator god (demiurge) who was hostile to him; this was not an authentic explanation of its origin, of Paul's gospel or even of the Old Testament.

The same is also true of Manichaeism, which emerged in the fourth century as quite a dangerous competitor for the church. In the context of the Manichaean dualism of light and darkness, the God of the Jews is the prince of darkness, and his law brings death instead of life. His prophets do not foretell the Christ, and his message is addressed only to the Jews. A favourite way of showing that the God of the Old Testament was different and alien was to quote all the passages which in a literalistic interpretation proved to be offensive in religious or moral terms, for example those that indicated that God was jealous (Ex. 20.5), that he brought damnation instead of salvation (Isa. 45.7; Amos 3.6), or that he had commanded the extermination of the Canaanites. The God of the Old Testament was not even omniscient, because if he had been, he would have foreseen Adam's sin. The laws of purity and the regulations about the sabbath and about circumcision either did not come from the true God, or they ought still to be observed by Christians. Above all, however, the Manichaeans objected – as others were to continue to do in later times – to the earthly and materialistic content of the Old Testament promises: the possession of land, fertility, a long and happy life. The sensual character of this promised salvation was matched by the morally reprehensible life of the chief figures of the Old Testament, of which examples could easily be cited. The arguments and attacks assembled and accumulated here kept recurring in subsequent periods, and have continued down to the present day. They have been used in an attempt to prove that the ideas and conceptions of the Old Testament world are inferior to those of Christianity and in any case show that by contrast the Old Testament portrays an alien religion. The line taken by the Manichees was continued by the Catharists (= the pure) in the twelfth century. This ascetic sect, which became particularly influential in southern France and northern Italy, used the same arguments to reject the Old Testament as the document of an un-Christian and unspiritual religion, which looked forward to a purely materialistic salvation. However, the extremism of this all-embracing understanding of the Old Testament simply seemed to justify the official line taken by the mainstream church with its allegorical interpretation. So the approach which began to make itself felt here, and which was no less correct for being heretical, was unable to progress very far.

It was only with the resolute return to the literal sense at the time of the Reformation that the veil spread over the Old Testament by allegorical interpretation, dogma, tradition and the authority of the church was ripped away. As a result, it could once again be seen just how alien this collection of writings was. It is easy to assemble, especially from Luther's writings, a collection of statements which, taken by themselves apart from other comments, sound so Marcionite that Harnack could argue that the failure to jettison the Old Testament ballast from the ship of the church was in the end simply a piece of inconsistency. For Luther, the law was the 'social code of the Jews', and even the ten commandments had a Jewish colouring, although they were in essence identical with the natural law which was common to all men. Christians had no interest in any of the Jewish elements in the Old Testament. Moses was the lawgiver for the Jews, not for the Christians. Remarks like this (cf. H. Bornkamm, *Luther and the Old Testament*, IIIA, which gives a representative collection of comments) express the recognition that the Old Testament is *also* the document of a particularist non-Christian religion and way of life. Despite this, Luther does not go as far as Marcion in rejecting the Old Testament completely, because he can also see the dialectic between law and gospel within the Old Testament, and does not simply identify the law with the Old Testament and the gospel with the New (see 51ff. above). However, we can hardly claim that this is a solution to the problem how the Old Testament can be – at least also – a document of another religion while at the same time remaining part of the Christian canon. The correct insight and fruitful approach represented by the dialectical distinction between law and gospel is concerned with the law and legalism generally, and does not need the Old Testament as a justification and a basis. Luther still failed to see that if the assessment of the Old Testament as 'the Jewish social code' were applied consistently, without any exaggerated emphasis, it could make the whole of the Old

Testament an alien document. Such a conclusion was obscured by the assumption that not only did the Old Testament contain the same dialectic between law and gospel as the New, but both testaments formed part of a greater whole, even if the Old Testament contained elements which were no longer of concern. Both testaments were concerned with the same God and his revelation, and *both bore witness to Christ*: the Psalter in particular, which stood high in Luther's esteem, spoke of Christ, his death, his resurrection and his ascension. Other Old Testament passages are proofs for the doctrine of the Trinity (e.g. Num. 6.22–27). The view put forward, for example, by Harnack in his book on Marcion, where he continually stresses that Luther and his followers were less than consistent here, is fully justified. The same is even more true of the other Reformers, especially Calvin. Inherited dogma and the weight of tradition were too heavy for any real progress to be made in epistemology, despite the profound advances made, for example, by Luther himself. Hardly had the veil been lifted from the Old Testament than it was put back by Protestant orthodoxy. The Old Testament was no longer seen as an alien document, and the dogma of verbal inspiration either made it impossible to discuss the hermeneutical problem of the Old Testament openly or banished such talk from the sacred haunts of theology and the church.

The consequence of this development was that the problem, once suppressed, began to emerge again as it were on the periphery, from where it forced its way back into theology and the church with great vigour. Socinianism, which provided powerful impulses in this direction, must be singled out for mention here. Faustus Socinus (Fausto Sozzini, 1539–1604) emphatically made sound reason (*sana ratio*) the criterion for biblical interpretation. Reason was to lay bare the rational element from the historical garb in which it had been decked by the Bible. Here we have a prefiguration of rationalism, with its anthropocentric approach; dogmatic prejudgments and prejudices are questioned as a matter of principle, though at the same time this approach is not developed to any great degree. In particular, sober consideration demonstrates the difference between the two testaments. There is a recognition that Old Testament thought is nationalistic and limited, whereas in the New Testament the gospel is proclaimed universally to all men and all nations. Here too, as earlier in Manichaeism, it is made quite clear that the Old Testament promises an earthly salvation. The recognition that the Old Testament, because it is nationalistic and historically conditioned, needs to be understood historically, points forward to future developments.

Whereas the church may interpret many psalms messianically, in terms of Christ, sound reason teaches that such psalms originally referred to David or to other earthly kings of Israel. For example, Psalm 22, which was thought to have special significance as a christological psalm, is to be understood as the lamentation of some unfortunate man whose name we do not know. The view generally held within the church, that the prophets foretold Christ, is largely toned down: they are said to have announced the future, but this was seen to refer to Christ only at a later stage and from a Christian perspective. Whereas the Old Testament is not said in so many words to be the document of an alien religion, its difference from the New Testament can be seen clearly. And although the Socinians could exercise little direct influence as a sect, because they were proscribed and exiled, their rationalistic and anthropocentric approach and their sense of historical distinctions continued to have some effect. Despite some crude errors and confusions – anti-Trinitarianism and rationalism mixed up with supranaturalism – this movement was ahead of its time and in the not too distant future the church was to learn that the theological and hermeneutical problem could not be solved by claims to power, persecution, and the burning of heretics (as for example Servetus in Geneva in 1553).

2. The devaluation and repudiation of the Old Testament

Reason, the instrument used by the Socinians in interpretation, and also commended and employed by Grotius and Spinoza, could not be suppressed. Spinoza himself was a Jew, so for him the Old Testament could not be a problem as the document of an alien religion over against Christianity, even though large parts of the Old Testament ceased to have any immediate value because he regarded them as mere popular opinion, which could in no way reproduce and comprehend adequately an absolute doctrine of God. Reason is not only the instrument of investigation, but also the screen which sieves out everything that is either really or apparently irrational. This tendency finds full effect where the freedom of reason is not limited in any way by concern for the synagogue or the church or by the ties of tradition and dogma. Thus the English free-thinkers who emerged in the second half of the seventeenth century and who were known as Deists proved, like Spinoza, to be an important stimulus to the free investigation of the Pentateuch (for example, Hobbes did not believe that Moses had written any of the Pentateuch except for parts of Deuteronomy). Although they furthered study of the first and most important part of the Old Testament canon, the idea of a natural and reasonable religion which they developed proved to be an inadequate criterion by which to assess the Old Testament. Judged by the criterion of reason, the religion of the Old Testament loses its character as revelation and proves to be no different from other particularist and nationalistic religions, the rites and ceremonies of which prove to be comparable with those of Israelite and Jewish worship. Such 'external' rites and ceremonies, especially animal sacrifice, could not be part of a truly rational religion, nor could they be ordained by God. The argument that true religion is concerned with the bliss of the immortal soul and not with earthly welfare recurs once more here; it is meant to indicate that the Old Testament with its material benefits cannot be regarded *in toto* as the document of the true religion. It is only a short step from the historical reflections and insights of John Spencer (1630–1693), who sought to derive a number of Mosaic laws and rituals from other Semitic religions and denied that at least this part of the Old Testament had the character of revelation (how could something be revelation that was also in vogue outside Israel?), to the position of Thomas Morgan (1680–1743). Morgan branded the Old Testament the document of a narrow-minded, nationalistic Jewish religion, and argued that the true religion of reason was embodied only in Pauline Christianity. Like Marcion in the early days, Morgan marshalled every conceivable argument which might indicate that the religion attested in the Old Testament was alien and inferior: the law is merely external, it threatens earthly punishment and knows of no retribution in the world to come. In fact, the Old Testament as a whole knows nothing of eternal life. The extermination of the Canaanites is morally reprehensible; the miracle stories are a cheat and a deception; the messiah looked for by the prophets has nothing in common with the Christ of the Christians. In short, Yahweh is the false god of an alien nationalistic religion.

We have already shown the influence that such ideas had on the continent and how they spread (see 69ff above). Semler's new 'free investigation of the canon' (IIIB) also led him to regard large tracts of the Old Testament as testimony to an alien religion which in some respects was even opposed to Christianity – seen as the embodiment of the 'rational' and the 'morally improving'. This new perspective could not fail to bring to light the difference between the two testaments. Historically speaking, the Old Testament canon is primarily a Jewish collection of Israelite and Jewish writings. They therefore have no immediate Christian content; they belong to the Jewish religion, which is by no means identical with Christianity. They have, rather, a particularist, nationalistic character, whereas the Christian message is directed to all individuals. Moreover, the content of the Old Testament promises is materialistic, whereas the Christian religion is concerned with 'moral improvement', i.e. religious and moral perfection and the fulfilment of human life. Semler's character-ization of the Old Testament, which takes its bearings from Spinoza, also excludes any idea of the combination of the two testaments in a history of salvation. The message of the New Testament is equally near to and equally remote from the worlds of the Old Testament and of paganism. Although Semler accepts that some things in the Old Testament might possibly be valid for Christians, especially those elements which in his view rise above the particularist, Jewish and merely this-worldly limitations which are characteristic of the col-lection as a whole, the logical conclusion of his view is the repudiation of the Old Testament as part of the Christian canon. In Semler's view, select extracts from the Old Testament writings might be a good solution. On the one hand, this would correspond to the way in which the Christian church has always used its traditional heritage: in fact Christians have always used only a limited selection from the Old Testament, for whatever reason. On the other hand, Semler's sug-gestion of an Old Testament anthology goes far beyond the church's usage, since it has never marked out a Christian canon within the Old Testament canon and rejected all the rest.

The criterion offered by moralistic rationalism may have proved to be inadequate, and rationalism may in some respects have got in the way of an adequate historical approach, despite the powerful stimuli which it gave to historical research. Nevertheless, once the course of historical and critical investigation had been embarked upon, there was no turning back. It was not just as a matter of practical con-venience that biblical theology soon divided itself into a theology of the Old Testament and a theology of the New. The historical approach of this new discipline necessarily led to such a differen-tiation. It was also inevitable that Old Testament theology should take the form of a history of Israelite and Jewish religion; in all honesty it therefore changed its name accordingly. Now that the different character of the Old Testament and its remoteness had been recognized once and for all, various consequences could be drawn with differing degrees of clarity. Once it has been discovered and brought to light more clearly, the difference between the testaments *can* lead to a more or less radical repudiation of the Old. Powerful new arguments seemed to have been discovered to support Marcion's repudiation of the Old Testament, and the historical research set in motion by Deism and the Enlightenment provided constantly new insights into the historical conditioning of Old Testament religion and its involvement with and also independence from the 'pagan' environment. These could be used in turn as further arguments for the devaluation and repudiation of the Old Testament. The Old Testament seemed to move further and further away from the New Testament not only because of its legalism (whether this legalism was real or supposed) but also because of the alien character of Old Testament religion and in particular its *nationalistic* and *this-worldly* character.

Thus for the young Georg Friedrich Wilhelm Hegel, the God of Israel was a demon of hate, and Israelite and Jewish religion was the dark counterpart to the splendour of the humanism that streamed forth from Greece. He condemned the prophets of Israel as narrow-minded fanatics who ventured to involve themselves in the routine politics of their time. The fate of the Jews did not even rouse him to pity; he simply thought it abhorrent (*Early Theological Writings*, V, 203f.). In short, 'There is no room for the infinite Spirit in the prison of a Jewish soul' (265). This negative judgment is toned down considerably in the great philosophical works, but even there Israel's 'lofty religion' is held to be inferior to that of the Greeks and Romans and is set alongside both of these in contrast to the 'absolute religion' which manifests itself in Christianity (cf. Kraus, *Geschichte*, Ic, 191ff.).

We have already mentioned Schleiermacher's judgment on Old Testament legalism (above, 119). However, his criticism is more comprehensive than that. In earlier times, the two testaments had been thought to be interconnected largely by the messianic prophecies, the fulfilment of which was proclaimed in the New Testament. This, however, has been shattered, because historical research shows that these prophecies did not refer to the Christ of Christianity but to a Jewish messiah. In his so-called *Second Letter to Lücke* (1829), Schleiermacher denies that there was a special divine revelation in Israel's history; Christianity does not need any support from Judaism. Schleiermacher's *The Christian Faith* (V), also accentuates the difference between the testaments (especially in § 132). Only deliberate or unconscious reinterpretation makes it possible to read a Christian message out of the prophets and the psalms. Similarly, in his *Brief*

Outline on the Study of Theology (V) written in 1811(§ 115), Schleiermacher had refused to recognize the Jewish canon as part of the Christian Bible. He did not deny the material and historical connection between Judaism and Christianity; he recognized that the church took over the Old Testament as a legacy and to begin with could not avoid making use of its heritage. At the same time, however, he recognized equally clearly that the historical connection between the two religions cannot provide a theological motivation and justification for a recognition of the Old Testament as the sacred scripture of Christianity in the present (*The Christian Faith*, § 132). There is some justification in claiming that Schleiermacher had an inadequate knowledge of the Old Testament and oriental studies, and one can fault his idealistic understanding of religion as an inadequate key for the interpretation of the Old Testament, but this does not alter the fact that he was right in principle to enquire what was the theologically valid justification for the reception and use of the Old Testament in Christianity, rejecting the historical connection between it and the New Testament as an insufficient foundation. In this respect Schleiermacher may be said to have aroused a critical spirit which has to take account of his hermeneutical judgment, even if it has a different, and higher, estimation of the Old Testament from his and may even wish to retain it as part of the Christian canon.

Questions which are left unanswered or suppressed tend to break out again in due course even more vigorously. Friedrich Delitzsch (1850–1922) launched a polemical attack which went far beyond Schleiermacher. In 1902, a lecture, later published as *Babel and Bible* (V), caused the so-called Bible-Babylon dispute, the vehemence of which can be seen as the expression of suppressed discontent with the situation. As with Schleiermacher, it is not important whether or not Delitzsch was mistaken in his assessment of the relationship between the Bible and Babylon, i.e. in his estimation of the influence of Babylon and the Near East generally on the Bible and the distinctive character of Israelite and Jewish religion. He doubtless exaggerated a good deal, and made things too easy for his opponents not only by his overstatements and distortions, but also by his hatred and bigotism. What is more important is that in his two-volume work 'The Great Deception' (*Die grosse Täuschung*), which appeared in 1920–1921 (Harnack's book on Marcion also appeared in 1921), he set out to read the Old Testament as an intelligent layman, critically and without ecclesiastical or dogmatic preconceptions. Here he displayed with relentless openness and a wealth of detail all the features which ran contrary to Christianity, or proved either to be sub-Christian or even historically untenable.

Those critics who took a negative view of the Old Testament were concerned not only with the incursions of the earlier prophets into politics and religious policy, but also with the cruel acts and the massacres narrated in the book of Joshua. Delitzsch regarded the whole of the Priestly account of the events on Sinai as a cheat and a deception, and included Deuteronomy in his condemnation. This book had been attributed to Moses, although it was in fact the product of a much later time. Christians were misguided in having a high opinion of the prophets; mature reflection showed them to be nationalistic fanatics. It was clear that the prophets could not be said to be inspired by God, if only because it was impossible that the Yahweh whose prophet incited Jehu to revolution should also have inspired the prophet Hosea to condemn Jehu's actions (cf. II Kings 10.30 with Hos. 1.4). According to Delitzsch, even the prophets do not represent an advance on Jewish nationalism and particularism. The statement in Isa. 56.7 that the temple is a house of prayer for all nations is not an expression of religious universalism: it in fact expresses the hope that one day everyone will become Jewish and accept circumcision. The hatred felt for foreign nations, which is expressed in many of the prophetic oracles, is certainly not transformed into a universal love of humanity. Delitzsch feels that even the psalms are almost all sub-Christian: they know of no life after death, which is an essential feature of Christianity, and their expectation of salvation is essentially materialistic. The only exception which proves the rule is Ps. 73.25f., where the psalmist to some extent goes beyond the confines of this life and seems to hope for an eternal life with God. There are far more expressions of hatred of enemies and prayers for vengeance than passages which Christians can take over and make their own. In short, although the Old Testament may have many linguistic felicities and provide important information about the history of religions, it cannot be considered as part of the Christian canon.

This consistent repudiation of the Old Testament has one significant consequence which is instructive, precisely because it seems so inevitable. Delitzsch is compelled to correct the traditional picture of Jesus, and in so doing follows in the train of both Marcion and Schleiermacher. Marcion became the founder of a new religion in which the Christ-event was transformed into a timeless and ahistorical myth, and Schleiermacher threatened to turn Christ into an equally ahistorical Christ-principle; the rejection of the Old Testament by both these theologians thus led to a view of Christianity with a distinctive understanding of christology. Delitzsch claimed that Jesus was a Galilean and not a Jew, thus making it clear that there cannot – or need not – be any link between Judaism and Jesus. The idea of the Aryan Jesus was born. It is evident that, just as Marcion was compelled to purge the New Testament canon, so any plan for a Christianity without the Old Testament must also leave its mark on the New Testament tradition. Of course, this insight does not tell against all the arguments of Delitzsch and his predecessors. Like many of those who engaged in polemic before him and after him, he may have made things too easy for himself and abused the role of the intelligent layman, choosing for his polemics material which more scholarly research and a better appreciation would show to be inappropriate. Nevertheless, if we leave aside his polemic, his exaggerations, his hatred and his anti-Semitism, it is clear that he gave an impressive demonstration of the alien character of the Old Testament and its independence from the New. Delitzsch gave a clear account of what the layman would feel if he were to read the Old Testament critically, and as a Christian – even if the way in which he expressed himself was less than attractive. However, his unprepossessing approach should not prevent us from studying his arguments and trying to answer them.

3. The alien character of the Old Testament as a scandal and a 'taskmaster'

The historical recognition of the alien character of the Old Testament can also be of use to theology. Emanuel Hirsch, who must be mentioned yet again here, is concerned, like Schleiermacher, Delitzsch and Harnack, with the legalism of the Old Testament both in relationship to the gospel of the New Testament and also in opposition to it. If it is read in its original sense, without being reinterpreted in Christian terms, the Old Testament proves for Hirsch to be the document of an alien religion, on the same level as other pre-Christian or non-Christian religions.

Hirsch rightly points out that so far the Old Testament could be accepted as a book of the church mainly because large parts of it tended to be reinterpreted in Christian terms. At the same time, however, Christianity had forfeited its original purity and was permeated with Old Testament ideas. This is what had made possible the preservation of its Jewish heritage. The earliest church had taken over the legacy of the Old Testament not as a concession to Judaism, but first and foremost because it sought to read the Old Testament as a prediction of Christ, thus demonstrating that its claim was justified and the Jewish claim was not. However, since the messianic predictions could not be applied to Christ, such a claim proved after an interval of two thousand years to be not only historically impossible but also theologically superfluous.

Hirsch now proceeded to draw out the theological implications of his legitimate historical insight. In his book 'The Old Testament and the Preaching of the Gospel' (IVB, 74), he said with the utmost clarity:

> The cross of Jesus Christ has condemned this nationalistic religion along with all other nationalistic religions. The New Testament conception of the kingdom of God and the Redeemer is radically different from the ideas of the Old Testament and of Judaism. As a result, there is a division between the people as a whole and the Christian community, the national law and the will of God that brings salvation; the dialectic between the kingdom of God and the kingdom of this world takes on quite a different meaning, unheard-of in the Old Testament and Judaism, and the relationship of the individual to God is now based purely on personal belief.

Christians can regard the Old Testament only as a stumbling-block and an irritation, but it retains its significance in this dialectical relationship. As a result, Hirsch, who lays the strongest emphasis on the totally legalistic and therefore utterly alien character of Old Testament religion, can recognize a way in which Christians can use this un-Christian and pre-Christian book: the religious attitude held out here as a model is in a horrifying way still characteristic of Christians, and is the attitude which is shattered by the proclamation of Christ.

It is clear that historical and theological considerations of this kind can easily become involved in the morass of anti-Semitic struggles and controversies, of politics and church politics. They can be – and have been – applauded loudly from the wrong side. Such a reaction does, however, call for continued careful consideration, to eliminate false polemics and excessively pro-Jewish sentiments which can lead to unbalanced theology. We should never forget where the line from Marcion, through Morgan, Semler, Hegel, Schleiermacher, Delitzsch and Harnack, to Hirsch ended up; nevertheless, the abysmal racist and religious misuse of the Old Testament, the *abusus*, is not necessarily a feature of its use, the *usus*. Those who recognize that the Old Testament is an alien document which may even be contradictory to Christianity do not necessarily end up in a state of murderous hatred! Radical historical criticism and sound Lutheran dogmatics can be reconciled and go hand in hand in an attempt to solve the hermeneutical problem of the Old Testament. The position adopted by E. Hirsch should be seen as such an attempt. In a similar way, Friedrich Baumgärtel can state quite explicitly:

> For the hermeneutical question, we cannot eliminate from our present-day thinking the fact that the Old Testament is a witness of a religion which stands outside the gospel, and is therefore an alien religion. Its historical context is not that of the Christian religion ('The Hermeneutical Problem of the Old Testament', IIIc, 135).

Nevertheless, according to Baumgärtel the Old Testament continues to be valid for Christians because it already presents the basic promise, 'I am the Lord your God', even though this was in fact misunderstood, objectivized and falsified by Israel. Above all, the Old Testament is still valid even for Christians because they constantly lapse into the pre-Christian attitude of Old Testament man.

Consequently, Baumgärtel can say,

> ... for those of us who are Christians and stand under the promise given in Christ, the word of the Old Testament is a word of God addressed to us in the present, which relates to us and concerns us. The Old Testament history of salvation and disaster is our own history of salvation and disaster.... The fact that the witness of the Old Testament speaks to our existence despite the fact that we are not bound by its testimony, and that we find ourselves forced back into an Old Testament situation, must affect us more deeply than those for whom the new covenant is still well-founded (*Verheissung*, IIIc, 65).

Franz Hesse makes a similar attempt to justify the validity of the Old Testament despite its alien character. He also remarks: 'The Old Testament religion is something qualitatively different from the faith of the New Testament. In the faith of Israel and in Christianity we are confronted with essentially different religions' ('The Evaluation and Authority of Old Testament Texts', IIIc, 300; he makes a similar comment in *Das Alte Testament als Buch der Kirche*, IIIc, 1966, where his language is rather less terse). But for Hesse, as for Baumgärtel,

> The entire word of God which lays claim upon us from the Old Testament demands authority also at the point where it lets us perceive the pattern of a 'line of obduracy' ... The Old Testament Word of God claims authority because and insofar as it warns us against going the way of error

and disobedience of Old Testament man, about which the Old Testament bears such a manifold witness in so many ways ('The Evaluation', 308; cf. also *Das Alte Testament*, 152 etc.)

In conclusion, mention must be made of Rudolf Bultmann. He begins his important article 'Prophecy and Fulfilment' (V) by showing how the way in which the New Testament resorts to the Old for proof from prophecy is impossible today. He then makes positive use of the theory of the Erlangen theologian J. C. K. von Hofmann (see below, 179ff.) that the prophecies of the Old Testament are not to be found in individual sayings: the Old Testament history as a whole has the character of prophecy. Bultmann then largely modifies Hofmann's theory by saying that in its essential features (as a history of the people of the covenant, as a history lived under the kingly rule of God and as the history of the people of God) the history of Israel is prophecy 'fulfilled in its inner contradiction, its miscarriage' (72). Thus the Old Testament as a whole fulfils its function as law: 'If we interpret Old Testament history in this sense, we are following Paul's interpretation of the law. The law is a taskmaster which leads us to Christ (Gal. 3.24), because it led man into this miscarriage of his endeavours' (74). According to Bultmann, of course *all* law and every moral demand can also take on this function: 'It can only be for pedagogical reasons that the Christian church uses the Old Testament to make man conscious of standing under God's demand ...' ('The Significance of the Old Testament', V, 17).

As Bultmann in particular makes clear, in theological terms the alien character of Old Testament religion, which makes it possible and indeed necessary for us to put the Old Testament alongside the other documents of the history of religion outside Christianity, is interpreted in terms of law. Seen as law, the alien Old Testament is then brought back into the dialectic of law and gospel and recognized as a necessary part of the canon. For Bultmann, this necessity is still only 'pedagogical', because in principle each and every law can take on the same function. This brings us back to a question which has already been raised, namely whether it is really appropriate to understand the religion of the Old Testament as 'law' in the narrow, theological sense and whether the situation of Old Testament man can really be interpreted in Christian terms only as the miscarriage of his endeavours. Right though Bultmann may be in showing the dilemmas in which Israel was entangled in wanting to become the people of God on the stage of human history, while remaining a particular empirical nation and a specific religious community, it is impossible to subordinate the whole of the Old Testament to the concept of law, however wide the understanding of this concept may be. Quite apart from the fact that the Old Testament is more than an account of history, for this reason alone the Old Testament presents more than a history of failure. The problems which are pointed out so impressively by Bultmann were already recognized within the Old Testament and pioneering attempts were made to solve them. Moreover, by no means everything which is thought to be a materialistic and objective feature of salvation need be condemned as a miscarriage or be branded as a falsification of the 'fundamental promise'. These considerations lead us on to a criticism of the criticisms which have been made of the Old Testament.

4. *Criticism of criticisms of the Old Testament*

The work of the history of religions school is a particularly good illustration of the fact that a recognition of the autonomous character of the Old Testament need not always lead to its devaluation and repudiation. Once the limitations of a purely rational and rationalistic approach, and of the morality of the Enlightenment, have been seen and a proper historical sense has been developed, it is possible to join the history of religions school in wondering at the primitiveness and originality of the ancient popular sagas, in trying to share in the jubilation and lament of the psalmists, and in holding up the lofty and strict ethical sense of the prophets as a model. Of course we may ask whether even this approach does not continue to regard the Old Testament as the document of an alien religion, which is not regarded as holy scripture in the strict sense because it has no message for the present. Does not such an approach fail to take seriously the claim of the Old Testament that 'thus says the Lord'? Does it not ignore this claim altogether? If the question is framed in precise terms, it can only be answered equally precisely, in the negative. For such an approach, the Old Testament becomes a 'source' for the reconstruction of a past religion.

We may follow H.-G. Gadamer by describing this mode of understanding in the following terms:

> The text that is understood historically is forced to abandon its claim that it is uttering something true. We think we understand when we see the past from a historical standpoint, i.e. place ourselves in the historical situation and seek to reconstruct the historical horizon. In fact, however,

we have given up the claim to find, in the past, any truth valid and intelligible for ourselves. Thus this acknowledgment of the otherness of the other, which makes him the object of objective knowledge, involves the fundamental suspension of his claim to truth (*Truth and Method*, IB, 270).

There would have been no lasting echo to the reaction of dialectical theology towards the alienation of the Old Testament (and scripture generally) which was brought about by historical criticism, but for considerable discontent over a historical approach which simply banished the Old Testament into the remote past while giving some satisfaction to those with aesthetic sensibilities and neo-Romantic dispositions. This reaction can be seen especially in Karl Barth's energetic attempt to get back 'to the subject matter' and to read the Old and New Testaments as a testimony to the Word of God which is both proclaimed and perceived in the present, without any concern for losses and gains resulting from historical criticism.

One particularly influential book which attempted to put Barth's approach into practice in biblical interpretation was *The Witness of the Old Testament to Christ* (IIc), written by the Barthian Wilhelm Vischer. It was especially popular among the clergy.

Vischer asserted that it was necessary for the life of the Christian church that the two testaments should be seen as one and that the Bible should be interpreted in such a way as to illuminate, rather than dismiss, its claim to have a valid message for today. Beginning from the premise that the messianic hope was as much the centre of the Old Testament for Jews as it was for Christians, and that if Jesus really was the Messiah and Christ, as Christians believe, both the Old Testament and the New Testament are the church's scripture, he interpreted the Old Testament in terms of the 'Christ event'. It is obvious that this mode of interpretation would discover in the Old Testament what was read into it on the basis of the premise.

Vischer's book was controversial from the start, and it was easy for biblical critics to show that his approach was illegitimate and impossible to carry through. Like Friedrich Delitzsch on the other wing, Vischer really made things too easy for his opponents. But his attempt should not be dismissed too lightly. The Old Testament was being repudiated in increasingly drastic terms and scholars were dissociating themselves more and more from the burning questions of its significance, validity and character: were these the only possible alternatives? Vischer offered an answer in a book which announced its intention of rescuing the Old Testament from its exile in the realm of alien religious documents, paying attention to its claims and promises, and expressing once again the significance of the biblical testimony for the present. This reaction to the negative approach of scholars and non-scholars alike, and to the neutral, quasi-objective perspective adopted by historians, was a necessary one. Nevertheless, there is no going back on history, nor on the history of scholarly research. Theologians like Barth in his *Church Dogmatics* may assert that the Old Testament is a book which belongs to the time before Christ and is a witness to the expectation of Christ, and that it is therefore different from the New only as the expectation is chronologically different from the fulfilment (*CD* I, 2, VIA, 70ff.), going on to interpret it accordingly; however, this does not remove at a stroke all the undoubted results of historical research over several centuries, or all their theological implications. Perhaps the attempts made by Barth, Vischer and others to pass over or to make light of the results of historical research where they did not fit into the right christological or dogmatic framework, on the grounds that the results were only 'relatively assured', were necessary in the particular situation of the time. If so, the necessity was a tragic one, as was already suspected by some people at the time, even if the full extent of the tragedy emerged only at a later stage. The struggle against National Socialism came to an end, and as it did so the excitement of battle declined: the bold flights of Christian and christological interpretation of the Old Testament gave place to a rather more mundane view. The cold light of day revealed an earthly land that was promised to Israel and not to the church, with earthly salvation, nationalistic hopes, a particularist theology, unsolved problems and endless tragedies: in short, the Old Testament was seen once again as the *Old* Testament, and all the old questions which had been put aside unsolved, came into the foreground once again.

This means that we have to summarize once again the real or apparent reasons against having the Israelite-Jewish Old Testament as the holy scripture of the Christian church, subjecting them to a careful historical and theological scrutiny. As we do this, we must remember that the undoubted historical connection between the Old and New Testaments and between Judaism and Christianity can no longer be cited as a reason why the church should recognize this ancient legacy: historical links and connections are not to be confused with normative validity. Furthermore, while those who continually stress that the New Testament cannot be understood fully without the Old are undoubtedly right, this is not the whole story. Most of the honorific titles given to Jesus, the concept of the kingdom of God and indeed the general religious conceptuality of the New Testament and its world of ideas, can only be understood in all their fullness when we take into account their Old Testament derivations. A theological wordbook of the New Testament is inconceivable without an Old Testament infrastructure. However, all these considerations do not add up to an argument that the Old Testament must be part of a canon of scripture. To understand the New Testament we need not only the Old, but also a grasp of the ancient Hellenistic world and of Graeco-Oriental syncretism, just as to understand the Old Testament in turn we need to see it as a specific product of the religion and world-view of the ancient Near East, which has countless links to the world of its time. Elements which may contribute to our understanding (and indeed may be indispensable for it) may be of great significance for present-day knowledge without in fact having canonical validity.

A careful scrutiny of this kind may also help us to distinguish merely polemical arguments against the Old Testament which are not really worth taking seriously. These include the view that in terms of culture, race and religion the Old Testament is *inferior* to Aryan civilization, the Greek world, Christendom or even the high culture of ancient Babylon. Quite apart from the fact that such judgments are merely subjective evaluations, there can be no serious doubt of the religious and cultural independence of the Old Testament over against its non-Israelite environment, despite the many wide-ranging and deep connections and even dependent relationships that it has with that environment. A work like the book of Job has just as much a claim to be counted among the great works of world literature as, say, the epics of Homer. There may be some parallel phenomena to the prophets, but with their eloquence and their profound concern for justice which leads them to pronounce devastating judgments on their own people and their own states, they are nevertheless a unique phenomenon in the ancient Near East. And although Israelite legislation is certainly impracticable for a modern European state concerned for the freedom of the individual, its moral seriousness, social awareness and particularly sensitive reticence in sexual questions are noteworthy, and can serve as a positive model for us. In the first eleven chapters of the book of Genesis, the depths of human guilt are plumbed and vividly illuminated by imagery which has now become classic; here too the literature of the other nations in Israel's world does not offer any truly comparable parallels. Even where Israel's dependence on great models from elsewhere is unmistakable – as in the story of the flood – an ability to assimilate and transform and to make something new out of traditional material can clearly be seen. Instances of this kind can be multiplied at will. Of course, taken by themselves, these too serve to refute the polemical assertion that the Old Testament is inferior and lacks originality, but they are not evidence in support of its validity. The canonical status of a work – including that of the New Testament – is not based on its real or supposed cultural value.

Nor do we need to spend a great deal of time refuting the argument that the Old Testament is a 'deception', a pious (or impious) *fraud*, despite the great emphasis laid on it by Delitzsch. Delitzsch made this a major theme and presented it in popular terms, but he did not really have scholarship behind him. It should be noted in this respect that most of the Old Testament books are anonymous; they do not claim to be the intellectual achievement of particular authors who are known to us by name, and they come from an age which knew no copyright law and no sense of personal authorship as we know it. Neither the Pentateuch, the prophetic books nor the historical works come from the pen of a single author; in their present form they are the end-product of a complicated process of oral and written tradition. Once the idea of a canonical period of lawgiving by Moses had become common currency, it became necessary to include all the legal material in the Sinai pericope and its surroundings, and this material was supposed to have validity as divine law. Where there is no deceiver and no one is deceived, it would be deceptive to talk of deception. The same is also true of the prophetic books. While they bear the names of particular prophetic figures, they are the literary product of whole schools of prophets and circles of tradition which collected together their message in the name of the prophet. These collections were enriched by the addition of material composed by these groups or taken from elsewhere, sometimes over a period of centuries. The collectors were not interested in history, nor did they seek to preserve the spiritual heritage of the prophets unchanged for posterity; the impulse towards the collection and reshaping of the material was provided by its significance for the present and for the future. Again, to talk here of deception is to misunderstand the real historical setting and the true interests and intentions of those who handed down the tradition. Moreover, the attribution of wisdom books to wise King Solomon is not an attempt to gain royal authority for these books at a late date by a pious fraud; it was thought that the wisdom tradition, which for long had been held in high esteem, must be connected with the wise king who was thought to stand behind the development of the wisdom schools.

For a long time it has been argued against the Old Testament that it contains many *acts of cruelty* which were committed or at least planned in the name of the God of Israel. We have already considered these and their background in our discussion of the law and the Israelite theocracy. At that point we already noted that the Old Testament in fact has considerable limitations and dubious features, and this feature should be conceded to the critics and not made light of. At the same time, however, it should have become evident that the aspect of law and theocracy is not the only possible and legitimate key towards an understanding of the Old Testament. Alongside and over against the extermination of the Canaanites – which did not really take place – we find the universalism of, say, Isa. 56.7. This does not require the forcible circumcision of all non-Jews and their observance of all the Jewish laws, as Delitzsch claimed; it declares that the temple is a house of prayer for all the nations on earth. The book of Jonah also protests against too narrow and nationalistic a view of religion, with its reproof of Jonah and his over-particularist view of salvation and its testimony to the one God who has mercy on Nineveh, 'that great city, in which there are more than a hundred and twenty thousand persons who do not know their right hand from their left, and also much cattle' (Jonah 4.11). One might point to Ruth 4.17, with its tradition that the family of David is descended from the Moabite woman Ruth (even if this tradition is secondary) and all the other material which goes beyond narrow-minded nationalism. Above all, however, the creation stories in Genesis 1–11 see Israel as just one constituent of the world of nations, and the curse which mankind brings down upon itself is succeeded by a universalist promise of boundless blessing (Gen. 12.1ff.). Of course, as with the covenant and the law, final clarity is not achieved here: the prior claims of Israel are not questioned, and 'all families on earth' are blessed only by virtue of their positive relationship to Israel. What, then, is finally at issue? What is the real goal? Is it the salvation of all men, or is that so to speak no more than a by-product of Israel's prosperity? Such questions take us out of the realms of polemic and bring us to the real problem of the alien character of the Old Testament.

Before we come to that, however, we must consider yet another feature of polemic against the Old Testament, the so-called '*cursing psalms*'. First of all, it should be noted that there is no such genre as the 'cursing psalm'. True, the psalms of lamentation often speak of 'enemies', against whom God is summoned to take action. This aspect of the Old Testament is also used as an argument which helps to demonstrate the inferiority of Old Testament religion and the hatred to be found in abundance in it. Here is not the place to consider in detail the much-discussed phenomenon of the enemies in the psalms of lamentation, but they should at least be presented in the right perspective. The mere fact that the mention of 'enemies' is part of the very stereotyped language of the psalms shows that what we have here is certainly not a series of individualistic, emotive outbursts of hatred directed against particular people or even a group of people who are specifically hated as enemies. The stereotyped form of expression suggests, rather, imaginary figures who are the counterparts of what the suppliant hopes to be and who seek to separate him from his God. Like the waves and floods (e.g. Ps. 42.8) and the wild beasts, bulls, buffaloes, lions and dogs (e.g. Ps. 22.13ff.) which appear again and again, the 'enemies' are an image and an element of chaos, which separates men from God, from life and the divinely ordained pattern of creation: they are a reflection of the suppliant's own anxieties and cares (so Othmar Keel, *Feinde und Gottesleugner*, V). Of course the ambivalence to be found in so many Old Testament statements is to be found here also, and cannot be gainsaid. Prayers about and against 'enemies' can also be understood and used in their superficial and direct sense as desires for vengeance.

All these arguments, then, are used against the Old Testament: deception and fraud, moral and religious inferiority, bloodthirstiness towards enemies and the lust for vengeance. However, when they are seen in their true historical context, they either become blunted and lose their sting, or prove to be of only relative significance when other aspects of the Old Testament which are more pleasant, cheerful, lovable, lofty or profound, are given the attention they deserve.

One need only remember that the God of the Old Testament who is so angry when it comes to his righteousness, is nevertheless prepared to spare countless evil men for the sake of ten righteous men. Those who criticize this God should themselves share something of his attitude and not find fault with the morality of the Old Testament authors because they do not divide people, and especially their great heroes and saints, into paragons of virtue and devils in human form, but remain aware of the intermediary colours, the ambivalence and the ambiguity of all human existence. To understand is not necessarily to excuse. The way in which Israel's national heroes, above all David and Solomon, are portrayed, is evidence enough of that: although they are committed by a great man, murder and adultery are seen for what they are – murder and adultery. And who would regard such a critical attitude as being normal and typical of both the past and the present? The Yahwist has Abraham, the pattern for the believer, telling a lie in an emergency (Gen. 12.11–13). As the continuation of the story (the endangering of the mother of future generations and with it the threat to all the promises and blessings) shows, Abraham's action is in no way condoned. His lie is more than morally offensive; it is unbelief, a lack of trust in the word which God himself gave; as a result of it, Abraham risks losing all that was to follow from the promise. The Elohist, who tells the same story in his own way, already understood it wrongly and made it a moral tale (Gen. 20.12), serving as a valid model for many critics of Old Testament morality and some Old Testament scholars who have failed to grasp the point.

5. *The question of the true nature of Israel*

The objections that we have just considered are for the most part a feature of polemic against the Old Testament, or in part rest on a deficient knowledge of the historical background and intention of the texts involved. They can therefore be refuted or put in their place fairly easily. There is, however, another argument which carries much more weight. It underlies as it were all the other objections that can be made to the Old Testament as part of a biblical canon valid for Christians. No matter whether it has a high or a low moral standing, whether it is wondered at or despised, loved or hated, is not the Old Testament the document of an *alien religion*? Is it not a catalogue of writings which were not collected by the church, a collection of writings which are in all respects pre-Christian and which are therefore something other than Christian? Does not the Old Testament relate specifically to Israel? This link with and reference to Israel includes the way in which the Old Testament, unlike the gospel, holds forth the promise of a this-worldly salvation (a feature which has often been severely criticized). Because of the link with Israel, the Old Testament keeps within the bounds of the nation and is sometimes nationalistic, only rarely and by way of exception taking a broader view; the most important feature of salvation is seen to be the promise of a particular land, a promise which was never lost sight of even in later Judaism (indeed it was particularly cherished then) and is even now staunchly defended as the final fulfilment of all desires and hopes in present-day Israel. Those who interpret this as an objectifying falsification of God's true promise, which is concerned with a life with God, with righteousness and sonship, like Friedrich Baumgärtel (*Verheissung*, IIIc) and Franz Hesse (e.g. in *Das Alte Testament als Buch der Kirche*, IIIc), are in fact saying, albeit reluctantly, that Israel's religion as a whole is a 'great deception'.

Now if the Old Testament cannot be understood as a great deception or a self-deception or even simply as a book of failures, are not these specific this-worldly features of people and land the equally specific limitations which distinguish Christianity from this religion which is alien precisely because it is bound up with people and land? There is no going back on the historical recognition of the alien nature and the autonomy of Israelite religion as it is evidenced in the Old Testament, nor can we reinterpret the texts in a way which would deprive them of this character. However, that is not the whole story. Above all, it can hardly be said that in the meanwhile historical scholarship has rehabilitated the heretic Marcion. What we need to do, rather, is to explain and understand the specific content of Israelite religion against the background of its own changing horizons.

It is easiest to begin our interpretation where the content of Israelite religion is described and understood as divine ordinances of salvation. This is the case first with the promises which the patriarchs receive on their wanderings. The earliest (and possibly the original) content of the patriarchal traditions seems to be the promise of land and descendants (Gen. 12.1–3, 7 J, etc.). P adds the special covenant relationship with God (Gen. 17.1–8). If Alt ('The God of the Fathers', 1929, in *Essays on OT History and Religion*, ET 1966, 1ff.) is right in seeing patriarchal religion with its cultic founders and bearers of the promise as a preliminary stage in the worship of Yahweh and Israelite religion generally – and this can hardly be doubted – at this point we already meet the two specific features, the themes, on which the religious life and thought of Israel is to be based from now on: the possession of territory and the promise of descendants, the land and the people. Furthermore, if it is true that the narratives about the wanderings of the patriarchs in Canaan reflect an early phase of the conquest (and again, this can hardly be doubted), it is easy to interpret both the elements of the promise in terms of the situation of semi-nomads wandering to and fro between the desert and cultivated land, who then gradually settle in this cultivated land. Those who own land are persons and citizens in the full sense. Even now, people in rural, agricultural areas who have no land of their own are thought of as being inferior; this was even more the case in antiquity, in the conditions of the patriarchal period and also during the later stages of the history of Israel. From this perspective, land is the basis for living, for humanity in its full sense; it makes possible not only physical life, but also intellectual life and the exercise of law. This is what was hoped for from the God of the fathers, and later from the God of Israel, and this is what the Israelites believed that they had been given. As a result, the link with a particular land is not a limitation: on the contrary, it is the symbol of an attitude to life which looks for, and receives, life itself from God.

The promise of descendants is to be interpreted from the same perspective. Life in the best and most fertile land has no *future* without descendants. Anyone who has no children, and in particular anyone who has no son, must echo Abraham's lament, 'I continue childless, and a stranger will possess my house' (Gen. 15.2). If the possession of land carries with it personhood and citizenship *in the present*, descendants are a concrete assurance *for the future*. With descendants, time has no bounds, and the future cannot be reckoned any more than can the stars in the heavens and the sand on the sea shore (Gen. 15.5; 13.16; 22.17). This prospect of an endless future is also the gift of God and is looked for from him. Are we to describe such a form of religion as merely this-worldly and earthly? It is true that the land given to Israel is an earthly land and that its descendants are physical descendants, the fruit of the body; yet the descriptions 'merely this-worldly' and 'earthly' are inadequate, because they fail to recognize the totality of existence in both present and future, which are believed to be a reality and a possibility given by God. It is not the faith itself which is earthly and limited to this world, but the perspective of the semi-nomads and small farmers, who cannot envisage more than a future in their own terms. However, within the one particular historical perspective in which it has to be viewed, this faith is by no means limited to earthly things in the context of this world, to inferior physical well-being, the quest for prosperity rather than true salvation. It embraces every conceivable kind of well-being and every kind of salvation, conceivable and even inconceivable – like the stars in heaven and the sand on the sea shore. So this universalist belief in salvation is not attested only at the end of the Old Testament and at its fringes; it can be found at the beginning of Israel's history and even before the beginning of Israelite belief, in that it formed part of the content of patriarchal religion which is a prelude to Israelite belief, just as the patriarchal period is the prelude to Israelite history. Paul did not need typology, much less allegorical interpretation, to find evidence for his belief in Gen. 15 (Rom. 4.1–3; Gal. 3.6). Of course, the testimony of faith is not itself pre-Israelite; it is an expression of Israelite belief. The fact that the Priestly Writing shows how God promises Abraham a covenant and a special relationship with him is a development which is significant for the way in which the horizon of belief is later widened: the perspective becomes broader, theological reflection becomes more profound, and God is removed into a distant, invisible realm. Now life in covenant with him becomes a special, 'spiritual' form of salvation: the horizon extends and moves back, the content of salvation begins to develop.

The history of Israel as a whole can be read as a continuous change of horizons which brings about ongoing processes of tradition, developments, transformations, realizations and shifts of accent. Yet at the same time, truly Israelite belief remains oriented on land and descendants, the people and their relationship with God.

However, history not only brings about changes of horizon which as it were represent an invitation to deeper and more comprehensive ideas of salvation; it also introduces the temptation to regard the salvation given by God as a possession at man's disposal, which in effect means that this salvation is forfeited. The state must be regarded as one such temptation, despite the fact that it opened up a prospect extending beyond peasant smallholdings and the hills and mountains of Israel; above all in Jerusalem, it proved to be the point of entry for Canaanite and indeed Near Eastern ideas and cultural features which disclosed new realms of thought. The land which Yahweh had given became a territory to be defended by the state; the people who had come into being through Yahweh's saving acts and his blessings became the members of a state organized on a basis laid down by the state; their relationship with God seemed to provide the guarantee for the elect character of a theocratic, political community with an impregnable centre – Zion. This gave rise to all the discrepancies and problems which we have already sketched out in another context.

The idea of the Davidic covenant on the basis of which the king rules in Jerusalem as the adopted son of God (II Sam. 7) can be seen as an attempt to overcome the difficulty of reconciling the nature of the people of God and life on the basis of the divine promise with the existence of a state based on political autonomy, though this was in fact an impossibility. The kingship, as a mediating institution between God and man, appointed by God to direct the human business of the state, basked in the splendour of its own divinity, which was taken over from the cultural pattern of the ancient Near East. In theory, the kingship was an attempt to put into practice an all-embracing ordinance of salvation and creation, but this attempt must once again be regarded as no more than a piece of secular politics, even if the kingship itself was not entirely reduced to being a mere political factor in the context of harsh political reality. Kingship is in fact an obvious illustration of the problem of Israel's existence. 'And Yahweh loved him' (II Sam. 12.24). Yet Solomon, this beloved son, had his father's most faithful followers murdered in their old age. Was this the religious answer to brutal tyranny? Or the political perversion of faith? Or both?

As with the question whether the Old Testament should be read as law or gospel, here too reality proves to be much more complicated. Here too it is impossible to outline a history of development leading from a pure Abrahamic faith and then a pure, original 'amphyctyonic' community through David and Solomon to Zedekiah, who is finally swept away by the judgment, as a history of ever-deepening decline and apostasy. Both land and people are the content of salvation for both the Yahwist and the oriental despot Solomon – in the view of many scholars these were in fact contemporaries. Are land and people the specific historical features which make salvation possible as a life lived under God's blessing and in the power of his redemption, or are they elements of salvation which can be acquired once and for all, and once acquired, remain at man's disposal and need to be defended?

The real point at issue is not the earthly reality of people and land, the special position of Israel and the this-worldliness of the Old Testament, the corporeal blessings of milk and honey, the fig-tree and the vine, and rejoicing before the Lord. We should not be asking whether these amount to a falsification of salvation. The question is whether Israel goes out again and again, like Abraham, 'as the Lord commanded him' (Gen. 12.1ff.), leaving behind his country, his people and his clan, prepared to abandon all possessions and all security and to look firmly forward; whether, like Abraham, Israel is prepared to receive salvation from God's hand, to sacrifice Isaac in order to receive him back again, along with all salvation in the present and the future, as a pure gift from God (Gen. 22).

The Old Testament certainly contains testimony which, even though the name of Christ does not actually appear in it, can be understood as a valid formulation and realization of the Christian kerygma without any reinterpretation, allegorical interpretation or typology. The church has always understood such testimony in these terms, and in it the Christian, like Paul, can see his own pattern of existence reflected and understand it as the gospel. Historical research also brings out such testimony: it does not only make the Old Testament an alien document, by disclosing its historical strangeness, but it can also kindle new understanding and 'restore' the Old Testament texts as testimony to the gospel. Other elements remain ambivalent and ambiguous; they may be thought to be particularist, nationalistic and a lapse into the temptation to look for tangible success and reward, or they can be seen as the overcoming of such limitations. Is the new exodus announced by Deutero-Isaiah only the restoration of people, state, city and temple? Is the hymnic exuberance of this proclamation no more than the expression of nationalism in a heightened form which, like the prophecy of salvation and outward success so despised by the great Old Testament prophets, is utterly sure of itself? Or can we see in this exuberance a struggle to express something that cannot be put into words, 'what no eye has seen and no ear heard', something which, although it is an earthly hope centred on Jerusalem, nevertheless transcends all that is earthly, particular and nationalistic? Can it therefore be proclaimed as a testimony to the salvation that has been clearly manifested in Christ? Yet other elements are obviously alien, the social code of the Jews, the national literature of the Israelites with its climaxes and nadirs, with its terrors and also – to mention the fact in passing – its amusing side. Anyone who enjoys a rough joke should read the story of Jacob's deceit or the account of how Samson tied together three hundred foxes by their tails, added burning torches, and drove them into the Philistines' corn (Judg. 15), which may well bring back memories of Till Eulenspiegel's pranks. The text may not be suitable for Christian preaching, but not everything in the Old Testament has to be preached about, and it should certainly not be seen only as material for sermons!

None of this amounts to 'Christian interpretation', but it does represent the application of the standard of what is Christian to the Old Testament. And after all, that is the only way of measuring what is alien and what is not, of showing what should be brought into prominence and what should be kept to one side.

Is the Old Testament, then, the document of an alien religion or is it – at the same time – a testimony for Christian faith, one which can stand the test of Christianity? The question cannot be answered in this form with reference to the whole of the Old Testament, but only in connection with specific texts. The ambivalence of the whole of the Old Testament, which can also be seen here, is in turn an expression of the ambivalence of the community which calls itself Israel and whose national and religious literature became the canon of the Christian church. Israel was called to life by God, who rescued it from slavery in Egypt and gave it form; yet it is one amphictyony among other amphictyonies, one people and state among other peoples and states, one ethnic and social group among many others with a national religion which at the same time can rise above all the limitations of particularity. But when is Israel really Israel? When it leaves these limitations behind and continues to exist without land or state – a pure community of faith and a 'church' –, or when it affirms these limitations as the indispensable historical form of its own specific mode of existence? The way in which this question is answered marks out the dividing line between Israel and the church, and makes the Old Testament appear to be either the document of an alien, nationalist religion or a collection of writings in which the true Israel of faith can find support.

This is not to shift the question of the alien nature of the Old Testament into the uncontrollable realm of arbitrary evaluations, any more than our discussion of legalism had such a result. On the contrary. The gospel of the free grace of God revealed in Christ, which is to be proclaimed to all peoples, serves as a clear criterion, and not only for those who believe it. It may be testified to in the New Testament in a variety of forms, formulations, nuances and facets, but it does offer a standard by which to judge whether Old Testament texts are and remain alien, or whether in this new light they disclose their truth, lose their alien character, transcend their limitations and so become testimony to the one God who is the Lord and Father of all mankind.

VI

THE OLD TESTAMENT
AS A HISTORY BOOK

1. Divine and human economies of salvation

If the Old Testament was and is a legacy from the time before Christ, it was – and is – natural to define its status as that of a *preliminary stage*, and the earliest church did in fact understand it in this way. For the first Christians, the Old Testament as law was essentially a stumbling-block and a problem, but as a book which prophesies the Christ who died and rose again according to the scriptures (I Cor. 15.3f.), and in whom Christians believe, though he has been rejected by the Jews, it was the holy scripture of the church and rightfully belonged to the church alone. In this way the Old Testament, taken by itself, without any clearly definable centre, and open on many sides to many kinds of interpretation, acquired another focal point than that which had become normative for Judaism. It was not seen primarily and predominantly as a law that was also preached and applied by the prophets (which is the way in which the tripartite Hebrew canon presents it), nor as a book which presented a comprehensive interpretation of history, extending from the earliest beginnings of mankind, by way of the present, into the hoped-for messianic future. The Old Testament became the church's book as a scripture containing prophecy and promise and their fulfilment. This understanding makes the testimony of the Old Testament a preliminary stage to the testimony to Christ, which announces the fulfilment of what had been promised and prophesied previously. Typical of this approach is a passage like Luke 4.21, where, after a lengthy quotation from the book of Isaiah, Jesus says, 'Today this scripture is fulfilled in your ears.'

This understanding of the Old Testament is maintained, though with a variety of nuances, from the very old, even pre-Pauline tradition, which asserts that the cross and resurrection of Christ are in accordance with the scriptures (I Cor. 15.3f.), down to the latest strata of the New Testament. Some predictions are in fact contained in the Old Testament, especially messianic promises like Isa. 9; 11; Micah 5; Zech. 9.9, etc., or the promise of a new covenant in Jer. 31.31–34, but there are also statements which were not originally meant as promises for the future. Passages like Pss. 2; 110, etc. refer to a contemporary king, whose enthronement they celebrate. Furthermore, there are passages which were interpreted contrary to their true meaning and even contrary to their actual wording – like Isa. 7.14, where the Hebrew text speaks of a young woman, whereas the Septuagint speaks of a virgin – as evidence and proof that the scriptures promised and prophesied Christ.

Typological interpretation, which Paul already made use of, presupposing a relationship between Old Testament types and Christian or christological antitypes, understands the Old Testament as a preliminary stage: the types are prefigurements and foreshadowings of what is to be fulfilled in Christ. Just as the prophecies foretell in words what is to come, so people, institutions and events in the Old Testament period point to the final event of Jesus Christ by their existence or by their occurrence. Indeed, even allegorical interpretation can recognize that the literal sense was valid during the history of Israel, but such interpretation contrasts this preliminary stage with a deeper, true, Christian or christological sense. For example, the Letter to the Hebrews presupposes that a 'commandment given earlier' had in fact been valid, although it was annulled because it was weak and useless (Heb. 7.18). It is only when allegorical interpretation denies the original text any literal meaning whatsoever and rules it out as the misunderstanding of incompetent and malicious Jews, as in the Letter of Barnabas (see above, 34), that the Old and New Testaments are put more or less on the same plane.

In the controversy with Judaism, this understanding of the Old Testament as a preliminary stage had some use: the church's claim to the Old Testament seemed to be supported by its assertion that the prophecies and promises which had been announced earlier the 'types' which had existed beforehand, were now fulfilled, and that a true, more profound, spiritual sense of scripture had only now been revealed. At the same time, the independence of the old legacy over against the new, final and therefore incomparable character of the Christ event could be preserved: the inherited scriptures were the '*Old* Testament', as they were described in a phrase which now became established as a technical term (see 35ff. above).

This definition of the relationship between the testaments also made possible a still more subtle view. Once the controversy with Judaism became less significant and drew to a close, and the Old Testament became an undisputed and indisputable first part of the Christian canon, attention was drawn to the historical line which seems to run from the Old Testament in the more remote past down to the New. Thus even for Luke, the 'mid-point of time' which is to be found in Christ is preceded by the period of Israel and succeeded by the period of the church. The Old Testament itself encourages such an interpretation. Although it may be described as 'law and prophets', it is certainly more than law and prediction; it is also a historical narrative extending from Adam and Eve down to a time shortly before Christ. It is followed by the history of Jesus and – in Luke – by the history of the church. This historical development contains various stages, and the chronological succession can be understood as a theological classification and evaluation.

It is instructive and significant that this extensive outline was prompted not by the controversy with Judaism and its understanding of scripture, but by the fight against Gnosticism and its rejection of both the Old Testament and the 'God of the Jews'. It made up an attempt to see the Old and the New Testaments as the documents of an on-going course of history directed by God. The anti-Gnostic theologian Irenaeus worked out this conception in the second century in his book which bears the title 'An Unmasking and Refutation of that which is wrongly called Knowledge'. In his view, one and the same God was at work in the mists of time and then especially in the history of Israel, before he revealed himself fully and universally in Christ. Regarded in this light, the Old Testament is no longer merely the prelude to the New; it is the written record of a salvation history which takes place in stages and extends over a long period. According to Irenaeus, it moves from stage to stage, from covenant to covenant, from Adam to Noah, to Moses, and then to the new covenant of Christ, in which the Word (Logos) becomes visible. The Pauline notion that the law is the taskmaster which leads men to Christ (Gal. 2.24) is largely reinterpreted: God is seen to have tried to educate men over a long period to make them mature and capable of receiving true salvation. Over this period he made use, above all, of the law, which, because of the hardness of men's hearts, first of all compelled them to be obedient to God, accustomed them to obedience and protected them from apostasy, so that when at last they became free, they could receive the revelation of Christ as children of God. Here, then, we find a comprehensive and profound, well-developed conception which makes it both possible and plausible to accept that the Israelite and Jewish Old Testament is and must remain, despite Gnosticism, the church's book. Testimony to Christ thus becomes one element (albeit the highest stage) in the course of a universal history which is understood *as such* to be God's action. Texts with specific testimony in each individual pericope now give way to an ongoing historical narrative in which each stage simply acquires a relative significance in the context of the whole. The apparent plausibility of this outline led to its being accepted as virtually the normative theology in a church in which in any case the proclamation of the word was beginning to be replaced by the realization of salvation in the present through the sacraments, and in which the course of the church's year and the liturgies reflected the course of salvation history (see 43ff. above).

However, Irenaeus' thoughts also exercised some influence outside the normative theology of the church. The idea of a series of covenants recurs prominently in Reformed theology (see 58f. above) and in the federal theology of Cocceius (see 163ff. above), to which it lends its name. Another idea which is often expressed is that in the childhood of mankind, God 'accommodated' himself to a particular stage of human knowledge, in order to educate the men of the time.

It is not surprising that this idea recurs in the Antiochene school. Here there was a retreat from allegorical interpretation, which passed over the literal sense and simply concealed the theological and hermeneutical problem of the Old Testament (see 40 above). Attention was once again drawn to the autonomy of the Old Testament. Theodore of Mopsuestia taught that the Old Testament was governed by the fact that it was the record of a preparation for the revelation of Christ, and his contemporary John Chrysostom, the great preacher, thought that he had found the reason why the great men of God spoke as though to children in the fact that here God was being loving and gracious to mankind. Even for Augustine, however, the law of the old covenant had a function in an all-embracing divine economy of salvation: it was intended to subdue the fleshly lusts of men and their hardness of heart and so to provide a way from the earthly city, the *civitas terrena*, to the city of God, the *civitas dei*. Indeed, it was Israel's task to be the image of the heavenly city. Augustine's significant contemporary Jerome, the experienced translator and philologist, was also well aware of the differences between the Old and the New Testament; one was dominated by transitoriness and the other by eternal grace; in one there was retribution ('an eye for an eye'), whereas in the other there was pure, forgiving love (cf. Diestel, 106ff.).

Just as covenant theology was later characteristic of the Reformed churches, so too the theme of the education of man recurs within them. Calvin thought that the language of the Old Testament was as though addressed to children, and that Moses in particular accommodated himself to 'the childishness of the people' (*puerilitas populi*), as when, for example, he writes that God himself made clothes for the first human beings. For Calvin, a divine pedagogy (*paedagogia Dei*) holds the two testaments together. The attribution of human characteristics and human feelings to God are seen above all as pedagogical attempts to communicate the beginnings of a revelation to a mankind which is still in a state of childhood (Diestel, Ic, 290ff.).

Just as Irenaeus was already advancing the idea of an economy of salvation and God's use of history as an educational process in his arguments against the Gnostic repudiation of the Old Testament, so those who defended the Old Testament against the rationalistic polemic of the Enlightenment in a comparable conflict returned to the same theme. Whereas for Semler, the pre-logical and pre-rational language of the Old Testament is accommodation, J. G. Eichhorn and J. P. Gabler understand its approach to be that of myth, and explain it as the specific way of thinking and imagining to be found during the childhood of mankind. The creation stories, in particular, are to be interpreted as such a myth, and the way in which this is to be done is demonstrated in Eichhorn's *Urgeschichte*, which was edited by Gabler (1792/1793).

Gabler observes (II, 62 n. 26, quoted from Kraus, Ic, 150):

> If the development of human understanding proceeds by stages, the divine revelation must take the same course: it will communicate, centuries earlier, some truths at which the human spirit will later arrive of its own accord, and do so in a form appropriate to the time. We can therefore understand why there are various economies of religion; the truth itself is eternal and unchangeable, but the form of truth, like the method of arriving at it, is subject to constant change and variation. In this connection Lessing's *Erziehung des Menschengeschlechts* [The Education of the Human Race, VIA] deserves special attention and study.

An interesting feature of this statement is the assumption that revelation does not bring any knowledge which human reason would not have arrived at even without revelation, albeit at a very much later stage. It can also be found in the work of Gotthold Ephraim Lessing, whom Gabler in fact mentions. Lessing had remarked that millions of years could have gone by had God not intervened to educate mankind. Since it had fallen victim to a barbarous form of polytheism, mankind had to be submitted to divine discipline. God achieved this by choosing the Jews and educating them to the point when the universal revelation of Christ could finally take place. He continues this education by drawing man on further and further even in the present, since mankind has still to arrive at the heights of reason and morality which are revealed in Christ and attested in the New Testament. It should be remembered that these ideas of Eichhorn, Gabler and Lessing were intended as a defence of the Old Testament (and indeed Christianity generally) in a situation in which both threatened to fall into disrepute because of the many irrefutable attacks that were being made on orthodoxy. Of course the presupposition that revelation is rational, and does not contain anything at which human reason would not be capable of arriving even without divine support, raises the question of the necessity of revelation and divine education in *any* form.

Similar comments can also be made about Johann Gottfried Herder, the other significant apologist and defender of the Old Testament, and of his 'Spirit of Hebrew poetry' (IIIB). He urgently demanded a sympathetic understanding of the Old Testament. People should put themselves in the situation of the old, childlike beauty of the East and sense its atmosphere, and should beware of the arid abstractions of rationalism. He advised them to enjoy, as far as possible in the spirit of naive children, what was meant in a naively childlike way. This approach had the same consequences as that of Lessing and others: it put in question the claim of scripture to convey revelation, and with it the position of the Old Testament as part of the canon of the Christian church. Hearing became enjoying, and 'Thus says the Lord' became Hebrew poetry. In this way divine economy and divine education can become a history of development which can be understood purely within its own frame of reference without recourse to God and revelation, and in which the Old Testament is no more than the documentation of a period prior to Christianity. Thus in Hegel's system, in which the absolute Spirit comes to itself by a progression which involves three stages, Old Testament religion is assigned to the second stage, after natural religion and before the absolute religion of Christianity. Once this speculation is given the form of a system, it amounts to a history of development in which one stage seems capable of being explained genetically in terms of the others. And the way is open for the genetic fallacy.

2. *Salvation history, the history of promise and typology*

It is, of course, also possible to think of *God* as the power which drives history on towards its goal and keeps it in motion. Once again, it is instructive and significant that the conception of salvation history was developed in a controversy, no longer with Gnosticism, but with an attitude which threatened to rob the Old Testament of its status as an expression of Christian revelation and truth. This development began as early as Irenaeus, but it was 'conservative' theology in the nineteenth century which in particular used outlines of salvation history to counter such tendencies. Thus Johann Tobias Beck (1804–1878), inspired by Bengel and others, argued that a history of salvation could be read off scripture, which had been written by inspired witnesses to God. Some ideas which have been revived in twentieth-century theologies of the Old Testament can already be found here in embryo. Beck's *Einleitung in das System der christlichen Lehre oder propädeutischen Entwicklung der christlichen Lehrwissenschaft* (Introduction to the system of Christian doctrine or a propaedeutic development of Christian education, 1838) describes how God's *promise* is the glorious power which keeps salvation history moving forward, a history in which every fulfilment bears within it the seeds of a new promise. The revelation which is already contained implicitly in the Old Testament is developed fully in the New, so that the Old Testament needs to be understood as a 'prefigurative document of revelation' (238). Here we have a new presentation of Irenaeus' ancient conception of salvation history, made with some transformations and different nuances, and with great passion for correct doctrine. As Irenaeus once protested against Gnosticism, so Beck now protests against historical criticism and its philosophical premises. Twentieth-century protest, with a similar passion for truth but sometimes with only half-hearted attention to criticism, could find a point of contact here.

Probably the best-known representative of the idea of salvation history in the nineteenth century was Johann Christian Konrad von Hofmann (1810–1877), who wrote 'Prophecy and Fulfilment' (VIA).

For von Hofmann, the Bible, Old and New Testaments together, is a *historia sacra*. This history has to be called sacred because it is directed in a unique way by God; the history narrated in the Old Testament is a history of preparation for Christ and prefigures a Christ who is still hoped for. Christ is the archetypal destiny of the world, towards which history is directed. History is itself revelation and revelation is history, not doctrine. However, the real significance of von Hofmann's theology does not lie so much in these ideas, which it shares with other outlines of salvation history. In his work the concept of prophecy is given a new content, or rather a new emphasis. Prophecy here does not mean what has been foretold in words; the history of Israel as such is interpreted as *a prophetic history*, which carries its destiny within it. Now if history itself is given the character of prophecy and revelation, the *proclaimed word* of the Bible threatens to lose its significance. Von Hofmann acutely recognized this inevitable consequence, which can also be seen in present-day theologies of history like that of Pannenberg (it is even to be found in the work of Gerhard von Rad, see 91f. above), and in theologies of society in which social interests, conflicts, solutions and concerns assume the character of revelation. Von Hofmann attempts to avoid it in his *Biblische Hermeneutik* (1888, VIA, 153). Here he seeks to distinguish within the Old Testament on the one hand a 'consecutive series of events which make up a historical line culminating in the appearance of Jesus and the formation of his community' and on the other a series of 'statements' about salvation, which begins to be realized in these events and is ultimately fulfilled in the 'statement' of the salvation that is finally achieved in the New Testament. According to von Hofmann, these two aspects must be assigned to the history of Israel and the theology of the Old Testament respectively; the first is concerned with revelation through actions, and the second with revelation through the word. Both, however, are concerned with the same salvation. He seeks to preserve the significance of the *Word* by arguing that history is shown to be salvation history only in the light of the knowledge of salvation in Christ. Still, this nevertheless gives the word of proclamation another, inferior quality: it does not bring the salvation that it *promises* (as the Word of the cross and the resurrection), but becomes the key for a proper understanding of history in which salvation develops by stages. The dilemma of von Rad's theology is here so to speak already 'prefigured in type', and as in von Rad's theology, no solution is found.

Difficulties have overburdened the idea of salvation history from the start, and any philosophy of history which attempts to understand historical reality – 'historicity' – as one stage in an ongoing process runs the risk of losing that reality and being left with only stages and phases which, while having relative importance within the totality, have no autonomous, individual significance. Nevertheless, we can understand how the outline first presented by Irenaeus could be readily accepted, especially in the most recent past and even in the present. After the dawn of historical consciousness at the time of the Enlightenment and the recognition of the historical remoteness and strangeness of Old Testament religion, at least those who had scholarly integrity found it impossible to put both testaments on the same level. It therefore seemed the obvious thing to do to attempt to overcome the theological difficulty produced by *historical* criticism *with the help of history*. As a result, biblical theology, born out of the rise of historical consciousness, changed itself into a history of Israelite and Jewish religion.

Accordingly books were no longer entitled *Theology of the Old Testament*, but 'Textbook of the History of Old Testament Religion' (R. Smend, 1893), or *Religion of Israel* (K. Budde, 1899, ET 1899). On occasion, when a new edition was published of an old, out-of-print 'Theology of the Old Testament', the editor turned the book into a 'History of Israelite Religion'. This happened when Karl Marti edited and revised August Kayser's 'Theology of the Old Testament' (1907). He justified his action with an instructive argument which I shall therefore quote here.

> Critics who were on the whole well-disposed to this book in its new form felt at the same time that in being given its old title it was really sailing under false colours. That is why I have retitled subsequent editions *History of Israelite Religion*. This new title corresponds much better to the structure of the book as a whole; it also demonstrates the impossibility of deriving a unitary theology from so pluriform and varied a book as the Old Testament (op cit., v).

This explanation deserves careful reading. The title had to be altered not so much because of the historical variety within the Old Testament, as because 'theology' was a false flag for the ship to sail under. Thus theology becomes history.

Once this terrifying and painful loss had been recognized, the only alternatives seemed to be either to return to a form of *systematic theology*, or to approach and evaluate *history itself* in theological terms and to pursue *history as theology*. Now it is certainly permissible to describe important Old Testament statements – the 'important views, notions and concepts' of which Ludwig Köhler's *Theology* (IIIc) speaks – in a systematic way: to present them thematically, or classify them in an instructive fashion, or group them around a particular centre and attempt to make them comprehensible (cf. 89ff. above). This makes good sense, and is useful for teaching and study. But such a systematic approach does not solve the theological problem of how some theological justification can be given for the value and validity of such 'important' ideas and concepts. By what criterion is their importance to be measured? How is the Old Testament once again to become a Christian witness which calls for a man's belief today, once it has been alienated by historical criticism and shown to be a work which demands consideration in its own right? A systematic approach does not even pose the questions sufficiently clearly. On the contrary, it runs the risk of overlooking the constant problem posed by history.

Without doubt, this is the point at which von Rad's *Theology* (IIIc) has done special service. He attempts to understand in relevant theological terms the process of the formation of tradition and indeed history itself as an ongoing testimony to Yahweh's saving institutions and a way of describing them which adapts itself to every historical period. We can hardly question the description of such a conception in terms of salvation history; von Rad himself uses the term frequently, and his basic statement about the relationship between the two testaments sees their connection in these terms. However, history has to be narrated, so another term which appears often in his work is that of 'retelling'.

It should not be seen as a slight on von Rad's resolute concern to maintain a historical approach and not to give way to the temptation of presenting a system based on the postulation of a particular centre to the Old Testament, if we go on to note that his *Theology* is caught up in the dilemma of all approaches which consider the Old Testament in terms of salvation history. The crucial word 'retelling' already hints at this. This verb presupposes a chronological sequence, a historical development. Retelling is important in connection with the *process* of history. Historical development is important as such and is only given its true importance, only becomes clear, in terms of the end of the historical process. Nor is it to belittle von Rad's achievements to understand his *Theology* as a particular expression of an approach and conception which can already be found in Irenaeus, but which has now been adapted to take account of modern historical research. Von Rad himself may be seen as a particularly distinguished representative of a view which in the meantime has found widespread acceptance.

This view represents a protest – made since the time of Irenaeus in the form of a refutation (Latin *Adversus haereses*, 'Against heresies') – against the threatened loss of the Old Testament to Gnostic denigration or alienation brought about by historical criticism, by means of an appeal to the *history* which links Old and New Testaments (though of course this appeal may take many forms).

In New Testament criticism and theology, no direct theological significance is attached to the actual course of history, though New Testament scholars certainly take account of historical research and the historical sequences and developments that form its subject-matter. Despite the reputation they have gained, New Testament scholars who put forward a view of salvation history, like Oscar Cullmann (*Christ and Time*, 1946, ET 1951; *Salvation in History*, 1965, ET 1967) or Ethelbert Stauffer (*New Testament Theology*, 1941, ET 1955), are the exceptions which prove the rule that salvation history is usually regarded with some scepticism. In any case, the amount of criticism directed against them should be noted. However, Old Testament scholarship has displayed a constant loyalty to salvation history, even when its heart has not always seemed to be in it.

All this is clear simply from the briefest of scrutinies of the discussion about the hermeneutical problem of the Old Testament which was carried on in the 1950s, especially in the journal *Evangelische Theologie* (cf. esp. volume 12, 1952/1953) and in the collection *Essays on Old Testament Interpretation*, edited by Claus Westermann (1960, ET 1963, IIIc). The questions discussed here have still not been solved and still largely govern contemporary discussion; they need therefore to be mentioned at greater length.

The various attempts made to win a way through to theology without abandoning history, and without being dishonest in denying the historical insights which had been achieved, are almost all characterized and motivated by a concern to provide a theological evaluation of the course of history. In almost all cases it is regarded as a preliminary stage to the Christ event and as a history which leads up to Christ; it is this goal which makes it a sacred history. Rather than quote in detail at this point, we may perhaps just mention that for Zimmerli it is a movement 'which presses from promise towards fulfilment' (VIA, 109). Granted, the Old Testament already knows of fulfilment, as towards the end of the book of Joshua (21.45), where we read: 'Not one of all the good promises which the Lord had made to the house of Israel failed; all came to pass.' 'Here,' Zimmerli writes, 'the brook seems to have come to a standstill. But in fact this is only

apparent; in what follows the book of Judges will make clear the
aspect of watching and waiting for the "helper" who will make room
and give Israel rest' (p. 112). But in that case, one might ask, why is
there so clear and extensive a mention of fulfilment if this fulfilment is
'only apparent'? Furthermore, does not this attempt to take history
seriously and not to lose sight of it lead to a way of dealing with the
texts which treats them as historical reports? However, before we
consider this question and the whole problematic nature of the enterprise, we must develop it in rather more detail. Zimmerli, too, has no
doubt that the history of promise and fulfilment to which the Old
Testament bears witness found its final fulfilment in Christ:

> All Old Testament history, in so far as it is history guided and given by
> Yahweh's word, receives the character of fulfilment; but in the fulfilment it
> receives a new character of promise ... No summons which would call
> this history to its conclusion can be heard in the Old Testament ... The
> New Testament message of fulfilment thus stands over against this situation
> in the Old (112f.).

The editor of the collection, Claus Westermann, has essentially the
same view. According to him, the situation is aptly described on the
one hand 'by the realization that we must inevitably speak of the Old
Testament theologically, answering the question of whether and in
what way the God of whom and for whom the Old Testament speaks is
the same God on whom Jesus calls in the New Testament and the
God of the creed of the Christian church' (44). After this adequate
description of the situation with regard to the hermeneutical problem,
he explains what all the new attempts have in common: 'Basic to all
approaches is the insight that the Old Testament reports history or a
story or events that happened' (44).

As instances, he quotes Martin Noth, Gerhard von Rad, Walther
Zimmerli, Martin Buber and G. Ernest Wright (44). It is particularly
interesting for our present situation that Westermann discusses the
possibility of a 'narrative' theology, the demand made by G. E. Wright
and cited by Westermann that true theology should be a 'theology of
recital' (*God who Acts*, 1952, 13; Westermann, 46).

Of course, Westermann does not use the term salvation history in
an unconsidered way and, with references to the scholars mentioned
above, he connects it with the *Word* of God.

Gerhard von Rad had begun his 1952 article, 'Das Alte Testament
ist eine Geschichtsbuch' (ET 'Typological Interpretation of the Old
Testament'), with the words: 'The Old Testament is a history book.

It portrays a history brought to pass by God's Word, from creation to the coming of the Son of Man' (Westermann, 25, where the statement is in fact made in section 5 of the article). Westermann quotes this remark with assent and elaborates on it, claiming it to be a new definition of the concept of history which seeks to correct the limited nineteenth-century approach to history and to make it clear that the history of mankind cannot be described appropriately 'by excluding the question about the working of God' (47). Thus the history recorded in the Old Testament is to be seen neither as the history of religion nor as salvation history 'in the sense of a sector of history', but as 'a part of world history' in which no single factor gives objective proof that it is concerned in a unique way with God's action, 'least of all the Word of God as a controllable and available entity' (47).

In Westermann's view, history does not simply speak the 'language of facts', a phrase which is later to be used by W. Pannenberg (*Revelation as History*, VIA, 153). Westermann recognized more clearly than others, even von Rad, that the relationship between history and the Word must necessarily become a problem in any conception of salvation history. That is why, like von Hofmann before him, he attempts to preserve the essential significance of history and the Word. It is the Word (significantly enough, understood primarily as proclamation) that qualifies history as a process of revelation.

He says this on the relationship between history and the Word:

> Only through the relation with the promising Word and solely through the relation with it does the historical fact become God's acting; it is only in this way that a 'history of God with his people' comes into being. The continuity of this history lies in nothing else than in the overarching connection which binds the promise to the happening of the promised. This is why in the present discussion about the interpretation of the Old Testament the double concept of promise and fulfilment stands in the foreground (48).

The concept of an 'overarching connection' which links the announcement with the occurrence now becomes the hermeneutical key and is therefore used quite regularly. In a later study (*Das Alte Testament und Jesus Christus*, 1968, VIA, 51), Westermann remarks:

> The relationship between the Old Testament and the New need not only be seen in terms of the Old Testament as the vehicle of the promise and the New Testament as the vehicle of the fulfilment; rather, the Old Testament contains the history of the promise which is fulfilled in the

New. Promise and fulfilment together form a total event which is recorded in both Old and New Testaments.

Like Westermann and those involved in his discussion, Klaus Schwarzwäller (*Das Alte Testament in Christus*, 1966, VIA) is also concerned with history, namely the history of God's self-disclosure. Similarly, Friedrich Mildenberger writes of 'our decision for the unity of God's history and therefore of scripture' (*Gottes Tat im Wort*, 1964, VIA, 93). It is said of this history that it has within it 'a connecting thread which makes the beginning point to the consummation and shows the consummation to be the consummation arising out of that particular beginning' (107). At this point Mildenberger rightly observes: 'A conceptuality of this kind always runs the risk of doing away with the contingency of historical events in the schematism of a hypothetical construction. However, this danger can be avoided if we keep to what the text says' (107, n.41). Mildenberger feels that we may and must speak of 'salvation history' because the linear development, the 'continuity of the divine action in history' (108), is so important. He chooses to express it by means of the term 'proclamation history' (81f., 107ff.).

For Walter Eichrodt ('Is Typological Exegesis an Appropriate Method?', VIB, 224ff., cf. 226), typological exegesis is appropriate because 'the type, like the entire salvation history of the Old Testament, indicates only a preliminary stage of the salvation in Christ and cannot attain to the completeness of the latter. Thus the element of intensification, even if it is not expressly stated, is always there in the background.' It is worth noting Eichrodt's remark that exegesis should not limit itself to discussion of the literal sense which may be arrived at by means of historical and philological criticism. Rather,

> ... exposition of the Bible has to go beyond the pure establishment of the literal sense, has to determine the significance of a passage in its wider setting in the history of thought, and has to assess its influence in later times. For the Old Testament this can be done appropriately only if the function of its history as a previous stage of the New Testament history of salvation is taken into consideration. For it is this that differentiates Christian exegesis from Jewish exegesis and from all other kinds of exposition: It believes and recognizes that the Old Testament is determined fundamentally by its directedness toward the New (242).

It is noteworthy here not only that faith functions as an epistemological instrument and that *faith* understood in this way is concentrated on 'the directedness of the Old Testament toward the New', i.e. *on a course of history*, but also that for such faith and the exposition which it produces the Old Testament becomes the document of a prior history and a 'prelude' to the New.

Typological interpretation (see 112f. above) also presupposes that history has a theological significance in itself, so it is not surprising that the discussion of the possibility of a new theology of the Old Testament on a historical basis also brought about a reconsideration of this early hermeneutical key, which was already used by Paul. Two things made it seem legitimate and indeed necessary to search out typological correspondences: first, the fact that typological analogies can be discovered within scripture itself (e.g. the typological understanding of the proclamation of the new exodus in Deutero-Isaiah as the antitype of the first exodus, and the occasional typological interpretations that can be found in Paul, see 22ff. above), and, secondly, the conviction that both testaments are held together by a historical connection, a purposive divine course of history. Like the pattern of promise (prophecy) and fulfilment and the idea of a progressive salvation history, typological understanding seemed to give value to the Old Testament as the Old Testament, the prelude and prehistory to the New. Unlike allegorical interpretation, which strives to find 'another' sense everywhere, typological exegesis did not do away with or dissolve the events, persons and institutions, which were seen as types. It allowed them their reality and their concrete historicity and yet interpreted this uniqueness as a prefiguration, a foreshadowing and a prelude to their fulfilment in the antitype. It is easy to see how the idea of salvation history and the method of typological exegesis belong together.

Thus Eichrodt writes ('Is Typological Exegesis an Appropriate Method?', 240):

> Typology ... emphasizes at central points the continuity and the purposefulness of the divine action. It is not exhausted by the correspondence of external facts of whatever kind, but relates itself to the intercourse between God and man made real through them. In this way it answers an urgent question which agitates Christian faith in relation to the problematic nature of history in general and of Old Testament history in particular: It points to the realization of salvation through a history which is moulded by the same divine will to fellowship in the Old Testament as in the New Testament communities, and which strives towards a final consummation.

After Leonhard Goppelt (*Typos*, 1939, IIc), Gerhard von Rad and Hans Walter Wolff above all have attempted to argue for the justification and necessity of a typological approach in Old Testament study.

In a controversy with (among others) Rudolf Bultmann ('Ursprung und Sinn der Typologie als hermeneutischer Methode', 1950, IIc) who attempted to explain typology in terms of repetition and the notion of the cyclical recurrence of the same event, and also with the theological programmes of Ludwig Köhler (IIIc) and Otto Procksch (IIIc), von Rad stressed that the Old Testament was primarily a history book, 'the picture book of a history of faith' ('Typological Interpretation of the Old Testament', VIB, 27), in which the New Testament Christ event is already prefigured everywhere.

> Typological interpretation will thus in a fundamental way leave the historical self-understanding of the Old Testament texts in question behind, and go beyond it. It sees in the Old Testament facts something in preparation, something sketching itself out, of which the Old Testament witness is not itself aware, because it lies quite beyond its purview (36).

It is clear both from this quotation and from von Rad's often criticized comment that for this sort of typological interpretation 'no pedagogical norm can or may be set up; it cannot be further regulated hermeneutically, but takes place in the freedom of the Holy Spirit' (38), that here typological interpretation threatens to become allegory and that in any case the boundary between the two is blurred. We cannot ignore the possibility that the freedom of the Spirit can easily be confused with the whim of the interpreter. H. W. Wolff ('The Hermeneutics of the Old Testament'. VIB) is therefore more careful in the way in which he expresses himself. In his view, there is no going back on the Reformation return to the literal meaning; arbitrary interpretations are impermissible. However, as in Wolff's view there can be no question that 'Israel, as Yahweh's covenant people, is, as a whole and in detail, a type of the *ekklesia* of Jesus Christ' (173), the relationship between Old and New Testaments cannot be defined exclusively in antithetical terms. There is an analogy between the Old Testament and the New:

> The old covenant moves forward toward the new; Israel is called for the sake of the Gentiles. The new covenant comes from the old; Jesus Christ is the Son of David and the Paschal Lamb. It is the analogy of journey and destination, of shadow and body, ... of engagement and marriage. This analogy in a historically unique relation, which is not without a decisive moment of intensification toward the eschaton, we call typology (180f.).

Another of his remarks makes it clear that here, too, typology as a

method is based on the assumption that the Old Testament is a prelude
to the New:

> The central question of typological exposition [is]: To what extent is the
> New Testament kerygma illuminated by the history that precedes it (or,
> apprehended only when the previous history is listened to along with it)?
> (190).

Of course typology can also be understood in a very different way,
as being independent of a linear understanding of history and without
any methodological link with the conceptions of salvation history:
here typology differentiates between the Old Testament and the New
by 'choosing as a basis for comparison the particularity of Being in
time' (Ernst Fuchs, *Hermeneutik*, Iʙ, 201). Of course, this understanding
cannot be regarded as characteristic of the typological method,
although it marks a suitable point at which to bring to a meaningful
conclusion the now defunct discussion over the justification of typological exegesis (see below 214ff., 230f.).

3. Revelation and the historical process

Whereas exegetical insights – and errors – often have very little
influence on systematic theology, the wide-ranging consensus that Old
Testament theology should be connected with salvation history or
oriented on a linear historical approach has had considerable effect on
modern systematic theology in a number of ways. First of all, we
should mention Jürgen Moltmann's outline of a *Theology of Hope*
(1964, ET 1967, VIA). Moltmann makes an apodeictic and programmatic declaration:

> But now the more recent theology of the Old Testament has indeed shown
> that the words and statements about the 'revealing of God' in the Old
> Testament are combined throughout with statements about the 'promise
> of God'. God reveals himself in the form of promise and in the history
> that is marked by promise. This confronts systematic theology with the
> question whether the understanding of divine revelation by which it is
> governed must not be dominated by the nature and trend of the promise
> (42).

Moltmann can therefore describe Old Testament religion as 'the
religion of promise' (43), and go on to interpret the event of the cross
and resurrection of Jesus Christ as the revelation of a promise:
' "Revelation" in this event has not the character of *logos*-determined

illumination of the existing reality of man and the world, but has here constitutively and basically the character of promise and is therefore of an eschatological kind' (85). Westermann's 'overarching connection', which extends from promise to fulfilment, here becomes a relationship between hope and promise, in which the promise culminates in hope and preserves a 'creative expectation' (to use Ernst Bloch's phrase) which gives men the drive to change society and which is the only approach to deserve the designation (again derived from Bloch) 'presentative eschatology' (335, with reference to Bloch's *Tübinger Einleitung in die Philosophie* II, VIA, 176). *Promise* (prophecy) and *fulfilment* become an Old Testament 'history of promise': 'In the gospel the Old Testament history of promise finds more than a fulfilment which does away with it; it finds its future' (147). The 'future religion of the Bible' (Bloch, loc. cit.) knows only an exodus community (Bloch, loc. cit.; Moltmann, 304ff.). We may simply observe in passing that these ideas, which derive from the particular understanding of the relationship between Old Testament and New that has been discussed here and which are based on the results of Old Testament *research*, have exercised considerable influence. The influence has been all the greater because this theology regards itself as a theoretical guide to the action to be taken by the church and even more significantly by society as a whole; it takes over the Old Testament (and later above all the Reformed) concern for the realization of the kingdom of God and attempts to reconcile the content of eschatological hope with Marxist aims in a kind of 'historical compromise'.

As its title implies, the programmatic study *Revelation as History*, edited by Wolfhart Pannenberg (1961, ET 1969, VIA), in which the Old Testament scholar Rolf Rendtorff played a significant part, is oriented on history and is inspired to a considerable degree by its understanding of the Old Testament as a history book. Rendtorff puts forward a view which is meant to overcome the old dilemma inherent in salvation history, of history and the Word, or the history of facts and the history of traditions. He argues that tradition itself is also history. Going beyond the position already reached by von Rad, which seeks to distinguish between history and the Word while maintaining harmony between them, this view made an important contribution towards laying the basis for the new outline of universal history put forward by the 'Pannenberg circle'.

This outline is developed fully and discussed with reference to the currently topical discussions of the philosophy of science in Pannenberg's *Theology and the Philosophy of Science* (1973, ET 1976, VIA).

Here it is not only the Old and New Testaments which are linked by a historical connection.

If the exegetical disciplines are treated as part of historical theology, the question of the canon has no more than secondary importance. There is a much greater awareness of the connection between the religion of Israel and the rest of the Middle East and of the importance for primitive Christianity of Jewish history in the 'intertestamental' period, and similarly the boundaries between primitive Christianity and the history of the early church become fluid. In this approach the formation of the canon is seen as a moment within the history of Christianity (375).

It is also significant for this theology that a normative *canon of scripture* led to normative significance being attached to the *earliest period* of Christianity (ibid.). History, as an extended period of time, acquires the character of revelation. In pointed polemic against the theology of the Word of God, 'kerygmatic theology', with its concept of God's revelation of himself which is given, proclaimed and believed in the Word, *Revelation as History* speaks of 'the language of facts' (153). Thus history as a whole is the revelation of God. As it is not yet at an end, it will be recognized as revelation only when it comes to an end (Rendtorff, ' "Offenbarung" im AT', VIA, col. 837). Now, however, this end has already taken place in anticipation in the resurrection of Jesus Christ from the dead, which is to be understood as the final event in terms of Jewish apocalyptic. The resurrection is the anticipation of the end and the goal of history, which sheds light on the whole of history as revelation.

Thus 'history' becomes the embodiment of reality in all its aspects. As in Moltmann, interest shifts from scripture as Word, from revelation as address, from the faith of the individual who hears the Word and believes it, in short, from what is supposed to be a limitation to individual human existence, and is now directed towards a horizon which embraces the whole of history or the whole of society. As the anticipation of the goal (*telos*) of history, the resurrection of Jesus Christ is a fact like all the true facts of history. Faith is directed towards this fact, of which there is a reliable tradition, and not towards a mere word. As the resurrection of Christ, which has actually taken place, is the anticipation – prolepsis – of the unique revelation in the full sense of this word and has universal historical significance, the character of revelation can be assigned only to universal history, and this rules out a particular history of revelation, for example in Israel. The special status of the Old Testament, therefore, is not based on its testimony to a special instance in history; it lies in the dawning within Israel of an awareness of history in the overarching connection of promise and historical fulfilment, without which Christianity could not even have a historical existence. So Pannenberg can say: 'The essence of Christianity is this history from the advent of God's future in Jesus to the future of the Kingdom of God to be inaugurated by the returning Christ' (*Theology and the Philosophy of Science*, 418).

If for Pannenberg – and similarly for Moltmann – faith is not essentially related to the word of God's self-revelation and in fact has its primary reference to the facticity of history, the language of facts, rather than to the Word, the scriptures which bear witness to the Word necessarily lose their central, canonical position. 'By scripture alone' (*sola scriptura*) turns into 'by history alone' (*sola historia*). The history to which the Old Testament bears witness is incorporated as a partial aspect into this total history. Similarly, the interpretation of texts and biblical criticism generally becomes part of a task which involves both theology and the history of religions, and has a universal scope. This helps us to understand how church history can be given a positive theological evaluation:

> Church history is not just a particular theological discipline, as biblical theology can be said to be. It embraces the whole of theology, whereas biblical theology as a discipline can only *per nefas*, and the individual exegete only by exercising considerable courage, transcend the limits of their own discipline in order to consider its contribution to theology as a whole ... Unless a fundamental distinction is made between the canonical scriptures (as in early Protestantism) or the whole apostolic age (as by Karl Barth) and the age of the church and its history, there is no reason for denying the discipline responsible for investigating the history of Christianity competence to study the beginnings of Christianity and indeed its prehistory, even though it is valuable to draw attention to a contrast, based on the uniqueness of the Christian faith, between the apostolic church and the apostolic writings as a significant constituent of the history of Christianity on the one hand and all later ages of the church on the other (*Theology and the Philosophy of Science*, 392).

This is understandable from Pannenberg's standpoint: the history of the beginnings of Christianity is a short period measured against the 'prehistory' to be found in the Old Testament along with all the rest of the prehistory of Christianity and its subsequent history lasting over two thousand years.

For the position we have just outlined, scripture and exegesis retreat well into the background, providing only the key words 'promise' or 'resurrection' as an anticipation of the end and goal of history. At the same time, however, other attempts have been made to find a way back to a theology which involves the whole of the Bible. Thus Peter Stuhlmacher ('Neues Testament und Hermeneutik', VIA, 43) regards the 'bisection of scriptural interpretation' into two separate disciplines, Old and New Testament exegesis, as 'very questionable theology'. He too thinks that 'the problem of universal history, which has been suppressed for a while, is now emphatically back with us and is, I believe, inescapable'. He therefore calls for 'renewed reflection on the process of universal history in which we are involved, by broadening our insights into reality and tradition and by a heightened interest in those outlines of the future which have proved decisive in particular periods of history' (40). In this perspective,

> Old and New Testament traditions in fact emerge as closely related phenomena which can no longer be fitted within the established historical or dogmatic approaches. It cannot be said that the New Testament is the true revelation by virtue of its proclamation of Christ, whereas the Old Testament, along with other evidence from the history of religions in late antiquity, is simply part of the New Testament environment and at best represents a preliminary stage to the New Testament tradition which is particularly important for the history of tradition (43).

Stuhlmacher leaves open here the question how the traditio-historical situation is to be understood, namely 'that the most important interpretative elements in New Testament christology, and most of the honorific titles given to Christ, along with, for instance, the conception of the resurrection, are derived from the Old Testament and from Judaism. In other words, New Testament christology was evidently conceived of, experienced and proclaimed in terms of the Old Testament.' This is something that we have to discover 'by further theological reflection' (loc. cit.). One way of achieving this would be to interpret the situation in terms of a linear history of tradition, seeing Old and New Testaments linked by their historical connection and then affirming the importance of this connection as such for theology and the history of religions. This would bring Stuhlmacher's position close to that of Pannenberg, and Pannenberg does in fact quote Stuhlmacher's article with approval (*Theology and the Philosophy of Science*, 382). Of course, the connection between the Testaments can be interpreted in another way, which can stand up to the test of historical and traditio-historical criticism; we shall have to discuss this later (223ff. below).

Stuhlmacher wrote a later article on the possibility of a new biblical theology, 'Das Bekenntnis zur Auferweckung Jesu von den Toten und die Biblische Theologie' (The Confession of the Resurrection of Jesus from the Dead and Biblical Theology, VIA). As the title indicates, this was intended as an outline of a biblical theology starting from the confession of the resurrection. At the same time, however, Stulmacher points out that the conception of the resurrection and the idea that God has power even over death was 'elaborated in Israel after a long period of independent work on the tradition' (146). 'The development of Jewish belief in the resurrection may be understood as a way of extending belief in Yahweh' (149). Consequently, 'The Christian confession of the resurrection expresses more precisely, in christological terms, an Israelite confession of belief in God which had been developed during a lengthy process of tradition, focussing it on the death of Jesus and his resurrection appearance.' For this reason, Stuhlmacher concludes, New Testament theology must be carried on as *biblical* theology, which is open towards the Old Testament (151ff.).

Once again, we can ask what is the *hermeneutical* and *theological* significance of this traditio-historical situation; does it lie in 'the long period of work on the tradition', that is, a history of development within the tradition leading up to Christ and the confession of the resurrection, or in the fact that the Christian proclamation, the kerygma, takes over the *language* of the Old Testament and reshapes it in the light of the Christ event? Here, too, there is apparently little concern for kerygma and language, and this 'approach to biblical theology' also leads towards an understanding of the historical process as revelation. Here, it is supposed, there is a drive towards 'establishing how far the Old Testament tradition of faith has come to its end and goal in the proclamation of Jesus ...' (154f.).

Here, too, one remarkable consequence that Stuhlmacher draws is that revelation can be discovered and made comprehensible by *historical research*:

> Historically speaking, there is no doubt that the revelation of God in both Old and New Testaments has been manifested in an ongoing process leading up to the resurrection of Jesus. Similarly, there is also no doubt that after the resurrection of Jesus a certain period of time and a variety of types of experience were needed for the understanding, exploration and proclamation of the revelation of God in Christ in terms which could demonstrate that this revelation applied to, and embraced, all realms of being in the past, present and future, even before time was and after the end of history (165).

At the same time, Hartmut Gese approached the problem of the unity of biblical theology and therefore the relationship of the two testaments from the perspective of Old Testament scholarship and from similar considerations (cf. his collection of articles, *Vom Sinai zum Zion*, 1974, VIA). Gese makes it even more clear than Stuhlmacher that the unity of biblical theology is to be based on 'the unity of the process of biblical tradition' (see the title of the first section of the book: 'Thoughts on the Unity of Biblical Theology', 11ff.). The New Testament 'forms the conclusion of a process of tradition which is essentially a unity, a continuum' (14). These considerations lead Gese to draw the following conclusion: 'Revelation is a process and the process can be grasped only as a whole. The process of revelation presupposes an ontological process which culminates in the event of the death and resurrection of Jesus, in which the bounds of being and non-being are destroyed. Being is, and the truth has become, historical' (30). The continuum which holds Old and New Testaments together is the unbroken process of tradition which began with the canonization of the Pentateuch but which was still completely open in the period of the New Testament. According to Gese, it was as a result of 'polemic directed against apocalyptic, against the wisdom tradition and above all against Christianity . . . that a significant part of this tradition was finally eliminated in AD 100, when the bulk of the apocalyptic and wisdom material was rejected. Christian theology can never approve of the Massoretic canon, since it interrupts continuity with the New Testament in a significant way.' Gese goes on: 'One of the influences of humanism on the Reformation seems to me to have been disastrous: the Pharisaic reduction of the canon was confused with the Massoretic tradition of the text to which the humanist tradition resorted, and apocryphal material was separated off' (16f.). The damage done by this reduction of the canon is to destroy the continuum of revelation (if that is humanly possible). Just as the theologians who contributed to *Revelation as History* rediscovered apocalyptic as the 'missing link' and used it to restore an uninterrupted historical continuity, so Gese is compelled to close the gap in the canon and as it were to become more canonical than scripture itself.

This viewpoint, too, was developed by means of and in controversy with von Rad's *Theology*. Whereas for von Rad the content of the kerygma, which is continually presented in new forms depending on the circumstances of the time, is related to history (except in the wisdom literature, some of the Psalms and apocalyptic), for Gese the kerygma is 'not a static entity; it develops continually along with the historical process of the tradition' (18). And as in Pannenberg's work, progress (to being with, at any rate, this word does not express a value judgment) consists in the involvement of the kerygma itself in the historical *process* so that this becomes the *process* of revelation. Unlike Pannenberg, of course, Gese understands this process only in terms of the scriptures of the Old and New Testaments; it is a process of revelation which does not extend to universal history, but is limited to the history of Israel, Judaism and Christianity. Gese differs from Moltmann, for whom the Christ event is itself essentially and primarily promise: 'Jesus went against the whole tradition of salvation history in its futuristic expectation of something other, and in its detachment from salvation, by proclaiming salvation here and now. This attributed the same sort of goal and end-point to the apocalyptic expectation of the future as did the Torah, and the conception within wisdom of a symbolic, derivative participation in salvation', because in the proclamation of Jesus 'the accomplishment of salvation is not merely hinted at, but actually realized' (28f.). Here too, however, for all the stress on the unity of the Bible and therefore the requirement of the unity of biblical theology, the Old Testament is understood as the written evidence of a prehistory, important though that prehistory may be.

4. *History and the Word: a critique of salvation history*

For all their differences in detail, all the attempts to solve the hermeneutical problem and to find a way back to a theology of the Bible as a whole have been at one in seeing the Old Testament primarily as a history book. In Westermann's words, 'Basic to all approaches is the insight that the Old Testament reports history or a story or events that happened' (*Essays*, VIA, 44; cf. 184 above). If we are to give this widespread opinion (which in fact has almost acquired canonical status) its due, assessing it within the context of the development and history of the hermeneutical problem, we have to take into account the following considerations. When Irenaeus outlined his view of a history of salvation in an attack on heretics (*Adversus haereses*) who disputed the validity of the Old Testament, he can hardly have been aware that his approach would encourage and pioneer an understanding of the Old Testament which went against the original concern of the early church with the scriptures, even if it cannot be termed heretical in itself. To begin with, we may ignore the fact that the Greek canon of the Old Testament taken over by the church was certainly not meant to be the written record of a prelude to Christianity and that the Hebrew canon was oriented on the law and its interpretation rather than on history. Leaving this aside, however, when the earliest Christian communities referred to the Old Testament as *scripture* (or 'the scriptures'), they were *not* referring to a *history* (in whatever form) which was 'narrated' or 'retold' by this scripture and which was to be found as it were underlying the texts. In the early tradition which even precedes Paul, Christ died and rose again 'according to the scriptures' (I Cor. 15.3f.), not at the end of a prehistory or a period of time to be regarded as an ongoing process of salvation history, which found its climax in the Christ event. Even where the New Testament speaks of the 'fullness of time' or the 'time' (*kairos*) which is fulfilled (Gal. 4.4; Mark 1.15; Eph. 1.10), there is no thought of a development, of a salvation which is gradually realized within history or of a process which progresses from promise to fulfilment. On the contrary, as is indicated by the term *kairos*, which usually occurs in such contexts (Mark 1.15; Luke 21.14; Eph. 1.10), the reference is to the decisive, eschatological moment, the end of time which is filled with the salvation brought by Christ. Even for Luke, 'this *scripture*' is fulfilled with the appearance of Jesus Christ (Luke 4.21). Luke is an evangelist who thinks 'chronologically', but not once does he see the *history* of Israel as a prehistory to Christ extending over several centuries. What is important for him is *scripture*, the significance of which lies especially in its character as prophecy and fulfilment. The continuity of time and history is unimportant, and the Old Testament is not seen to be the church's book for the reason that there is a continuous history of this kind which connects Israel and the church. On the contrary, the church acknowledges the Old Testament because it sees it as *scripture* which has been fulfilled. If we seek to retain the idea of continuity at any cost, we should see it in terms of the *Word* and of *language* generally. In the light of the Christ event the old word becomes the new Word; it acquires new significance and discloses its full truth. In short, 'Today this scripture is fulfilled in your ears' (Luke 4.21).

It is to the credit of Günter Klein, above all, that he has drawn attention to this quite different use of scripture and this quite different understanding of the Old Testament in the early church. He has made the point energetically in a number of writings, to which sufficient attention has yet to be paid. The point has been accepted and developed further in the context of systematic theology by H. G. Geyer ('Zur Frage der Notwendigkeit des Alten Testaments', VIA).

Of course, the way in which the primitive community accepted the

Old Testament and dealt with the scriptures cannot be regarded without further ado as normative for all times, particularly as its approach was far from uniform and many of its theological implications had not been fully explored. Nevertheless, the quite different understanding of the Old Testament, which is not in terms of a linear history, shows that anyone who dissociates himself from the circles of those who interpret the Old Testament as a history book parts from quite respectable company to find himself in the even better company of the New Testament writers. For them, the legacy which they had taken over from the fathers was first of all 'scripture', 'the law', and above all 'the prophets'. We have already demonstrated that this was a one-sided view; the Old Testament cannot be described wholly as law, nor can it be understood in its entirety as prophecy, prediction or promise. Because of this, the question could arise whether the understanding of the Old Testament as salvation history, predominantly in linear terms, which had emerged again and again since the time of Irenaeus, was not a more appropriate approach. There is no denying that the Old Testament tells a history and that it is possible to pursue a line beginning with Adam and extending on to the post-exilic period.

This clear insight should not be blurred by references to the discrepancies between what in fact happened and the reports contained in the Old Testament, between the historical facts and kerygmatic narrative, between the historical picture arrived at by historical criticism and the picture of history which is drawn by the Old Testament for the purposes of its kerygma. There is no need to stress the enormous differences between the two in order to produce a *reductio ad absurdum* of any kind of salvation history, by pointing either to a supposed course of history which never in fact took place or to a kerygmatic history with no basis in reality. For all this, there is no disputing the real historical basis of the most important 'saving facts': the wanderings of the patriachs, the exodus from Egypt, the conquest, the formation of the state, the Davidic kingship, the post-exilic restoration. All these are part of a history which took a linear course.

Now because there is a discrepancy between the biblical picture of history and the actual course of events, it has been thought that a decision has to be made either theologically, in favour of the biblical picture (G. von Rad), or in terms of the actual course of history (Franz Hesse; Hesse later changed his mind, see *Abschied von der Heilsgeschichte*, 1971; id., 'Zur Profanität der Geschichte Israels', 1974, both VIA). Alternatively, on the assumption that the history of tradition is itself history, it has been supposed that the two should be combined (R. Rendtorff, 'Hermeneutik des Alten Testaments als Frage nach der Geschichte', VIA; similarly O. Cullmann, *Salvation in History*, VIA, 75, 91f.). This once again discloses the difficulty of all forms of salvation history, which consists in the association of history and the Word (interpretation, narration, testimony), leading to a threat to the Word or its actual loss. However, this loss could be got over and even regarded as a gain if the Old Testament spoke the 'language of facts' and proved to be the kerygma even without the Word. Consequently, malicious reference to the difficulties in which von Rad (on the one hand) and F. Hesse (on the other) are entangled (see G. Klein, 'Bibel und Heilsgeschichte', VIA) should not be taken to rule out salvation history as a possible structure for biblical thinking. The problem could indeed lie in the fact that the nature of the 'facts' or of salvation history had not been thought through consistently enough.

Leaving behind the difficulties confronting Hesse and von Rad, both Moltmann and the Pannenberg group attack the theology of the Word with a new concept of revelation in facts and in history.

Moltmann seeks to liberate the concept of revelation from the supposedly restrictive 'fetters of the reflective philosophy of transcendental subjectivity' (*Theology of Hope*, 76). For him it is the Word *per se*, which is always promise, that sets in motion the process of history which leads towards fulfilment. Old Testament scholarship has already demonstrated that revelation in this sense should always be understood as promise (42). Here Moltmann refers to the understanding of revelation to be found in the Pannenberg group, which had been worked out above all by R. Rendtorff. Thus although both approaches are similar in having a starting point in a particular understanding of revelation, for which the Word is above all promise and a pointer to history, their ways part when it comes to developing the system. Whereas for Pannenberg, revelation understood in this way takes place against a background of universal history, for Moltmann 'the apocalyptic outlook which interprets the whole of reality in terms of universal history is secondary compared with this world-transforming outlook in terms of promise and missionary history' (83).

On closer and more matter-of-fact consideration, however, it proves that the enthusiastic systems of a theology of hope and of a theology of history generally, which have in turn generated so much enthusiasm, rest on a very narrow and indeed inadequate exegetical basis. There is certainly no reason for claiming that 'the more recent theology of the Old Testament' has shown that 'God reveals himself in the form of promise and in the history that is marked by promise' (42).

At the same time, a protest has developed against this at least one-sided understanding of revelation in the Old Testament which needs to be taken very seriously. Shortly after the appearance of *Revelation as History* in 1961, W. Zimmerli called attention to the one-sidedness of its approach in his article ' "Offenbarung" im Alten Testament' ('Revelation in the Old Testament', 1962, VIA). Although Zimmerli himself had said in an earlier article in 1957 that 'the truth of God's revelation is manifested from within historical happening' ('Das Wort des göttlichen Selbsterweises (Erweiswort), eine prophetische Gattung', VIA, 126), and there seemed to be support for the view put forward by Rendtorff that in the last resort the historical event itself was the important thing and that revelation took place only in history and as history, Zimmerli stressed in his criticism of Rendtorff that the Word itself is already a happening which gives motive power to the world and history and that this happening is the realization of the Word, the accomplishment of the proclamation (' "Offenbarung" ', 25). It is, of course, obvious that Zimmerli's own position (see 183f. above) landed him in considerable difficulties, if Rendtorff could refer to Zimmerli in the way that Pannenberg could refer to von Rad! If revelation is an event between promise and fulfilment, how can there be any talk of the primacy of the Word?

R. Knierim made a thorough exegetical and theological critique of the new understanding of revelation ('Offenbarung im AT', 1971, VIA). In it he recalled 'that history as such, in whatever way it may be conceived, was certainly not the only category in which reality was experienced in the Old Testament; indeed it was not even a universal way of comprehending reality' (228). Yahweh is revealed in actions and processes not only within history but also in nature, especially in his direction of creation, in his wise ordering of the world, in the sequence of morning and evening, being born and dying, the abundance of earthly gifts, fertility and so on (229). Above all, however, there is a clear distinction here between the general Near Eastern conception of 'manifestations of the divine in all realms of human experience' and therefore also in history (a conception in which Israel shared) and the identification of this *general presence of the divine* in a revelation of this name which cannot in any way be read out of history. The specific feature of the name has a linguistic character; it is a word-event.

Knierim rightly observes: 'There can be no doubt that the making known of a name (whether this happens in the form of a person introducing himself and giving his name, in a proclamation or in an acclamation) is always a word-event, whether or not it is related to another event, announces it beforehand or interprets it afterwards' (222). These exegetical observations demonstrate that two different processes of revelation coincide in the revelation of Yahweh as the God he is in truth. There is the manifestation of a divinity who is experienced as a transcendent power outside man's control and extending far beyond his capacities, which is a general phenomenon in the history of religions; in contrast, the fact that Yahweh reveals himself in such manifestations can only be perceived from the making known of his name (cf. 223f.).

It emerges from this that Pannenberg's sketch of universal history, which looks to the Old Testament and its understanding of revelation for a norm by which to orientate itself, in fact derives its universalism from history of religion in general. Israel certainly shared in this, but it is not a specific feature of belief in Yahweh and of Old Testament faith. Similarly, Moltmann's understanding of revelation, with the distinction (vital for his approach) between 'epiphany religions', for which the present is sanctified and qualified by the presence of a deity and for which salvation is experienced as the involvement of eternity in the present, and what he supposes to be the genuine Old Testament religion of promise, proves to be an instance of excessively narrow-minded exegesis. Whether in any case it is legitimate for Christian theology to have the norm for its understanding of revelation prescribed by the Old Testament is another question, the answer to which again presupposes a particular understanding of the relationship between the two testaments. It makes no difference whether or not the Old Testament is made to provide a particular concept of revelation which can be supported by exegesis: the question needs to be thought through carefully in a way which does not happen here. It is also evident from a historical perspective that assertions that one phenomenon or another is genuinely Israelite and has no parallels outside Israel are becoming increasingly perilous, especially in view of our knowledge of Israel's environment, which is still steadily increasing. A look at the texts coming from this environment refutes any claim that Israel was the first or only people to discover history as the locus of revelation, or even as revelation itself, on the basis of its particular belief in the promise, or that as a hearer of that promise Israel experienced history as a repeated departure from the present, which knows only the need for fulfilment and not fulfilment itself.

B. Albrektson (*History and the Gods*, 1967, VIA) has made this clear, but it can also be discovered from an unprejudiced interpretation of the Old Testament.

The Old Testament, then, cannot be subsumed under the concept of history. At the same time, however, there is no denying that it narrates history. The general consensus that the Old Testament is a history book is not completely unfounded. Is the history narrated here to be understood as salvation history? The concept of salvation history is an evasive one, and anyone who uses it, even to reject it, must first offer as good a definition as possible. Whereas the term 'saving event' is meant to indicate that salvation enters into history and into human destiny in a historical form and is received and experienced by men each in a particular period of history, 'salvation history', if the term is intended in its conventional meaning, refers to a historical continuum in which salvation gradually becomes possible in one way or another or in which God guides history towards some form of salvation. It is necessary, therefore, to distinguish between saving event and salvation history, though in fact the two terms belong together: where salvation is experienced in history in one way or another, as deliverance from distress, as the gift of land, fertility, well-being, blessing etc., a horizon can open up in which each individual saving event is linked together into a historical chain. For example, the individual themes of the Pentateuch, which were originally independent (the promise to the patriarchs, the exodus, the wandering in the wilderness, the conquest), have now been combined in a continuous historical narrative. It cannot, however, be said that salvation is realized in a gradual development or that it is finally achieved at the culmination of some historical process. It cannot even be claimed that according to the account in Genesis the patriarchs, say, who lived in the promised land as bearers of the promise and aliens, had a smaller share in salvation than the generation which took possession of the land for themselves. Indeed, it is questionable whether the authors of these narratives were concerned in any way at all with a *continuum* and a *course of events* as such. They were not like modern man with his historical consciousness. The line of historical development has no value in itself: the self-contained character of the pericopes, each of which can always be clearly distinguished (right down to New Testament times), shows that every one has a message of its own. They do not seek a hearing as mere phases, which derive their 'status' only from the whole of the narrative in which they are set. The linear course of history which holds them together has an auxiliary function.

By linking together past and present it serves to make the past relevant to the present or, to put it another way, serves to identify the present generation with the past. Where no sequence of historical events can be described, genealogies and uninterupted family trees serve the same purpose: what happened to the patriarchs was also relevant to the descendants who were incorporated in them and who were already contained in their 'seed'. The sons are their fathers' heirs, and inherit what was given to the fathers. Consequently it can even be said that Yahweh did not conclude his covenant with the patriarchs, but 'with us, who are all of us here alive this day' (Deut. 5.3). Anyone who describes such a view as salvation history understands the term in an unusual sense, to say the least.

When it comes to the great Deuteronomistic history work, one might be more inclined to talk in terms of a history of disaster. However, the arguments which tell against using the concept of salvation history also apply to such an approach. Even for the account of events in the Deuteronomistic history work, disaster does not develop and is not realized in a gradual process. Rather, the repeated apostasy from Yahweh which can already be found in the early period is continued in the period of the monarchy. The kings, as is said with a regularity which amounts to monotony, did 'what was evil in Yahweh's sight'. Similarly, the conclusion of the work represents the whole of Israelite history from the exodus from Egypt as a repeated succession of apostasy and disobedience: the Israelites 'walked in all the sins which Jeroboam did; they did not depart from them' (II Kings 17.22ff.). This characteristic expression has in mind the repetition of the same wickedness, rather than a development.

There are also other places where it is impossible to read out of the Old Testament a historical progression from promise to fulfilment, if the texts are understood as they are meant to be, rather than in terms of an 'education of the human race' or a history of religious development. The protagonists of the Old Testament story never achieve complete fulfilment: the patriarchs remain itinerant strangers, Moses is not allowed to enter the promised land, and even David has to defend his kingdom against his own son and against other usurpers. As early as the reign of Solomon, the kingdom begins to crumble at its frontiers, as we have been led to expect by earlier indications of Israelite failure to take possession of the land (Judg. 1.21, 27–35). However, the message of all these indications of 'not yet' is not primarily that of a new promise; they convey an awareness of sin and guilt, of personal guilt and the guilt of ancestors, which means that the people have

never been able to enjoy salvation to the full. Thus the Deuteronomistic history work, which narrates a history of disaster leading up to
the fall of Jerusalem, can *also* stress that *Yahweh* did not leave a single
promise unfulfilled (Josh. 21.45; 23.14). But it is *Yahweh* who brings
about complete fulfilment, whereas *man* brings down evil on himself
(Josh. 23.15). It is certain that this awareness of human guilt and
inadequacy, which always falls short of complete salvation, can also
be supported by hope for an ultimate eschatological fulfilment;
however, this is not a characteristic of the Old Testament historical
works, but is more a feature of prophecy.

Accordingly, for the New Testament, the Old Testament is not the
written record of a continuous history leading up to Christ. It is
scripture, which promises and prophesies Christ. The New Testament
refers back above all to prophecy, and to those texts which can be
reinterpreted in prophetical terms.

This applies to Paul more than anyone else. F. Hesse, who after
some bitter experiences with salvation history, took his farewell to it
in *Abschied von der Heilsgeschichte* (VIA), rightly remarks: 'There is no
passage in which the apostle begins from a continuity in terms of a
development in salvation history; he never talks in terms of a
continuous sequence of events. There is certainly a continuity
between, for example, Abraham and the present-day believer, which
is known only to faith, but this is not a historical connection' (32f.).
In fact it would be better to talk of continuity rather than analogy.
Furthermore, while Paul may occasionally attempt typological
exegesis, as in I Cor. 10, type and antitype are not stages on a course
which is followed according to plan, a 'history of the tradition of divine
salvation', for there are, significantly enough, no intermediate stages
whatsoever between the time of Moses and the Christ event (or the
time of the Christian community). Nor is there any indication of
salvation history: the decisive feature is that whatever was written,
was 'written down for our instruction' (I Cor. 10.11, op. cit., 33). And
although the evangelists write a history of Jesus and present the
kerygma of Jesus in narrative form, they do not regard the Old Testament as the written evidence of an early salvation history. Luke does
not attach any importance whatsoever to the continuity between the
history of Christianity and that of Israel and Judah: 'Luke
is concerned only to demonstrate that Jesus' way towards the cross
and resurrection took place in accordance with a divine plan of which
God granted a glimpse to one Old Testament prophet or another'
(34).

Popular though it may be, the view that the Old Testament is a history book proves untenable if history is understood as a continuous course of events which is important *as such* (whether as a sequence of cause and effect or as a series of events directed by God towards some final consummation). Granted, the authors of the books of the Old Testament may describe wider historical implications, but their narratives are never concerned with historical developments which take place under divine control and might be combined to form a salvation history, unless God retreats to the background and human beings take over the action (as in the Succession Narrative).

Theological significance is not to be found in the history – or histories – outlined by the Old Testament itself, much less in the 'real history', including the history of tradition, which can be reconstructed by biblical criticism; rather, as historical changes occur and horizons shift, the most important feature is the ever-repeated attempt to interpret Israel in the past and the present in terms of Yahweh's concerns: the present needs to be compared with the beginning of Yahweh's activity in judgment and in salvation, and Israel needs to be seen as the people of God which it supposed itself to be from the beginning, so that it might again become what it once was.

Thus in retrospect the *Yahwist* presents Abraham as the ancestor of Israel (and therefore as Israel itself). He abandoned all his possessions and set out in faith, in accordance with Yahweh's command. For this he received a blessing. This story is no mere 'prelude': it reminds Israel of its true nature and shows what it was and is, what it should be and can be.

Deuteronomistic theology is different, but nevertheless comparable. After a long and tragic history, Israel finds itself once again in the wilderness, there to be admonished and comforted by Moses so that 'today' it may receive its true salvation and serve Yahweh. In yet another way, which is still comparable, at a late stage the *Priestly Writing* draws a picture of the early days of Israel in the wilderness, showing how the Israelites gathered together around the tent of meeting and experienced the presence of Yahweh with them. This is narrated as history, yet it is not salvation history: it is at the same time both a programme and a reason for consolation: *today* Israel can be given the form of Israel as it was *in the beginning*, the form given by God in the wilderness; the community as it is here and now is the innermost sphere within that area which has been marked out from the waters of chaos.

Finally, we come to the work of the *Chronicler*. Although it begins with Adam, it does not present a salvation history, but a kind of developed aetiology and legitimation of the post-exilic community in Jerusalem and the Jerusalem temple. Established by Yahweh through the mediation of the holy king David, this is the place where Yahweh now 'brightens the eyes' and 'grants a little reviving' (Ezra 9.8). Such a life before God is not the end and the goal of a historical continuum, but a new gift of salvation after the collapse of the nation and the disaster of divine judgment. The work of the Chronicler is notorious for its historical unreliability. In this respect, however, it is only marginally different from the earlier historical works. Anyone who hopes to be able to detect a language of facts, or thinks that the Old Testament ought to be described as a *history book* because of the many narratives which it contains, can only be amazed and disappointed at such an apparently reckless treatment of facts. As things turn out, the interest of the Old Testament in the periods to which its contents are addressed (which makes it 'anachronistic' and shapes every detail of its descriptions of the past, in contradiction of any linear understanding of history) suggests that it is much more appropriate to describe the Old Testament as *a book concerned with achievements in the present.*

Of course the recognition that in so far as the Old Testament is concerned with narrative and history, it does not present a historical continuum or a line which leads up to Christ, does not rob its narrative of all value. It makes it possible to discover the particular message of different historical works and individual texts. In view of such 'resistance' to the idea of salvation history (G. Klein, 'Bibel und Heilsgeschichte', VIA), it seems clear that the concept of salvation history should be abandoned. At the same time, however, it is clear that inappropriate means are being used to articulate a particular concern: as the systematic theologian Karl Gerhard Steck puts it (*Die Idee der Heilsgeschichte*, 1959, VIA, 12), salvation history and linear history in general 'serve to prevent a purely speculative justification and exposition of Christian truth, which is at the same time purely anthropological, existential and philosophical, by making it impossible and unnecessary'. However, Gnosticizing speculations and anthropological reductionism cannot be countered by speculations in terms of a linear history and an idea which has no basis in exegesis. Quite apart from its faulty exegetical basis, this idea is questionable in a number of respects. From the perspective of systematic theology, faith and salvation are involved in a reciprocal relationship, but not faith and a historical continuum. 'On the contrary, because they are divine mysteries, incarnation and resurrection are inaccessible by means of a historical approach. If we ignore the historical materialism of more recent generations, this has always been the view of Christian doctrine' (60).

'Salvation history' is also questionable from the perspective of the philosophy of history. If it is understood as God's salvation, salvation does not appear in history any more than God does. Only a historical supernaturalism, which goes beyond 'the historical materialism of more recent generations' for the sake of religion, can presume to demonstrate and delineate the progression of God's action from one saving event to another. Theologians in particular should take a sober view of history (which is not the special domain of the God of Israel, or the only place in which he speaks and acts and brings about salvation) and see it for what it is: it is the embodiment of human action and experience, which needs to be investigated by historians in all its interconnections and complexity, its continuity and discontinuity, its necessity and contingency.

This is also the case with the most recent attempt made by Gese and Stuhlmacher to develop the history of traditions in theological terms and to identify the process of the formation of the tradition with the event of revelation. It culminates in Gese's statement: 'Revelation is a process, and can only be understood in the dynamic process which unfolds towards a goal' ('Anfang und Ende der Apokalyptik', VIA, 230). He can even claim that 'New Testament tradition is grounded in the Old and brings it to its unsurpassable conclusion' (loc. cit.). In fact, this statement is true only in its reference to the New Testament as the *formation of tradition*. However, the New Testament cannot and may not be understood primarily or even exclusively as the formation of tradition; it cannot even be understood as the conclusion of the process of the formation of a tradition. It is to be understood not only as the end-product of the formation of a tradition, but also (in accordance with its own claim) as the written record of the earliest, authentic *proclamation of Christ*, which while referring back to scripture (the law and the prophets), does not refer back to history. The New Testament in fact presents the Christ event as a saving event for the whole world without deriving it from any history or eschatology, involving it in no history and making it independent of any historical development. That the New Testament is the 'unsurpassable conclusion' to the Old is true only from a traditio-historical perspective which surveys the course of the formation of tradition. The fact that the *other* continuation of the tradition, in the synagogue, is played down to such a degree, is not a consequence of hostility towards the synagogue. It *has to be* passed over, so that the Christian 'conclusion' may be shown to be the only legitimate one and may be given theological value because it is 'unsurpassable'. Here the formation of tradition is identified both as a process which can be reconstructed by historical research, and as the revelation of God, which is accessible only to faith. This identification makes revelation into a historical process and a historical process into revelation. So this approach, too, attempting to justify the theological significance of the Old Testament and the possibility and necessity of a theology of the whole Bible by means of a linear construction – 'process' – leads to the loss of revelation and reduces the Old Testament to a written source of the prehistory to Christianity. The claim and the promise of particular texts exchange their intrinsic value for a relative value because they have now to be seen in a relationship with the course of history in which they are set.

Note should also be taken of the other implication (whether deliberate or unintentional) of a philosophy and theology of history for which history and revelation are simply regarded as a process. In any process, man can have only a 'relative value'. A particular picture of man goes with this understanding of revelation or history. Once man is caught up in this process, he is no longer addressed for his own sake, and is no longer taken seriously and justified as a unique individual; he derives his merely relative value from the morass of history, which is identified with the revelation of God. He is involved in a never-ending exodus, led on by the processes of a history which progresses from promise to promise. Anyone who makes history into God's medium and even into God himself, discovers that this God is a Moloch. What J. T. Beck wrote more than a century ago has lost none of its topicality: 'Today history is the god whom everyone runs after, yet history is emptiness' (cited by K. G. Steck at the beginning of *Die Idee des Heilsgeschichte*). History may not be emptiness – the horrors of more recent history, in particular, can hardly be said to be 'empty' – but it would be appropriate if we were to return to a more sober, theological consideration of it. History ought to be understood in theological terms as an aspect of 'this world', so that we can say of it:

> Christ is the end of history, because in its character as the world, as living in the flesh in accordance with the flesh, history is the product of sinful man's hunger for life. There is a great difference between this hunger for life and the testimony of those who live by virtue of the fact that they have

come to understand absolutely everything as God's gracious gift (Rom. 8.32) (E. Fuchs, 'Christus das Ende der Geschichte', VIA, 95f.).

5. *Critique of the argument from prophecy and typology*

We can well understand how after the dawn of historical consciousness and the discovery of the way in which even biblical religion was caught up in history, there was an almost unanimous consensus that the hermeneutical problem posed once again by the rise of the historical approach should be tackled by means of history and that a solution should be sought in terms of a historical connecting link. The revival of typological interpretation should also be seen in this context. The discovery of the original meaning of Old Testament texts through historical criticism, not to mention academic integrity, made it impossible in the future to deal with the texts in a way which had been possible for the New Testament authors, in all honesty and in accord with the exegetical methods of their time.

This situation has often been described, and there is no dispute over it in scholarly interpretation; we need not therefore discuss it in any detail here (cf. especially R. Bultmann, 'Prophecy and Fulfilment', and H. Braun, 'Das AT im Neuen Testament', both VIB, and see above 74f.). It should be sufficient to site a few examples which can be recognized without further comment as erroneous citations or quotations that distort the original meaning. In particular, it is impossible to quote prophetic and quasi-prophetic passages as messianic prophecies in the way in which this was done in the past. Isaiah 7.14 is used as evidence for the birth of Jesus (Matt. 1.23), Jer. 31.15 as evidence for the massacre of the innocents in Bethlehem (Matt. 2.17f.), Isa. 53.4 for Jesus' healing miracles (Matt. 8.17), Zech. 11.9f. for Judas' thirty pieces of silver (Matt. 27.9). Even Paul treats the texts with utter abandon – by present-day standards: according to Rom. 10.18 the mission to the Gentiles is prophesied in Ps. 19.5. Psalm 8.7, which speaks of the glorious status of mankind generally, is said to prophesy the consummation of the lordship of Jesus Christ (I Cor. 15.27). Such instances can easily be multiplied.

The conclusion which Bultmann draws at the end of his survey of the Old Testament quotations in the New Testament is therefore an obvious one:

It is clear that in all these cases the writers in the New Testament do not gain new knowledge from the Old Testament texts, but read from or into them what they already know. If one follows their intention one is obliged to say that the Old Testament becomes clear as prophecy as a result of fulfilment. And so prophecy is recognized as such in fulfilment! But what would be the point of such a proceeding on the part of God?.. Is that theologically tenable? Can the offence of the cross of Jesus be overcome by recognizing it as long-prophesied and decided upon by God – or only by grasping its meaning and significance? ... In reality this method of finding prophecy – whether with or without allegorizing – abandons the text of the Old Testament to the mercy of arbitrary choice, and the grotesque examples in the apostolic fathers are simply the consequence of the method of the New Testament authors (54f.).

(Cf. the similar argument in F. Baumgärtel, *Verheissung*, 75 etc.) In fact one can hardly avoid such a recognition and the conclusions that need to be drawn from it.

Nevertheless, this is still not the last word on the theme of prophecy and fulfilment. For although we cannot have a burning interest of this kind in demonstrating from scripture itself the Christian claim to the scripture which it has inherited, and in demonstrating the utterly new character of the revelation in Christ while keeping hold of scripture the phenomenon of an intensive preoccupation with scripture has other aspects which we must consider at a later stage (see 234f. below).

Thus while it seemed to have become impossible to deal with the Old Testament in the fashion of the New Testament writers while at the same time giving history its due in a theological context, there was inevitably a good deal to be said for a method of interpretation which was already prefigured in scripture itself, and which promised to bring out a deeper theological significance when oriented on a historical approach. So the discovery of history and the desire to take it seriously, the historical and theological impossibility of the argument from prophecy, and the concern to master the newly-posed hermeneutical problem by means of history, together brought about a revival of typology.

Although the concern to do justice to the Old Testament as the Old Testament – the type –, while at the same time expressing the new elements in the New Testament, is clear and correct in itself, a number of substantial and incontrovertible objections must be raised against such an approach. This has been shown by F. Baumgärtel in particular. Referring to W. Vischer's *The Witness of the Old Testament to Christ* (IIIc), which abandoned the pattern of prophecy and fulfilment, but revived typology and used it to place Christ at the centre of the Old Testament, he wrote: 'Typological interpretation has the right aim. But it can no more be used as a hermeneutical principle than the principle of prophecy and fulfilment' (*Verheissung*, IIIc, 138). His arguments are as follows:

> A demonstration that New Testament events are foreshadowed in the Old Testament does not affect my own existence, or rather, it forces me into the role of an intellectual onlooker. The insight that there is a correspondence between the New Testament event and its foreshadowing in the Old Testament does not matter and does not concern me in the slightest ... I can only look at typological correspondences in a detached way; they are quite irrelevant to my life of faith. The type lacks the element of facticity, quite naturally, because facticity implies an action by God towards me and with me. The types are not events, but abstractions. In the types God acts neither towards Israel nor towards me. The types were inaccessible to Israel; they could only be seen in the light of Christ, and the Old Testament knows nothing of that. Nor do they have any compelling power for me as a Christian, because that is true only of God's action in Christ (138f.).

(Cf. also his discussion of various 'typologies', 86ff.)

Anyone who feels that this stress on the existential irrelevance of a correspondence between type and antitype is too subjective might like to consider the following argument against typology. The attempt to rescue the Old Testament theologically by means of this hermeneutical principle involves so many contradictions that it is bound to collapse of its own accord. Theological significance is sought for the Old Testament, but in the attempt it is reduced to a type = foreshadowing = prefigurement = preliminary stage. The type only *seems* to have a significance of its own; in reality it simply conveys what is communicated more validly and more truthfully by the antitype. For example, when Joseph says that his brothers had had evil intentions, but that God had used their evil for good purposes (Gen. 50.20), his remark has no significance as such with reference to the situation described here. It is not even what the author of the Joseph story wanted to say to his readers by means of words put into Joseph's mouth. Only the antitype of the Christ event, the cross which does not save but which represents salvation, brings to light the truth of the type. There is no answer to the question of the significance of the shadow in such a light. On closer consideration, it is unsatisfactory to reply that typological correspondences and the purposeful extension of time as it moves from type to antitype rule out the possibility of the revelation in Christ being a mere coincidence, express a progression in God's action and thus preserve the roots of Christianity in history.

For although actual history and specific historicity are not denied, they do not go to make up the character of the types; the essential feature of typology is the way in which it makes events, institutions and figures of the Old Testament into shadowy pointers. This is no answer to the methodological question, namely *how* typological interpretation is to be used as a *method*. How does one discover and justify typological correspondences? Exception has often been taken to von Rad's remark that no theoretical norms can be applied to the typological treatment of individual texts, which takes place without any hermeneutical regulation 'in the freedom of the Holy Spirit' ('Typological Interpretation of the Old Testament' VIв, 38). It is not, however, an exception or an extreme. It is characteristic of a hermeneutical principle which cannot be controlled, cannot be taught, cannot be learnt, cannot be checked by any academic assessment. This means that in the strict sense it is not a hermeneutical principle at all. Von Rad's experience in interpretation and his extensive historical knowledge mean that he himself can use the approach with discretion; in the hands of less gifted disciples, the typological key proves to open all the doors of fantasy.

Baumgärtel's passionate protest against this approach was justified:

> Think of all the students and pastors, whose name is not von Rad, who will grub around in this mystery which gives such free rein to their own pneuma (better: understanding, or even misunderstanding). I suspect that this way of preaching, e.g. that the conquest is the foreshadowing of the Christ event or the eternal salvation which it contains, will sound very fine and very pious to the simple people who sit under the pulpit because it is so mysterious. Intellectual audiences (and we should not forget them) will suspect this way of preaching and find it empty for the same reason: because it is so mysterious. The former have too little intelligence to avoid falling victim to it – without having any idea of what is meant; the latter have too much intelligence not to dismiss the approach immediately, as being insignificant for their life of faith ... For the believer, the land of Palestine seen as a foreshadowing of the salvation to be found in the gospel is like a Thule veiled in everlasting clouds. It will never be discovered! (*Verheissung*, IIIc, 124f.).

6. *The analogous structures of the testaments*

After the long and sometimes bitter debate over typology, promise and fulfilment, salvation history and the problem of history in general, we might possibly draw the following conclusions. Historically speaking, and in terms of the history of religions, there can be no doubt that there is a historical line which connects the Old Testament and the New, and that this line is stronger and more significant than any other connection, whether between Israel and the world of the ancient Near East, or between primitive Christianity and Hellenism or Gnosticism. The attempts made by, for example, Stuhlmacher and Gese to emphasize this more strongly are very much to be welcomed. It is in fact less possible to understand the New Testament without the Old than was once supposed. Consequently, the concern to give an exaggerated theological significance to this legitimate historical insight which can be found in different forms in the works of von Rad, Zimmerli, Pannenberg and more recently Gese, has proved all the more disastrous. Each of these writers has identified a line of development which can be drawn through history and reconstructed by historical criticism with a process of revelation. Granted, this has shown in a new way, and more clearly than before, the way in which Old and New Testaments belong together. Moreover, we may ask how this connection is to be interpreted if the line of development as such cannot be called revelation and if the nature of history cannot be understood primarily as a series of events (which are to some degree, if not always, clearer in retrospect), but is to be seen as consisting in a specific happening, experience, suffering, encounter, decision, venture, success, mistake or failure.

Does that mean that such a line, by means of which historically conscious man subsequently interprets events, is simply a construction, a secondary product of reflection? Without historical order and sequence, does man not lose his bearings in the present and find himself without support for the future? Or, in terms of the hermeneutical problem of the Old Testament: what is the theological relevance of the connection between the testaments which is demonstrated so clearly by history, if it cannot be regarded in directly theological terms as a history of development or a salvation history, a process of revelation or revelation as a process (no matter how many processes and developments, of whatever kind, can be reconstructed by historical criticism and the history of traditions)?

Once the idea of salvation history in its various modes and transformations, extending from Irenaeus to Pannenberg, and the pattern of promise (prophecy) and fulfilment linking Old and New Testaments, proved to be no longer viable because they were historically inadequate as a principle of interpretation, there was a return to typological interpretation. There can be no qualifying the criticisms made above – especially in view of the comments made by F. Baum-gärtel – but it may be that a better understanding of typology than has been presented so far may put the element of truth contained in this hermeneutical approach in a proper light. In an earlier section we discussed typological interpretation in the wider context of the theme of the history and prehistory leading up to the New Testament; our treatment belonged with this theme, since it was clear that the modern revival of typology was connected with the discovery of history generally and the history of Israel as a prelude to the Christ event in particular. As we indicated above (22f.), Paul himself already used typology, but not to explain scripture or the history attested by scripture as an early stage of salvation history in which types were present. It is easy to see from the way in which Paul gives pride of place to the Abraham texts and interprets Abraham as a believer to whom faith is reckoned as righteousness (Rom. 4.3; Gal. 3.6), that he does not mean to 'retell' a continuous salvation history; on the contrary, he seeks to show that the historical continuity between Abraham and the Jews is spiritually and theologically irrelevant (Rom. 4.13; Gal. 3.7; cf. Rom. 9.7f.). Of course this treatment of the text is not typological. It does, however, show that neither Paul's typology (22f. above) nor his understanding of scripture are oriented on salvation history or indeed on any linear history at all. This has already been demonstrated by P. Vielhauer ('Paulus und das AT', VIA) and G. Klein (e.g. in 'Bibel und Heilsgeschichte', VIA). When Paul remarks, as in I Cor. 10.1ff., that the wandering in the wilderness is a type of the Christian church (10.6, 11), he is not thinking of a *history* which links type and antitype together. The stress is laid on the fact that something is *written* as a type and indeed as a type *of the community* (I Cor. 10.11; cf. Gal. 3.7f., where the function of scripture consists in having foreseen the event of justification). What comes first is not history, but *scripture!*

Thus Paul's typological interpretations are not intended to form the basis of anything like salvation history or a linear continuity. This was made clear as early as 1954 by E. Fuchs in his *Hermeneutik* (IB):

What drives Paul to use typology? Evidently the apostle is not content with salvation-historical thinking of a 'linear' kind. He is wholly concerned with the present time in which he appears, during which God means to bring 'all' men together through his grace (Rom. 11.30–32). Now the working of God's grace and his call have an unquestionable validity (Rom. 11.29; 15.8f.). As apostle to the Gentiles, Paul orients himself on God's innermost character (Rom. 10.12f.; 3.29f.) and therefore on the unity of the Word of God (Rom. 3.2; 9.4) ... At no point did Paul envisage this character in Gnostic terms, as though it were some metaphysical element in man. He saw it as that characteristic by virtue of which man resembles God; as the obedience which looks for everything from God's own assurances ... (198f.).

Thus typology can be described as a method which 'differentiates between the Old and the New in such a way that it takes as the basis of comparison the innermost character of Being in time', whereas the pattern of promise or prophecy and fulfilment represents an attempt at linear interpretation of history (201).

It is astounding that the concern for the hermeneutical problem of the Old Testament has hardly, if ever, thrown up such insights; evidently the long-standing familiarity with a linear idea of history as being the only generally valid way of understanding history has led to an occupational blindness which prevents Old Testament scholars from being able to see what is going on in the neighbouring field of New Testament studies.

However, H. D. Preuss has attempted to give a new definition of typology without any recognizable reference to Fuchs' remarks ('Das AT in der Verkündigung der Kirche', VIA). After a short survey of the various hermeneutical positions from Vischer via Hirsch down to Baumgärtel and Hesse, Preuss finally comes to the conclusion that the possibility of typological exegesis is the only one left. Of course, the objections to typology raised above (210ff.) are taken fully into account. Preuss therefore suggests that we should speak of a *typology of existence*. It would be concerned to discover the analogies of structure, the analogous situations, the historical relationships between Old and New Testaments. It can discover them because the Old Testament is 'the place of the incarnation', 'the language of incarnation and the necessary means for interpreting it': 'The Old Testament is the tradition within which Christ becomes incarnate' (78). This article, which is unfortunately quite short, in fact demonstrates the relative claims of typology, and although it fails to break the spell of salvation-historical thought in linear terms completely, the approach outlined represents real progress (not least in its reference to the significance of the language of the Old Testament) into new territory which deserves to be cultivated more thoroughly (see 232ff. below).

7. *Summary and prospect*

To describe the Old Testament as written evidence of the prehistory leading up to Christ and as a history book is one way of presenting the hermeneutical problem of the Old Testament as the *Old* Testament. It is understandable that after the rise of the historical consciousness this 'old' could easily be understood in chronological terms, as that which emerged at an earlier stage. Once historical insights had developed so considerably and a prospect of vast historical expanses and long epochs had opened up, it was inevitable that history should be understood generally and primarily in terms of historical investigation instead of in terms of the historicity of human existence. Some of the theological outlines of history, which are concerned to regain and preserve the theological significance of the Old Testament, therefore take such an understanding of history for granted and apply themselves first and foremost to 'history'. It has seemed as though the Old Testament could retain its significance only as a history book, by virtue of its historical connection with the New Testament. The pattern of prophecy and fulfilment, salvation history, and even typology oriented on the upward slope of salvation history, are different expressions of this approach to the theology of history, which resemble one another to a considerable degree. Apparently obsessed with history, this approach has continued to have a captivating effect on scholarship. Its effect is on *scholarship*, since in fact the reconstruction of historical developments and interconnections is an enterprise which captivates and enthrals those who are occupied with it, and is and remains an indispensable preliminary for a relevant and competent interpretation of specific historical traditions, and thus of the texts of Old and New Testaments. There is no doubt, however, that the enterprise is less fascinating for the church and its preaching and instruction than it is for the historical critic. The objection made continually by Baumgärtel to the theology of history and to typology, namely that it does not affect 'me' and is existentially irrelevant, and the suspicion voiced by Preuss that texts interpreted in these terms (if texts have any scope, value, claim or promise for this approach) only provoke the reaction 'So what?', describe the disastrous situation in hermeneutics very aptly. History does not dismiss its pupils, but those who are worn by other than historical cares and take delight in other than historical joys – those who listen to sermons and undergo instruction in Christianity – have a right not to be interested in historical developments or in the traditio-historical connection between the testaments. At this point, however, we find not only a problem of communication but the hermeneutical problem itself: from this perspective, once specific texts have been arranged in a historical series, incorporated into the 'process' of revelation and thus made phases within an all-embracing totality, they no longer have a specific message to express. And because their specific historicity is reduced to constructed and reconstructed historical developments and processes of revelation which have as much continuity as possible, the man who understands their language is left in the lurch when it comes to his own specific, living, fleshly and spiritually historical existence, in which he can live only from the bread which he receives anew every day, and not only from bread, but also from the Word which he receives anew every day and which is a light for his feet. It is as though the scintillating music of a Mozart symphony were made a phase in the history of music between Haydn and Beethoven – interesting for the musicologist, but silent and un-melodious for the concert-goer.

Of course the fact that anyone who involves himself in history *in this fashion* loses touch with specific texts and a specific audience does not mean that, conversely, anyone who tries to keep to the text will necessarily lose touch with history. Paul's way of dealing with the Old Testament is already evidence of this. The possibility here is also evident from the various contributions towards tackling the herme-neutical problem of the Old Testament which have been made from the side of New Testament scholarship and general hermeneutics. It is further evident from the attempt to reshape the concept of typology which has been sketched out above. Insights into analogies of structure and typologies of existence, and the significance of the language which holds the two testaments together, will take us further. They therefore also form the point of transition towards the next and final chapter in our hermeneutical reflections.

THE OLD TESTAMENT AS PART
OF THE CHRISTIAN CANON

1. *The New Testament as a criterion of the canonical validity of the Old*

We shall not at this point be pursuing the history of the formation of the canon and the origin of the bipartite canon of scripture. Those who are interested can find accounts in *Introductions* to the Old Testament and in H. Freiherr von Campenhausen's *The Formation of the Christian Bible* (IIA), and we have already touched on the subject in chapter II. Nor shall we follow K. Schwarzwäller (*Das Alte Testament in Christus*, VII) in attempting to establish a standpoint from which the Old Testament can properly be understood only as part of the canon of the Christian church, namely in the light of Christ, because there is no going back behind the fact that the Old Testament is part of the Christian canon. Here dogma becomes dogmatism, and the question *how* the testaments belong together and what the nature of their connection is becomes forbidden territory, instead of being given an answer.

One might argue – with A. Jepsen – that any scholarly concern with the Old Testament is *ipso facto* concern with the Christian canon, because one can talk meaningfully about the *Old* Testament only in relationship to the *New* (see 'The Scientific Study of the Old Testament', VII, 250). Judaism had 'the law, the prophets and the writings' or 'the law and the tradition', but not an 'Old Testament' in the strict sense, even if Jewish scholars occasionally use the term. The datum, the undeniable fact of the twofold canon, needs to be taken seriously and should not be left out of consideration or bracketed off from academic study of the Old Testament. However, that the Old Testament is a datum and a fact does not mean that it is the starting point for consideration and investigation on which there is no going back. On the contrary, the association of the Old and New Testaments in the canon is itself the real hermeneutical problem. The question is (to recapitulate it briefly yet again) whether there is *theological* justification for this *historical* fact, this situation which has come into being in the course of time.

This book has attempted to classify and give a critical survey of the various attempts to solve the problem, old and new. It has emerged that none of the approaches described so far has been able to produce a satisfactory and generally accepted solution. The reason for this is above all that the collection of Israelite and Jewish writings which have become the Old Testament in the Christian canon are so varied that they cannot be reduced to a common denominator, nor can they be dealt with by means of some universal hermeneutic concept. The only attempt which was thought to have appropriated the *whole* of the Old Testament for Christianity, namely the allegorical approach practised in the early church, proved to be a pseudo-solution; it no longer allowed the Old Testament to have a message of its own, but attributed to it a different, Christian sense. Both the insights of the Reformation and historical criticism have shown this method to be impossible and impermissible. The other approaches which have been attempted since then could produce no more than *partial* solutions. To contrast the Old Testament as law with the New Testament as gospel has only *partial* justification, i.e. with reference to those passages which are in fact law and have a legalistic significance. Such a contrast fails to explain all those texts which are not legalistic in any sense: prayers, expressions of joy, laments, narratives, interpretations in terms of the present, words of consolation, promises, threats. What relationship do they have to the New Testament? True, the contrast between law and gospel involves a dialectic which is an indispensable criterion for the evaluation of Old Testament texts. But as this dialectic can also be found *within* the Old Testament, it does not of itself offer any justification for accepting the *whole* of the Old Testament as the first part of the Christian canon; it can only be applied critically once the validity of the Old Testament has already been accepted in principle.

The same thing may be said about the understanding of the Old Testament as the document of an alien religion. Certainly the religion of Israel is not the Christian religion; there is no Christianity without Christ. But quite apart from the fact that the primitive community and the early church which demarcated and authorized the canon is very different from the church today and from modern Christianity generally, and in this respect could also be considered an alien religion (as far as its world-view and historical and social situation are concerned), there are so many close relationships, connections and analogies between Christianity and the holy scripture which it took over from Israel and Judaism, that there are problems in describing the Old Testament as the document of an alien religion. This is no reason whatsoever for excluding the Old Testament from the canon; in any case, as history shows, that inevitably leads to an abbreviation of the New Testament canon. Of course, the indisputable historical connection, which makes it impossible to repudiate the Old Testament on these grounds, does not in itself provide a positive justification for the validity of the Old Testament. While the religion of the Old Testament may not come into the category of an alien religion, it is still pre-Christian and – without Christ – un-Christian.

The varied attempts to find a way out of this dilemma which we considered in the previous chapter, in which the Old Testament was regarded as a history book, sought as it were to make a virtue of the necessity imposed by the influence of history on theology by producing a theology of history. I attempted to show that this virtue is not particularly virtuous and that by the standards of the New Testament treatment of the Old Testament it amounts to an innovation.

It seems, then, that these approaches cannot offer any satisfactory answer to the question of the validity of the Old Testament as the first part of the Christian canon. We can understand this when we reflect on what is meant by 'validity'. 'Valid' can – and may – simply be understood as defining what has a claim to validity *within the sphere of the Christian church*. In this strict sense, validity is Christian validity, whatever can be regarded as valid by the standards of Christianity. That means, however, that validity and non-validity can only be assessed and decided in Christian terms, on the basis of and by means of the New Testament. Such an approach once again makes it clear that the search for a theological centre to the Old Testament is a hopeless one. This is not only because one can hardly expect to find a centre to so varied and manifold a collection of literature, but also because such a search is a theological mistake (if theology is understood here strictly as Christian theology) and will never come to a satisfactory end. The reason is that it begins with the Old Testament rather than the New, despite the fact that only a Christian criterion can be the deciding factor over what is Christian and can claim Christian validity.

At the same time, we need to guard against a possible misunderstanding. It is not as though Christian *faith* is sitting in judgment here over the statements of the Old Testament. True, F. Hesse is quite right in saying:

> Thus it is a nonderivative decision of faith when we say that in the Old Testament ... the Word of God is addressed to us, just as it is addressed to us in the New Testament. It cannot be the task of theology to offer grounds for this statement or to reject it because it cannot be proved. We can only affirm that anyone who is not able to join in this statement of faith (the positive answer to the question of the authority of Old Testament texts) simply has a different faith ('The Evaluation and the Authority of OT Texts', IIIc, 292).

Nevertheless, although this observation is correct in itself, when related strictly to belief in God's Word in the existential sense as a personal encounter in faith, it should not mislead us into handing over judgment on what does or does not have Christian validity to faith or even to the realm of subjective assessment. Can the practice of putting captured enemies to the ban in Yahweh's holy war or – less gross, but still offensive enough – a prayer for vengeance like Ps. 109, or even (since we are not concerned solely with an ethical evaluation) the dogma of retribution presupposed in the Chronicler's history, be reconciled with the Christian ethos of the Sermon on the Mount or the doctrine of justification? This is not a question for faith, which can be answered only by faith. The non-believer too can note and observe these differences and tensions, and such observations can lead Christians, Jews and atheists alike to conclude that the conflicting standpoints cannot be reconciled.

If the criterion of what is Christian is used to assess the Old Testament, it is in fact an alien standard, since a Christian criterion is being used to judge a non-Christian religion. That such assessment and evaluation is illegitimate must be stressed again and again, especially in view of the frequent and apparently self-evident belief that the God of Jesus Christ and the apostles was the God of the Old Testament. However, although the historical connection between Israel and the church is indubitable, an assumption of this kind is only apparently correct. Is the God who marched before Joshua and the Israelites in their bloody battles and commanded them to exterminate the enemy the God of Jesus Christ? In any case, to talk of *the* God of the Old Testament would be to limit the Old Testament to one picture of God – e.g. Hos. 2.19f.; 11.8f.; Isa. 66.13 and some other passages. This God has many names and such varied characteristics that any talk of *the* God of the Old Testament runs the risk of becoming an empty formula. To talk of the God of the Old Testament who is the Father of Jesus Christ by-passes the hermeneutical problem and presupposes something that first needs to be established. As we have seen, the foundation for this can come only from the New Testament. To apply such a criterion to the Old Testament is not to interpret the Old Testament in Christian terms. Allegorical and typological interpretations set out to do this. But it is impossible to give a Christian interpretation of something that is not Christian; Christian interpretation of something that is not Christian is pseudo-interpretation. Proper interpretation is concerned, rather, to let the Old Testament have its own say and to interpret it and understand it in the light of the present. The goal of historical and critical exegesis is achieved when what a particular text says is interpreted and understood in the light of the present. Historical and critical exegesis is not made Christian and theological by ascribing a Christian, spiritual, higher meaning to the text after the fashion of allegory or typology. Nor does it lead into spiritual interpretation – whatever that may be understood to mean – or to Christian meditation – however that may be done. And it certainly does not hand over the texts that it has interpreted to dogmatic theologians for them to pass judgment – according to whatever criterion or by whatever means they may choose. Rather, the historical–critical exegete is a *theologian* by virtue of the fact that he has learnt to understand the text in the light of Christianity and is able to interpret it in this context. It is here, and not in the common historical work of reconstructing continuous lines which unite Old and New Testaments (important though this work may be), that Old Testament scholarship requires the help of the New Testament theologian. At this point interdisciplinary work can prove fruitful.

To assert that the Old Testament is part of the Christian canon is a factual statement. The history of the canon is an investigation and description of the way in which Israelite and Jewish writings became and could become the holy scripture of the Christian church. Thus whether and to what degree this canon may still claim canonical validity today is a question to be dealt with by a theological evaluation on the basis of historical reconstruction and interpretation.

If a decision on the validity or non-validity of Old Testament texts in the Christian sphere is made in the light of the New Testament, in other words, if the New Testament is the criterion for the canonicity of the Old, and if this judgment can only be made in particular instances with regard to specific texts and their interpretations, it has to be acknowledged that it is impossible to make any decision on the Christian canonicity of the Old Testament half of the canon which can be applied generally to all its parts. Only a differentiated approach which simply passes judgment in each particular case, and must also reckon with the possibility of revision if a better historical insight or deeper theological understanding is achieved, can correspond to the lack of uniformity, the variety, the riches and the plurality of meaning of the writings collected together in the Old Testament. The task of a theology of the Old Testament is to work out and describe their spiritual content, view of faith, religion and theological conceptuality. Such a theology is not worthy of the name simply because it proceeds not only historically, but also systematically or on the basis of some centre to the Old Testament, however that may be defined; it needs to make a critical examination of the material in the sense described above. In this way it will provide important and indeed indispensable preliminary work towards a theology of the Bible as a whole, which is so desirable and so urgently necessary. And of course, if it is to be Christian, it can only be developed in the light of the New Testament.

2. *Scripture, language and monotheism*

As we have said, it is simple to remark that the Old Testament is part of the canon. Such a remark by no means claims that all the writings belonging to the Old Testament enjoyed and will continue to enjoy the same standing in the canon without any gradation, omission or differentiation from the beginning of the Christian church into the conceivable future. Because the writings contained in the Old Testament are so varied and so ambivalent even in the New Testament they were made use of in accordance with a strict principle of selection – Christians preferred Genesis, the psalms and the prophets above all. They were certainly not interpreted in accordance with a unitary scheme (see above, 21ff.). Consequently, when it was argued earlier that once we have asserted that the Old Testament is the first part of the canon, we can only decide on its validity for Christians by examining it and evaluating it text by text, in each particular instance, we are in principle simply following the procedure used by the New Testament itself in dealing with the Old, even if we can no longer legitimately use the particular exegetical methods that were customary at that time. In every instance, however, no matter whether scripture is interpreted in accordance with a pattern of prophecy and fulfilment, or typologically or allegorically, or in accordance with its literal meaning, or simply referred to in more or less literal allusions, it is always considered as holy scripture. Translated into Greek, which was then the language of the civilized world, the Old Testament provided the vocabulary for the proclamation of the Christ event; in other words, Christian proclamation created a new language for itself, capable of doing justice to the eschatological newness of the Christ event, but it did so by resorting to the language of the Old Testament. This approach was a necessity: the historical contingency of the Christ-event, the paradoxical once-for-allness of the eschaton which had entered history, the Word which had become flesh, was matched by the contingency of this language which Christians used from the beginning – a language for which there was no substitute. It is because the first preaching of Jesus Christ took up this language and became involved with it, that the Old Testament *texts* have to be regarded as canonical. If the Christ-event is essentially a happening which was *proclaimed* and needs constantly to be *proclaimed* anew, it is essentially concerned with language, and language is something different from, something more than the verbal exterior to the content that is to be communicated, an outer packaging which can be changed at will. So we can see quite clearly the essential, material connection between the message of the New Testament and the language of the Old. Language as such is always an interpretation of the world and human existence – though it needs to be investigated by means of a meta-language. This is even truer and even more particularly the case with a language which makes the claim 'Thus says Yahweh' and 'Yahweh said to . . .,' and which when translated into Greek becomes, 'Thus says the Lord' and 'the Lord said to'. This claim, made in the name of a God who was believed to be more radically transcendent than all other gods, was given permanent form in a written text. Its language articulates an understanding of human existence and the world which, for all its dependent relationships, cross-connections and analogies to the culture of surrounding nations, is nevertheless unmistakably different. Moreover, this understanding of human existence is the same as that of the New Testament, the same as the Christian understanding of human existence as opposed to Greek, humanistic or idealistic under-standings. Bultmann has given a classic description of it:

> *Thus in the Old Testament man is seen in his temporality and historicity.* To understand himself, he is not referred to the universal, the cosmos, so that he may see himself as a part of this realm, nor is he referred to the Logos so that he may find true being in the timeless. Rather, he is directed into

his concrete history with its past and future, with its present that lays before him the demand of the moment in concrete relation with the 'neighbour'. He does not find himself within a cosmic rhythm which moves according to eternal laws and in which all struggle, all strife, is at eternal rest in God the Lord – here man's highest possibility would be to become aware of this God in *theoria*. But rather he finds himself put by the divine will in a particular place in the stream of temporal occurrence which for him holds the possibility of either judgment or grace depending on whether he acts in obedience to what God requires of him. Thus the relation to God is not one of seeing but of hearing, a fearing and an obeying of God, an act of faith. That is, instead of being an optimistic world view, it is an appropriation of the past in faithfulness, a trustful waiting for God in the face of the future, a steadfast obedience in the present ('The Significance of the Old Testament for the Christian Faith', V, 20).

We may not wish to put so one-sided a stress on the will and demand of God as Bultmann does; in the last resort he in fact seeks to understand the Old Testament from the Christian standpoint as law (31, and see 157f. above). We may wish to stress more than he does the primacy of God's *saving will*. Nevertheless, we can accept that here we have an essentially appropriate description of the Old Testament attitude towards human existence.

The Old Testament conception of God corresponds to this view of man. The manifold attempts to establish and describe a centre of the Old Testament have pointed towards Yahweh's lordship, his transcendence, his exalted status, his uniqueness, his zeal; they may not have succeeded in their primary aim, but they have given·a true indication of Yahweh's basic characteristics. It can be said that a consistent and radical *monotheism* is a specific feature of the Old Testament.

Now monotheism is an arid concept for a specific, concrete experience which stamps the whole of human existence. The juxtaposition of many gods necessarily qualifies their divinity. Where one rules there is no room for another. Similarly, polytheism necessarily leads to the narration of stories about gods who feud with one another, make alliances, become reconciled; these gods are men writ large, among whom men may appear as gods writ small. Israel may occasionally speak of Yahweh in mythological terms, but such mythology is in fact alien to him. He does not have any role in myth; he does not die like Baal when nature dies, to rise again as nature and fertility revive. He is not both god and natural event, a figure and at the same time a cyclical natural process, Lord and yet dependent on the correct performance of rites which depict and put into effect his mythical life. In quite a different way he stands over against everything that is not himself as its God and Lord. To use an abstract term which was not in Israelite vocabulary, he is transcendent. He is the Creator of all that exists, and as Creator, he is also its Lord. Because he is Lord, because he is other, he is said to be 'holy, holy, holy'. As the Holy One he is unapproachable. The fact that he nevertheless comes near to man is a sign of his condescension, whether he comes near bringing terror, or a blessing, or both at once. The fact that both these aspects are possible and real is the reason why his character cannot be defined once for all in such a way that man can deal with him as an entity whose features he can calculate. He has some characteristics in common with the gods worshipped by other nations and by the Israelite patriarchs in the earliest times; however, his uniqueness consists in the fact that he can combine in his person features which are otherwise irreconcilable. Like the supreme God El he is exalted, gracious and distant, but as the God of the fathers he *appears*, he condescends, he joins in wanderings, and his word of promise embraces the whole of human existence in the present (the conquest), the future (descendants), and in a covenant. As Yahweh he intervenes in history, with a mighty hand to rescue and liberate, to give his people somewhere to live and a way of life (*torah*).

In this connection, it makes no difference whether the monotheism of the Old Testament only developed in the course of a long history, and if so how, and whether the Old Testament still contains passages and strata which merely reflect a development which eventually led to pure monotheism. This makes no difference, because the church did not adopt a development in religious history but a collection of writings, and when this collection assumed its present form, monotheism was already taken for granted. Indeed, the community which recognized the Old Testament took this heightened form of monotheism so much for granted, that those who believed in Christ could assert his divinity without running any risk of lapsing into the polytheism of their environment, as long as they held on to the Old Testament as holy scripture.

To retain scripture was to affirm monotheism and the creatureliness of the world and man, in controversy with polytheistic mythology and the mythological speculations of Gnosticism. It was also to offer a front against the contemporary philosophy and ideology which, like Gnosticism and Marcion, sought to dissolve 'the permanent personal union of the work of the creator god with that of the redeemer god'

(Ernst Bloch, *Atheismus im Christentum,* 1968, VII, 62), for the sake of ushering in the perfect society of the future. Not least, the anchoring of the primitive Christian message in Old Testament monotheism and a belief in creation protects the New Testament against a 'Jesuology' which seeks to replace God by the man Jesus (cf. W. Schrage, 'Theologie und Christologie', VII).

In fact we can accept H. Grass's remark: 'The Old Testament is the church's monotheistic conscience. Even today it affords protection against anti-theistic movements which seek to do away with God, to declare that he is dead and to make do with a Christ understood in one way or another, who finally descends to being a mere representative of cohumanity' (*Christliche Glaubenslehre* II, VII, 97f.).

Without question, then, this specific monotheism and the aniconic image of God which it presents are the presupposition and basis for the Christian proclamation. The appearance and the ministry of Jesus and the proclamation of Christ after Easter in the primitive church were never understood as a correction or a criticism of this monotheistic understanding of God. The criticism of the Old Testament to be found in the New and the way in which it can sometimes even be seen to dissociate itself from the Old (see 30f. above) do not affect the unqualified affirmation of this part and this aspect of the Old Testament heritage. The proclamation of the salvation which has appeared in Jesus Christ presents this event as the action of the one God to whom the Old Testament refers when and in so far as it speaks of the free Creator and Lord of Israel and the world. The Christ event does not put *this* God of the Old Testament in question; it is proclaimed as his own, true, final work. As the final, eschatological act of God, it of course puts all the other works of the same God in the shade. In the light of the revelation of Christ we can also ask whether all the actions and properties attributed to God in the Old Testament really were divine actions and divine properties, or whether it is not the case that human self-assertion, egoism, nationalism and short-sightedness, in short our all-too-human failings, are not presented as divinely willed and divinely justified. However, even the criticism that we must apply in accordance with the criterion of what is Christian and the antithesis is the Sermon on the Mount, 'You have heard that it was said to those of old time; but I say to you', does not put in question this specific feature of monotheism and its equally specific implications, which are heightened by the Old Testament. Christian proclamation therefore always understood itself to be the preaching of the action of the one God, beside whom there is no other. That is why the Old Testament was preserved, even after the Christian mission had gone far beyond the bounds of Judaism. The Israelite and Jewish law could no longer retain its validity for Gentile Christians, but even the abrogation of the law did not mean the abrogation of the Old Testament, far less the dethronement of the one God to whom scripture bears witness. At the same time, we should not forget that as a result the special feature of Christianity – the message of eschatological salvation in Jesus Christ – could even retreat into the background, and the Christian mission in the Gentile world could be understood as the proclamation of an ethical monotheism purged of its legalistic Jewish accessories – which made it easier to accept. It was the apologists of the second century who stressed the monotheism and the moral character of Christianity, and from their time down to modern theological liberalism there have always been periods when Christianity has appeared primarily as an ethical monotheism and a theistic moral philosophy, and when Jesus has been regarded as a prophetic reformer of Judaism. Christianity has become a reformed Judaism on the basis of an Old Testament that has been purged by criticism. Indeed it can be asked in all earnestness whether, leaving all theological theorizing, philosophy and ideology aside, this is not the character of the popular understanding of Christianity: believe in the Lord God and always be faithful and honest! Still, even such vulgar simplifications and ideological restrictions contain an element of truth which they put in one-sided isolation: this element is in fact the indispensable grounding of the whole of Christianity in ethical monotheism, in a specific form which cannot be dissociated from the Old Testament. Apart from Yahweh there is no God (Isa. 43.11; 44.6; 41.4; 48.12). But in the speech of the Hellenistic synagogue, the name Yahweh had already been replaced by 'Kyrios' = 'the Lord'. 'The Lord' is a much simpler designation than Yahweh (a name which had long been incomprehensible in its original form) to express the uniqueness and the transcendent power of God.

The use of 'Kyrios' in the New Testament shows how close the links are between the Old and New Testaments. Where the Old Testament is quoted, Yahweh has become the Kyrios; in Christian manuscripts of the Septuagint the tetragrammaton YHWH, which was still preserved in older manuscripts of Jewish origin, is replaced by Kyrios. Now Jesus Christ is also Kyrios (1 Cor. 12.3; Phil. 2.11), so that statements originally applying to Yahweh can now be applied to him: the christological hymn in Phil. 2 (2.10f.) takes up what is said of Yahweh's lordship in Isa. 45.3, that every tongue will confess that Jesus Christ is the Kyrios (see also Rom. 10.15; I Cor. 1.2; Acts 2.36).

God the Lord and Jesus Christ, his eschatological bringer of salvation, belong so closely together that both can be given the same honorific titles (cf. e.g. Matt. 11.25; Luke 10.21; Matt. 9.38; I Tim. 6.15; Acts 17.24; and right alongside Acts 2.36 see 2.39!), because God the Lord has given the Lord Christ all power on earth (Matt. 28.18; cf. I Cor. 11.3; 15.28).

The New Testament does more than presuppose the monotheism of the Old and proclaim the Christ event as the action of this one Creator God and Lord. This proclamation develops out of – and also enters into – the wide areas of creation, the earth, mankind, the history of the nations and of Israel, the blessing, the fertility and the wisdom which are *disclosed in the language* of the Old Testament; at the same time it also shares its longing for a final consummation after sin and the curse, God's remoteness and man's despair, confusion and rejection. The New Testament presupposes all these 'themes', which are as numerous as the aspects and facets, contents and forms of human life; it affirms them, denies them, corrects them, sets them right. Because it is concentrated on the one necessary fact of Christ and his salvation, it does not always need to make all these themes explicit. But the proclamation of Christ echoes round an area which has already been disclosed by the Old Testament. This proclamation is also made through an interpretation of the world and human existence which is expressed in the language of the Old Testament: the *Word* – also – became *this flesh.*

Monotheism and Old Testament belief in creation do not represent an addition to belief in Christ – an eschaton which needed to be supplemented would be a contradiction in terms. Thus the themes to which we have referred above do not represent an enlargement of the New Testament, as H. Grass supposes in his understanding of the relationship of the two testaments, which in other respects is much akin to my own view, as a 'supplementary hypothesis' (VII, 99). It would be more correct to speak of an '*implication* hypothesis', as I have suggested elsewhere (Gunneweg, 'Sola Scriptura', VII, 9).

Thus in principle the New Testament presupposes the validity of the Old even to the point of offering arguments to the contrary from the Christian side in specific instances; in so doing it *implies* the Old Testament talk of the one God, the Creator, the fall of man, God's will to redeem him and all the numerous individual themes which relate to this.

H. Grass rightly observes:

What a wealth of attitudes and destinies, of individuals and groups in the most varied situations and relationships, are to be found in the Old Testament! And what a human book it is! Politics and social concern have a role, in the prophets and elsewhere; there are wars, victories, defeats, hunger, exile – and good times as well. We find a dramatic and eventful history with all its ups and downs, a concern with the common life of the people and with the question of righteousness. The psalmist speaks of transitoriness (Ps. 90), Job accuses God in his suffering, and Proverbs and Ecclesiastes echo wisdom and resignation. And in all this God is at work; it all takes place *coram Deo* (98).

We must add that these stories, prayers, reflections, rejoicings and laments before God (*coram Deo*) are not motives and themes *alongside* the Christ event which have been *added to* the proclamation of Christ. Rather, in the Christian sphere they are understood 'biblically' in the light of the revelation in Christ. Thus they become *texts* (in the sense indicated in I Cor. 10.11) which give an interpretation, true or false, of human existence in all its unfathomable depths (just try to give an exhaustive interpretation of the creation stories in the first eleven chapters of Genesis!) and in its earthly, eating and drinking, loving, hating, dying, this-worldly and yet onward-looking reality *under God*, who is called Kyrios, and now *in the face of Christ*, who is called Kyrios. This is done so that God's final Word, the gospel, can have a specific reference and gain a hearing.

This is the element of truth in that solution of the hermeneutical problem which stresses that the testimony of the Old Testament represents a *preliminary stage* and serves as a preparation. This, too, is the correct insight contained in typological interpretation: the Old Testament interprets the world and human existence *before* Christ, *before* the consummation, *before* the eschaton. It is what it is in relation to the penultimate, to this world, to everything that without Christ remains incomplete, unclear, ambivalent, and lacks a final valid answer. With the appearance of Christ, however, the penultimate does not become a mere preliminary stage which is only of noetic significance, and does not pale into insignificance as a mere foreshadowing. Rather, in the light of the ultimate, the Christ event, the penultimate is seen clearly – and here we have the element of truth in that solution which attempts to understand the Old Testament as *law* in a dialectical relationship with the gospel. It is weighed and tested, it becomes transparent to the failure and sin which crucified Christ or to the ultimate salvation which (like the name of Christ) may not be spoken in the Old Testament, but is suspected, hoped for, promised and really meant. In the light of the New, those things which in the Old

Testament are understood as Yahweh's saving gifts – land, descendants, good government, vine and fig-tree, health and prosperity, do not simply become merely this-worldly reductions and falsifications of a 'basic promise' to be understood purely in religious terms, albeit as foreshadowings of the true salvation. They remain what they always were: a specific possibility of life in this world in the present and future on the basis of trust in God alone, creation, preservation and blessing by the God 'who did not spare his own Son but gave him up for us all. Will he not also give us all things with him?' (Rom. 8.32).

All this earthly glory is not devalued if it is put in the context of the 'as though ... not' (I Cor. 7.29–31); the 'as though' is only possible in the light of the ultimate salvation of Jesus Christ, which is not transitory. Instead of being devalued, the saving benefits of the Old Testament are first clearly seen as the gifts of God, from whose love even the cessation of these transitory benefits cannot save men in their new relation to the salvation which has appeared and been given in Christ (Rom. 8.38f.).

The eschaton, with its finality and ultimacy, puts all other gifts and benefits in their proper, penultimate context in yet another respect. The gift of land, descendants, national existence and law remain what they are; they do not fade away and dissolve into mere prefigurements and foreshadowings, but can now be seen once again in their original significance: they make life possible, disclose the future and offer salvation in a sphere which is the gift of God, as life given by God and lived before him.

Of course this salvation which embraces the whole of existence was expressed in the conceptions and ideas of the time. For that reason it is not limited for ever to that particular horizon, and therefore to the concepts of land, descendants and a Davidic kingship.

When people began to objectify the benefits of salvation, election turned into being a chosen people, and the assurance of Yahweh's presence became the false security of a support which was under man's control. At that point the great prophets who pronounced judgment on Israel were already proclaiming the end of all the ordinances of salvation, and a new salvation which would come after the divine judgment (see e.g. Amos 3.2; 8.1f.; Hos. 1.9; 2.19f.). In the light of the collapse of the state and nation which did in fact take place, and of all that had once been thought to provide security as the saving gift of Yahweh, Jeremiah proclaimed a salvation from Yahweh that would be given in the midst of disaster to those who recognized and accepted the catastrophe of the destruction of the temple and the exile as God's just judgment (Jer. 24; 29; 32 as these texts were originally composed). This is the beginning of a theology of the cross, but it is not maintained, and those who handed on the tradition made it a mere announcement of salvation for the future. Towards the end of the exile, Deutero-Isaiah proclaimed a new exodus in his hymns; this so transcends Yahweh's earlier act of deliverance in the exodus and at the Red Sea, and indeed so far transcends all imagining, that it can become *the* picture of divine salvation, which can no longer be expressed in human words (cf. Isa. 55.12: 'the mountains and the hills before you shall break forth into singing, and all the trees of the field shall clap their hands').

Even within the Old Testament, the horizon, formerly so narrow, is widened, the restrictions on salvation are lifted, and an attempt is made to think of it and express it as the beyond in this world, the totally other. In the New Testament, everything that was proclaimed in the Old Testament as an element of salvation is put in a new light by the Christ event: the language of the Old Testament proclamation becomes the language of Christian proclamation.

3. *The language of Christian proclamation*

In this connection we must return yet again to typology and to the pattern of prophecy and fulfilment. A look at Paul's typological approach to Old Testament texts and the understanding of typology by E. Fuchs which is based on them has already shown that typology need not necessarily be bound up with a linear understanding of history (see 214f. above). On the basis of the encouragement of no less a figure than Paul, typology can be brought into our present concern, instead of being oriented on a linear view of history. In that case typology is a method which seeks out analogies and is based on the fact that such analogies occur within the historical sphere. History is unique and contingent, and never repeats itself. Nevertheless, comparable features are to be found. The traditional pattern of typological interpretation calls these comparable features type and antitype. Leaving aside its arbitrariness and its distortions, typological interpretation was able to discover these correspondences because it was based on the presence of analogies in historical life. The way in which the features of which typology makes use are heightened in the course of time cannot be derived from a general process of development and growth; that is not a basic characteristic of typology, which is conditioned by the fact that in the specific relationship between the two testaments, the antitype is the ultimate and final event of Jesus Christ, the eschaton, which puts everything else, past, present and to come, in the shade. This also explains the emergence of typology in primitive Christianity: seen in the light of the death and resurrection of Jesus Christ, the scripture which the church inherited, and whose validity is not abrogated, makes 'typical' statements. These typical features are not just put in the shade. Rather, the eschaton puts them in the right perspective. Just as the kingdom of God can be spoken of only in parables, so the last thing, the eschaton, can be spoken of only in terms of the penultimate. Therefore the types do not lose their importance after the antitype has appeared (by fading away into mere shadows and schemes as the course of time extends beyond them); they become the possibility of making an eschatological proclamation.

Thus a text like Gen. 12, without any reinterpretation, allegorizing and typological mistreatment, becomes a model of the meaning of faith. It shows how the present and future are disclosed to the believer who is prepared to abandon anything that may be called a possession. The land remains land, the basis of all life, the source of all prosperity, and descendants remain what they are: life for the future. All this is seen in the light of God, and is not just a prelude that has now passed; it is present, the present concreteness of the salvation which has been given in Christ, and which at the same time goes beyond all these concrete expressions, transcends them and is not bound by them.

To give another example, the message of the great prophets is also a type and can therefore be understood as the correct form of Christian preaching. The prophets also proclaim to the Christian community that the end has come – upon pride, godlessness, hard-heartedness and idolatry. Salvation, the forgiveness that renews life, is promised only to those who will accept this judgment; life and happiness are given to the humble only at the nadir of human failure. Now the language of a Deutero-Isaiah, which strains at the limit of what words can express, can become the preaching of the gospel of the salvation that has appeared in Christ. He announces the exodus from Babylon, from what Babylon always was (as a type!) from sin, disaster and judgment, to Zion, the place of encounter with the living God of salvation, who at the same time refuses to commit himself to any place.

In this way all the oracles of salvation – always interpreted and understood in a literal sense – and all the 'messianic prophecies' become a proper proclamation of the ultimate salvation – even though they may fail to understand it and may prove to be inappropriate.

They proclaim the ultimate salvation which alone deserves the name, and the saviour without whom there is no salvation. The kerygma of this salvation is always directed towards a particular situation; parts of the Old Testament help to make this kerygma specific, because the Old Testament is the tradition 'in which Christ became incarnate' (H. D. Preuss, VIA, 78, see above, 216).

In addition to reconsidering typology in these terms, we must look once more for the last time at the so-called argument from prophecy. It has been made sufficiently clear, here and elsewhere, that this way of dealing with the texts is no longer possible and legitimate today. However, as I hinted above, that does not mean to say that this comment is the last word on the subject (see 210 above). The concern expressed in this way of using scripture is not just to assert and to justify the Christian claim to scripture in controversy with Judaism, by using exegetical violence in order to make the scriptures prophesy Christ. Although a superficial consideration might suggest that this was the significance of the so-called argument from prophecy, we need to probe further. What was and is the importance of *scripture* which could not and cannot offer a support for Christian faith in any decisive respect because it does *not* proclaim the death and resurrection of Jesus Christ as a saving event? In any case, even the proclamation of earliest Christianity can dispense with the language of the Old Testament, as Paul himself shows; he only refers back to the Old Testament in four of his letters (Romans; I and II Corinthians and Galatians), and I John also gets by without the Old Testament.

However, leaving aside the exceptions, the fact that the church retained the Old Testament and sought to defend its claim against Judaism by exegetical means, doubtful though these may have been, shows the real and genuine interest of the church in scripture, even when it is far removed from any dispute over it with Judaism, and even when such a dispute has long since lost its topicality. In the last resort this interest is grounded in the belief and proclamation of the constancy of God: if the scripture is at all times testimony to the *one* God, the *Creator and Redeemer*, it also had to bear witness to the Christ event, and therefore Christ had to fulfil scripture. Scripture bears testimony to Christ by providing a language, and a *content* shaped by that language, with the help of which testimony to Christ can now be formulated. That is why Christ is born of a virgin, sees the light in Bethlehem and has to flee to Egypt, so that the prophecy may be fulfilled that God has called his Son out of Egypt (Matt. 1.23; 2.1; Luke 2; Matt. 2.15, 18; and Isa. 7.14; Micah 5.1; Hos. 11.1; Jer. 31.15).

In the first sermon that he preaches in Nazareth, he himself proclaims that the scripture is fulfilled in him (Luke 4.16–21). For his great, fundamental sermon he ascends a mountain, like Moses, whose law he fulfils and transcends (Matt. 5.1). As is well known, the passion narratives in particular have been shaped with the help of Old Testament quotations and allusions. According to Zech. 9.9, Jesus enters Jerusalem even riding on two animals, because that is what the prophet is said to have foretold. Judas betrays him for thirty pieces of silver because this is written in Zech. 11.9f. (Matt. 21.5; 25.15; 27.3–9). Otherwise the account follows the details of Ps. 22. It is in fact meant to demonstrate that the scripture was fulfilled even in detail, and how this came about. The scripture had prophesied, and in Christ the prophecy was fulfilled.

The evidence is well known, and the impossibility of such an interpretation of scripture today is clear, but the purpose of the procedure has not been interpreted. Indeed, the remarks made above do not really give a proper description of the evidence. What we have here is not *history which really happened* in this way, shown to be a fulfilment of scripture with the help of a questionable interpretation of scripture. Rather, the Christ event was first *narrated* in such a way as to show that it can be regarded as the fulfilment of scripture. The account shows how Christ, who in fact was born in Nazareth or elsewhere, was born in Bethlehem of a virgin as Son of David and Messiah, and fled to Egypt, where it is certain that he never lived. He is made to ride on two animals at once (and so on) so that his career may be shown to be in accordance with the scriptures. If it is impossible to produce such an argument from prophecy today, then a historiography which seeks to use these means to present a life of Jesus is even less acceptable. But if the story of Jesus is presented in this way, in accordance with scripture, are we concerned here with a historiography and a life of the historical Jesus at all? To pose the question is to answer it. We do indeed have a life of Jesus here, but what happens is that the proclamation of Christ is made in the form of a life of Jesus which is not intended to be read and proclaimed as an accurate biography, but as the proclamation of Christ. And this proclamation of Christ is made in language which was formed by the Old Testament, as testimony to the one and unique and constant God, and then taken over by the New Testament proclamation of Christ.

Can the proclamation ever be detached from this language? Is it possible to break the *linguistic* connection, 'the continuum that links faith with Abraham', which has verbal rather than temporal character

(G. Klein, 'Bibel und Heilsgeschichte', VIA, 30)? In that case, is the Old Testament in principle not an inalienable Christian possession? Is it not necessarily part of the Christian canon?

This question must be answered in the negative. Certainly proclamation and faith are not bound to one language once and for all – this is clear from the very fact that the early church read and canonized the Old Testament in a translation. Nor are they bound to a particular interpretation of the world and human existence which goes with that language. Proclamation and faith are and remain – *sola scriptura* – bound to the original testimony of the New Testament. However, for the most part the New Testament speaks the language of the Old and therefore presupposes its validity as a testimony to one and the same God. Thus the rejection of the Old Testament would not only make the message of the New Testament incomprehensible, but curtail its content. That is why Marcionitism – in its ancient and more recent forms – is always an attack on the very substance of Christianity: Marcion's Christ, a Christ shaped by his concern with Paul, is no more the Christ proclaimed by the apostle than is the Aryan Jesus of a purified German Christianity or the socially active representative of a dead God in modern times.

True, those actively concerned with the church cannot be premature in declaring that reflection on hermeneutical theory has come to an end. But a consideration of what actually happens in the church can reveal the purely theoretical and academic character of a form of reflection which fades away into idle speculation. Just imagine a church with a bowdlerized Old Testament and a similarly bowdlerized New Testament, with a bowdlerized service book and a bowdlerized hymn book, without 'Lift up your heads!', without the cradle at Bethlehem, without the oxen and asses which have wrongly found their way in, without the Canaanite and Israelite feasts of the church's year in the form in which the church celebrates them. Without the language of the Old Testament, the church would lapse into silence and find no way of fulfilling its calling to proclaim the testimony to Christ.

However, a critical hermeneutical theory does not force us to these lengths. On the contrary, along with the New Testament witnesses, and thanks to the criterion they provide, it encourages us to translate once again, on a better historical and hermeneutical basis, the old language of the Old Testament into the proclamation of the one act of God in Jesus Christ.

ABBREVIATIONS

AHAW.PH	Abhandlungen der Heidelberger Akademie der Wissenschaften. Philosophisch-historische Klasse
ASGW.PH	Abhandlungen der Sächsischen Gesellschaft der Wissenschaften. Philosophisch-historische Klasse
ATANT	Abhandlungen zur Theologie des Alten und Neuen Testaments
AVTRW	Aufsätze und Vorträge zur Theologie und Religionswissenschaft
BEvTh	Beiträge zur Evangelischen Theologie
BFChTh	Beiträge zur Förderung der christlichen Theologie
BGBH	Beiträge zur Geschichte der biblischen Hermeneutik
BGLRK	Beiträge zur Geschichte und Lehre der Reformierten Kirche
BHTh	Beiträge zur historischen Theologie
BT(N)	Bibliothèque théologique, Neuchâtel
BWANT	Beiträge zur Wissenschaft vom Alten und Neuen Testament
BZAW	Beihefte zur *Zeitschrift für die alttestamentliche Wissenschaft*
BZ NF	*Biblische Zeitschrift*. Neue Folge
CB.OT	Coniectanea biblica. Old Testament Series
D	Deuteronomist
DtPfrBl	*Deutsches Pfarrerblatt*
E	Elohist
ELKZ	*Evangelisch-lutherische Kirchenzeitung*
ErF	Erlanger Forschungen
ET	English translation
EThS	Erfurter theologische Schriften
EvTh	*Evangelische Theologie*

EZS	Evangelische Zeitstimmen
FGLP	Forschungen zur Geschichte und Lehre des Protestantismus
FRLANT	Forschungen zur Religion und Literatur des Alten und Neuen Testaments
FS	Festschrift
FV	*Foi et Vie*
GNT	Grundrisse zum Neuen Testament
GTB	van Gorcum's theologische bibliotheek
HNT	Handbuch zum Neuen Testament
HThS	Harvard Theological Studies
HUTh	Hermeneutische Untersuchungen zur Theologie
J	Yahwist
JAC	*Jarhbuch für Antike und Christentum*
JLCR	Jordan Lectures in Comparative Religion
KAI	*Kanaanäische und aramäische Inschriften*, ed. H. Donner and W. Röllig, Wiesbaden 1962–1964, ²1967–1969
KBANT	Kommentare und Beiträge zum Alten und Neuen Testament
KIG	Kirche in ihrer Geschichte
KuD	*Kerygma und Dogma*
KuD.B	*Kerygma und Dogma*. Beiheft
KVR	Kleine Vandenhoeck-Reihe
LuJ	*Luther-Jahrbuch*
NERT	*Near Eastern Religious Texts relating to the Old Testament*, ed. W. Beyerlin, ET 1978
NStB	Neukirchener Studien-Bücher
NTS	*New Testament Studies*
NZSTh	*Neue Zeitschrift für systematische Theologie und Religionsphilosophie*
OTS	*Oudtestamentische Studiën*
P	Priestly Writing
RGG	*Die Religion in Geschichte und Gegenwart*, Tübingen 1900–1913, ²1927–1932, ³1956–1965
SBM	Stuttgarter Biblische Monographien
SBS	Stuttgarter Bibelstudien
SBT	Studies in Biblical Theology
SKG.G	Schriften der Königsberger Gelehrten Gesellschaft. Geisteswissenschaftliche Klasse
SNT	Supplements to *Novum Testamentum*
StANT	Studien zum Alten und Neuen Testament

StGen	*Studium Generale*
SVT	Supplements to *Vetus Testamentum*
TB	Theologische Bücherei
TBT	Theologische Bibliothek Töpelmann
TDNT	*Theological Dictionary of the New Testament*
TEH	Theologische Existenz heute
TGI	*Textbuch zur Geschichte Israels*, ed. K. Galling, Tübingen 1950, ²1968
THAT	*Theologisches Handwörterbuch zum Alten Testament*, ed. E. Jenni and C. Westermann, Munich and Zurich 1971
TLZ	*Theologische Literaturzeitung*
ThR	*Theologische Rundschau*
ThSt	Theologische Studien
TWAT	*Theologisches Wörterbuch zum Alten Testament*
ThWiss	Theologische Wissenschaft
TKTG	Texte zur Kirchen- und Theologiegeschichte
TThS	Trierer Theologische Studien
TU	Texte und Untersuchungen zur Geschichte der altchristlichen Literatur
UTB	Uni-Taschenbücher
VF	*Verkündigung und Forschung*
VT	*Vetus Testamentum*
VoxTh	*Vox Theologica*
WdF	Wege der Forschung
WMANT	Wissenschaftliche Monographien zum Alten und Neuen Testament
WPKG	*Wissenschaft und Praxis in Kirche und Gesellschaft*
ZAW	*Zeitschrift für die alttestamentliche Wissenschaft*
ZKG	*Zeitschrift für Kirchengeschichte*
ZNW	*Zeitschrift für die neutestamentliche Wissenschaft und die Kunde der älteren Kirche*
ZSTh	*Zeitschrift für systematische Theologie*
ZThK	*Zeitschrift für Theologie und Kirche*
ZZ	*Zwischen den Zeiten*

BIBLIOGRAPHY

The number and letter following short titles in the text indicate the section of the bibliography where the work is to be found.

I *Introduction: The Old Testament as a Hermeneutical Problem*

IA. *On the methodology of exegesis*

G. Adam, O. Kaiser, W. G. Kümmel, *Einführung in die exegetischen Methoden*, ⁵1975

H. Barth, O. H. Steck, *Exegese des Alten Testaments, Leitfaden der Methodik*, ²1971

R. Barthes, F. Bovon, F. J. Leenhardt, R. Martin-Achard, J. Starobinski, *Analyse structurale et exégèse biblique*, BT(N), 1971

G. Fohrer, H. W. Hoffmann, F. Huber, L. Markert, G. Wanke, *Exegese des Alten Testaments. Einführung in die Methodik*, UTB 267, 1973

K. Koch, *The Growth of the Biblical Tradition*, ET 1969

K. Lehmann, in *Einführung in die Methoden der biblischen Exegese*, ed. J. Schreiner, 1971, 62ff.

W. Richter, *Exegese als Literaturwissenschaft. Entwurf einer alttestamentlichen Literaturtheorie und Methodologie*, 1971

IB. *On hermeneutics*

E. Betti, *Zur Grundlegung einer allgemeinen Auslegungslehre*, 1954

O. F. Bollnow, *Das Verstehen*, 1949

R. Bultmann, 'The Problem of Hermeneutics', ET in *Essays Philosophical and Theological*, 1955, 234ff.

W. Dilthey, 'Die Enstehung der Hermeneutik', *Gesammelte Schriften* V, 1924, 317ff.

— 'Erleben, Ausdruck und Verstehen', *Gesammelte Schriften* VII, ⁴1965, 191ff.

— *Leben Schleiermachers* II, posthumously edited by M. Redeker, 1966

G. Ebeling, 'Hermeneutik', *RGG* III³, 1959, cols. 242ff.

— 'The Significance of the Critical Historical Method for Church and Theology in Protestantism', ET in *Word and Faith*, 1963, 17ff.

E. Fuchs, *Hermeneutik*, 1954, ²1958

— *Marburger Hermeneutik*, HUTh 9, 1968

H.-G. Gadamer, *Truth and Method*, ET 1975
M. Heidegger, *Being and Time*, ET 1962
O. Loretz, W. Strolz (eds.), *Die hermeneutische Frage in der Theologie*, 1968
K. H. Miskotte, *Zur biblischen Hermeneutik*, ThSt 55, 1959
F. Mussner, 'Geschichte der Hermeneutik. Von Schleiermacher bis zur Gegenwart', in *Handbuch der Dogmengeschichte* I, 1970
F. D. E. Schleiermacher, *Hermeneutik*, newly edited from the manuscripts and with an introduction by Heinz Kimmerle, AHAW.PH, 1959, 2
J. Wach, *Das Verstehen. Grundzüge einer Geschichte der hermeneutischen Theorie im 19. Jahrhundert*, 3 vols, 1926–1933, reprinted 1966

Ic. *On the problem of hermeneutics and the history of the Old Testament in the church*

L. Diestel, *Geschichte des Alten Testaments in der christlichen Kirche*, 1869
G. Gloege, 'Zur Geschichte des Schriftverständnisses', in *Das Neue Testament als Kanon*, ed. E. Käsemann, 1970, 13ff.
E. G. Kraeling, *The Old Testament since the Reformation*, 1955
H.-J. Kraus, *Geschichte der historisch-kritischen Erforschung des Alten Testaments*, ²1969
— *Die biblische Theologie. Ihre Geschichte und ihre Problematik*, 1970
N. Lohfink, *Das AT in historischer und christlicher Auslegung*, 1966

II *The Old Testament as a Legacy*

IIA. *On the formation of the canon and the use of the Old Testament in the New Testament*

W. Bauer, *Das Johannesevangelium*, HNT, ³1933, esp. 31
K. Berger, *Die Gesetzesauslegung Jesu. Ihr historischer Hintergrund im Judentum und im Alten Testament*, WMANT 40, 1972
J. Blank, 'Erwägungen zum Schriftverständnis des Paulus', in *Rechtfertigung*, FS E. Käsemann, 1976, 37ff.
G. Bornkamm, G. Barth, H. J. Held, *Tradition and Interpretation in Matthew*, ET 1963
H. Braun, 'Das AT im NT', *ZThK* 59, 1962, 16ff.
R. Bultmann, *The Gospel of John*, ET 1971
— *Jesus and the Word*, ET 1958
— *Theology of the New Testament* I, ET 1952
H. von Campenhausen, *The Formation of the Christian Bible*, ET 1972, esp. 1–146
H. Conzelmann, *The Theology of St Luke*, ET 1960
— *History of Primitive Christianity*, ET 1973
D. Daube, *The New Testament and Rabbinic Judaism*, JLCR 2, 1956
W. D. Davies, *Paul and Rabbinic Judaism*, ²1955
Martin Dibelius, *From Tradition to Gospel*, ET 1934

242   Bibliography

C. Dietzfelbinger, *Paulus und das Alte Testament*, TEH 95, 1961
— *Heilsgeschichte bei Paulus?*, TEH 126, 1965
J. W. Doeve, *Jewish Hermeneutics in the Synoptic Gospels and Acts*, GTB 24, 1954
— *Christian Origins and Judaism*, 1962
O. Eissfeldt, *The Old Testament. An Introduction*, ET 1965
E. E. Ellis, *Paul's Use of the Old Testament*, 1957
H. Flender, *St Luke: Theologian of Redemptive History*, ET 1967
L. Goppelt, *Christentum und Judentum im ersten und zweiten Jahrhundert*, BFChTh 2, 55, 1954
— *Apostolic and Post-Apostolic Times*, ET 1970
— 'Israel und die Kirche, heute und bei Paulus', in *Christologie und Ethik. Aufsätze zum NT*, 1968
E. Grässer, 'Die antijüdische Polemik im Johannesevangelium', *NTS* 11, 1964–1965, 74ff.
R. H. Gundry, *The Use of the OT in St Matthew's Gospel*, SNT 18, 1967
A. von Harnack, *Marcion. Das Evangelium vom fremden Gott. Eine Monographie zur Geschichte der Grundlegung der katholischen Kirche*, 1921
— *Das AT in den paulinischen Briefen und in den paulinischen Gemeinden*, 1929
C. Haufe, 'Die Stellung des Paulus zum Gesetz', *TLZ* 91, 1966, cols. 171ff.
F. Hesse, *Das Alte Testament als Buch der Kirche*, 1966, esp. 37–66
R. Hummel, *Die Auseinandersetzung zwischen Kirche und Judentum im Matthäusevangelium*, BEvTh 33, ²1966
F. Jacob, *Principle canonique et formation de L'Ancien Testament*, SVT 28, 1975, 101ff.
A. Jepsen, 'Kanon und Text des Alten Testaments', *TLZ* 74, 1949, cols. 65ff.
— 'Zur Kanongeschichte des Alten Testaments', *ZAW* 71, 1959, 114ff.
O. Kaiser, *Introduction to the Old Testament*, ET 1975
G. Klein, 'Lukas 1,1–4 als theologisches Programm', in *Zeit und Geschichte*, FS R. Bultmann z.80. Gerburtstag, 1964. 193ff. = *Reconstruktion und Interpretation, Gesammelte Aufsätze zum Neuen Testament*, 1969, 237ff.
— 'Präliminarien zum Thema "Paulus und die Juden"', in *Rechtfertigung*, FS E. Käsemann, 1976, 229ff.
W. G. Kümmel, 'Jesus und der jüdische Traditionsgedanke', in *Heilsgeschehen und Geschichte, Gesammelte Aufsätze 1933–1964*, 1965, 15ff.
— *Introduction to the New Testament*, ET ²1975
J. C. H. Lebram, 'Aspekte der alttestamentlichen Kanonbildung', *VT* 18, 1968, 173ff.
B. Lindars, *New Testament Apologetic. The Doctrinal Significance of the Old Testament Quotations*, 1961
O. Michel, *Paulus und seine Bibel*, BFChTh 2, 18, 1929
S. Pancaro, *The Law in the Fourth Gospel*, SNT 42, 1975
M. Rese, *Alttestamentliche Motive in der Christologie des Lukas*, dissertation, Bonn 1965

J. A. Sanders, *Torah and Canon*, 1972

J. Schmid, 'Die alttestamentlichen Zitate bei Paulus und die Theorie vom sensus plenior', *BZ* NF 3, 1959, 161ff.

H. J. Schoeps, *Theologie und Geschichte des Judenchristentums*, 1949

— 'Paulus als rabbinischer Exeget', *Gesammelte Aufsätze*, 1950, 221ff.

A. Suhl, *Die Funktion der alttestamentlichen Zitate und Anspielungen im Markusevangelium*, 1965

A. C. Sundberg, *The Old Testament of the Early Church*, HThS 20, 1964

R. V. G. Tasker, *The Old Testament in the New Testament*, ²1954

W. B. Tatum, 'The Epoch of Israel: Luke I–II and the Theological Plan of Luke-Acts', *NTS* 13, 1966–1967, 184ff.

W. Trilling, *Das wahre Israel – Studien zur Theologie des Matthäus*, StANT 10, ³1964

P. Vielhauer, 'Paulus und das Alte Testament', in *Studien zur Geschichte und Theologie der Reformation*, FS E. Bizer, 1969, 33ff.

IIB. *On the use of the Old Testament in the ancient church*

C. Andresen, 'Justin und der mittlere Platonismus', *ZNW* 44, 1952/1953, 157ff.

— *Geschichte des Christentums I. Von den Anfängen bis zur Hochscholastik*, ThWiss 6, 1975

A. Bengsch, *Heilsgeschichte und Heilswissen. Eine Untersuchung zur Struktur und Entfaltung des theologischen Denkens im Werk 'adversus haereses' des Hl. Irenäus von Lyon*, EThS 3, 1957

G. N. Bonwetsch, *Der Schriftbeweis für die Kirche aus den Heiden als das wahre Israel*, 1908

W. Bousset, *Jüdisch-christlicher Schulbetrieb in Alexandria und Rom*, FRLANT 23, 1915

N. Brox, *Offenbarung, Gnosis und gnostischer Mythos bei Irenäus von Lyon*, 1966

H. von Campenhausen, *Ecclesiastical Authority and Spiritual Power in the Church of the First Three Centuries*, ET 1969

— 'Das AT als Bibel der Kirche vom Ausgang des Christentums bis zur Entstehung des Neuen Testaments', in *Aus der Frühzeit des Christentums*, 1963, 152ff.

A. von Harnack, *The Mission and Expansion of Christianity in the First Three Centuries*, ET, 2 vols., 1904–1905

J. Hoh, *Die Lehre des Heiligen Irenäus über das Neue Testament*, 1919

K. Hruby, *Juden und Judentum bei den Kirchenvätern*, Schriften zur Judentumskunde 2, 1971

H. Karpp, 'Antijudaism', in *Viator* 2, 1971, 355ff.

W. Maurer, *Kirche und Synagoge*, Franz Delitzsch-Vorlesungen, 1953

P. Prigent, *Justin et l'Ancien Testament*, 1964

B. Seeberg, 'Die Geschichtstheologie Justin des Märtyrers', *ZKG* 58, 1939, 1ff.

M. Widmann, 'Irenäus und seine theologischen Väter', *ZThK* 54, 1957, 156ff.

IIc. *On typology*

R. Bultmann, 'Ursprung und Sinn der Typologie als hermeneutischer Methode', *ThLZ* 75, 1950, cols. 205ff. = *Exegetica*, 1967, 369ff.

J. Daniélou, *From Shadows to Reality. Studies in the Biblical Typology of the Fathers*, ET 1960

E. Fascher, 'Typologie auslegungsgeschichtlich', *RGG* VI³, 1962, cols. 1095ff.

L. Goppelt, *Typos. Die typologische Deutung des Alten Testaments im Neuen*, BFChTh 2, 43, 1939.

F. Hesse, 'Typologie im At', *RGG* VI³, 1962, col. 1094f.

H. Nakagawa, 'Typologie im NT, *RGG* I¹, 1909, cols. 354f.

For further literature on contemporary typological exegesis see VIB below.

IId. *On allegorical interpretation*

B. Baentsch, 'Allegorische Auslegung', *RGG* I¹, 1909, cols. 255ff.

G. Chappuzeau, 'Die Exegese von Hohelied 1, 2a.b und 7 bei den Kirchenvätern von Hippolyt bis Bernhard. Ein Beitrag zum Verständnis von Allegorie und Analogie', *JAC* 18, 1975, 90ff.

J. Christiansen, *Die Technik der allegorischen Schriftauslegung bei Philo von Alexandrien*, BGBH 7, 1969

E. von Dobschütz, 'Vom vierfachen Schriftsinn. Die Geschichte einer Theorie', in *Harnack-Ehrung*, 1921, 1ff.

L. Goppelt, 'Allegorie im AT und NT', *RGG* I³, 1957, cols. 239f.

H. Gunkel, 'Allegorie im AT und Judentum', *RGG* I¹, 1909, cols. 354f.

W. Hagemann, *Wort als Begegnung mit Christus, Die christozentrische Auslegung des Kirchenvaters Hieronymus*, TThS 23, 1970

R. P. C. Hanson, *Allegory and Event. A Study of the Sources and Significance of Origen's Interpretation of Scripture*, 1959

A. von Harnack, *Der kirchengeschichtliche Ertrag der exegetischen Arbeiten des Origenes*, TU 42, 3.4, 1918/1919

E. Kuypers, *Der Zeichen- und Wortbegriff im Denken Augustins*, 1934

III *The Old Testament in the Light of the Reformation and under Fire from Historical Criticism*

IIIA. *On the Reformation understanding of the Old Testament*

H. Bornkamm, *Luther and the Old Testament*, ET 1969

J. A. Cramer, *De heilige schrivt bij Calvin*, 1926

— *Calvijn en de heilige schrift*, 1932

G. Ebeling, *Evangelische Evangelienauslegung. Eine Untersuchung zu Luthers Hermeneutik*, FGLP 10,1, 1942

G. Ebeling, 'Die Anfänge von Luthers Hermeneutik', *ZThK* 48, 1951, 178ff.
— 'The Significance of the Critical Historical Method', see IB above
K. Galling, 'Die Prophetenbilder der Lutherbibel im Zusammenhang mit Luthers Schriftverständnis', *EvTh* 6, 1946/1947, 273ff.
J. Hempel, *Luther und das Alte Testament*, 1935
V. Herntrich, 'Luther und das Alte Testament', *LuJ* 20, 1938, 93ff.
G. Krause, *Studien zu Luthers Auslegung der Kleinen Propheten*, dissertation, Zurich 1960
W. Niesel, *Die Theologie Calvins*, 1938, esp. 86ff., 98ff.
H. Østergaard-Nielsen, *Scriptura sacra et viva vox. Eine Lutherstudie*, FGLP 10, 10, 1957
F. K. Schumann, 'Gedanken Luthers zur Frage der Entmythologisierung', in *FS R. Bultmann*, 1949, 208ff.
H. Sick, *Melanchthon als Ausleger des Alten Testaments*, BGBH 2, 1959
O. Weber (ed.), *Calvins Auslegung der Heiligen Schrift*, 1937
H. H. Wolf, *Die Einheit des Bundes. Das Verhältnis von Altem und Neuem Testament bei Calvin*, 1958 ([2]1959)

IIIB. *On the history of scholarship*

J. A. Bengel, *Ordo temporum*, 1741, German edition by C. F. Werner, 1853/1854 ([5]1932)
— *Gnomon Novi Testamenti*, 1742 ([8]1891)
E. Busch, 'Der Beitrag und Ertrag der Föderaltheologie für ein geschichtliches Verständnis der Offenbarung', *Oikonomia*, FS O. Cullmann, 1967, 171ff.
J. Cocceius, *Summa doctrinae de foedere Dei et testamento explicata*, 1653
L. Diestel, see IC above, especially 555ff.
O. Eissfeldt, 'Israelitisch-jüdische Religionsgeschichte und alttestamentliche Theologie', *ZAW* 44, 1926, 1ff., cited from *Kleine Schriften* I, 1962, 105ff.
H. Faulenbach, *Weg und Ziel der Erkenntnis Christi. Eine Untersuchung zur Theologie des Johannes Coccejus*, BGLRK 36, 1973
J. G. Herder, *Vom Geist der ebräischen Poesie*, 1782/1783, ed. H. Hoffmann, 1890
H. E. Hess, *Theologie und Religion bei Johann Salomo Semler. Ein Beitrag zur Theologiegeschichte des 18. Jahrhunderts*, dissertation, Berlin 1974
E. Hirsch, *Geschichte der neuern evangelischen Theologie*, five volumes, [5]1975
H. Karpp, *Das Alte Testament in der Geschichte der Kirche. Seine Geltung und seine Wirkung*, 1939
E. G. Kraeling, *The Old Testament since the Reformation*, London 1955
H.-J. Kraus, see IC above.
W. G. Kümmel, *The New Testament. The History of the Investigation of its Problems*, ET 1973
E. Ludwig, *Schriftverständnis und Schriftauslegung bei J. A. Bengel*, 1952

M. Noth, *The History of Israel*, ET ²1960
— *The History of Pentateuchal Traditions*, ET 1972
L. Perlitt, *Vatke und Wellhausen*, BZAW 94, 1965
G. von Rad, *The Problem of the Hexateuch and Other Essays*, ET 1966
G. Schrenk, *Gottesreich und Bund im älteren Protestantismus, vornehmlich bei Johannes Cocceius*, 1923
J. S. Semler, *Abhandlung von freier Untersuchung des Canon* (1771–1775), ed. H. Scheible, TKTG 5, 1967
R. Smend, *W.M.L. de Wettes Arbeit am Alten und Neuen Testament*, 1958
W. Vatke, *Die biblische Theologie wissenschaftlich dargestellt*, Vol. 1: *Die Religion des Alten Testaments nach den kanonischen Büchern entwickelt*, 1835

IIIc. *On more recent theologies of the Old Testament*

F. Baumgärtel, 'Zur Frage der theologischen Deutung des Alten Testaments', *ZSTh* 15, 1930, 136ff.
— 'Erwägungen zur Darstellung der Theologie des Alten Testaments', *TLZ* 76, 1951, cols. 257ff.
— *Verheissung. Zur Frage des evangelischen Verständnisses des Alten Testaments*, 1952
— 'The Hermeneutical Problem of the Old Testament', ET in C. Westermann (ed.), *Essays on Old Testament Interpretation*, 1963, 134ff.
— 'Gerhard von Rads "Theologie des Alten Testaments"', *TLZ* 86, 1961, cols. 801ff., 895ff.
— 'Das Offenbarungszeugnis des Alten Testaments in Lichte der religionsgeschichtlich-vergleichenden Forschung', *ZThK* 64, 1967, 393ff.
B. S. Childs, *Biblical Theology in Crisis*, 1970
H. Conzelmann, 'Fragen an Gerhard von Rad', *EvTh* 24, 1964, 113ff.
W. Eichrodt, *Theology of the Old Testament*, ET London I, 1961; II, 1967
O. Eissfeldt, see IIIb above
G. Fohrer, *History of Israelite Religion*, ET 1973
— *Theologische Grundstrukturen des Alten Testaments*, TBT 24, 1972
G. F. Hasel, *Old Testament Theology: Basic Issues in the Current Debate*, 1972
— 'The Problem of the Center of the OT Theology Debate', *ZAW* 86, 1974, 65ff.
F. Hesse, 'Die Erforschung der Geschichte Israels als theologische Aufgabe', *KuD* 4, 1958, 1ff.
— 'The Evaluation and the Authority of OT Texts', ET in C. Westermann (ed.), *Essays on Old Testament Interpretation*, 1963, 285ff.
— 'Kerygma oder geschichtliche Wirklichkeit? Kritische Fragen zu Gerhard von Rads "Theologie des Alten Testaments I Teil"', *ZThK* 57, 1960, 17ff.
— *Das Alte Testament als Buch der Kirche*, 1966
— 'Bewährt sich eine "Theologie der Heilstatsachen" am Alten Testament? Zum Verhältnis vom Faktum und Deutung', *ZAW* 81, 1969, 1ff.

M. Honecker, 'Zum Verständnis der Geschichte in Gerhard von Rads Theologie des Alten Testaments', *EvTh* 23, 1963, 143ff

L. Köhler, *Theology of the Old Testament*, 1936, ET 1956

K. H. Miskotte, *When the Gods are Silent*, ET 1971

L. Perlitt, *Bundestheologie im Alten Testament*, WMANT 36, 1969

O. Procksch, *Theologie des Alten Testaments*, 1949–1950

G. von Rad, *Old Testament Theology* I, II, ET 1962, 1965

— 'Offene Fragen im Umkreis einer Theologie des Alten Testaments', *TLZ* 88, 1963, cols. 401ff.

W. H. Schmidt, ' "Theologie des Alten Testaments" vor und nach Gerhard von Rad', *VF* 17, 1972, 1ff. (with further bibliography)

— *Alttestamentlicher Glaube in seiner Geschichte*, NStB 6, 1975

E. Sellin, *Alttestamentliche Theologie auf religionsgeschichtlicher Grundlage* I, II, 1933ff.

R. Smend, *Die Mitte des Alten Testaments*, ThSt 101, 1970

C. Steuernagel, 'Alttestamentliche Theologie und alttestamentliche Religionsgeschichte', in FS K. Marti, BZAW 41, 1925, 266ff.

W. Vischer, *The Witness of the Old Testament to Christ*, ET 1949

T. C. Vriezen, *An Outline of Old Testament Theology*, ET 1958

C. Westermann (ed.), *Essays on Old Testament Interpretation*, ET 1963

E. Würthwein, 'Vom Verstehen des ATs', in FS G. Beer, 1935, 128ff. = *Wort und Existenz, Studien zum AT*, 1970, 9ff.

— 'Zur Theologie des Alten Testaments', *ThR* 36, 1971, 185ff. (with further bibliography)

W. Zimmerli, *Grundriss der alttestamentlichen Theologie*, ThWiss 3, 1972

— 'Erwägungen zur Gestalt einer alttestamentlichen Theologie', *TLZ* 98, 1973, cols. 81ff. = *Studien zur alttestamentlichen Theologie und Prophetie, Gesammelte Aufsätze* II, TB 51, 1974, 27ff.

IV *The Old Testament as Law and as a Covenant Document*

IVA. *On the understanding of the canon*

V. E. Hasler, *Gesetz und Evangelium in der alten Kirche bis Origines*, 1953

P. Katz, 'The Old Testament Canon in Palestine and Alexandria', *ZNW* 47, 1956, 191ff.

J. L. Koole, 'Die Bibel des Ben-Sira', *OTS* 14, 1965, 374ff.

J. C. H. Lebram, see IIA above

M. Limbeck, *Die Ordnung des Heils. Untersuchungen zum Gesetzesverständnis des Frühjudentums*, KBANT, 1971

A. C. Sundberg, see IIA above

IVв. *On the understanding of covenant, justice and law*

A. Alt, 'The Origins of Israelite Law', in *Essays on Old Testament History and Religion*, ET 1966, 79ff.

K. Baltzer, *The Covenant Formulary*, ET 1970

K. Barth, *Evangelium und Gesetz*, TEH 32, 1935

F. Baumgärtel, see IIIc

J. Begrich, 'BERIT. Ein Beitrag zur Erfassung einer alttestamentlichen Denkform', *ZAW* 60, 1944, 1ff., cited from *Gesammelte Studien zum Alten Testament*, TB 21, 1964, 55f.

J. Behm, 'DIATHEKE', in *TDNT* II, 1964, 106ff.

H. Braun, see IIA above

P. Buis, 'La nouvelle alliance', *VT* 18, 1968, 1ff.

R. E. Clements, *Prophecy and Covenant*, SBT 43, 1965

W. Eichrodt, 'Bund und Gesetz', in FS H. W. Hertzberg, 1965, 30ff.

G. Fohrer, 'Altes Testament – "Amphiktyonie" und "Bund"?', *TLZ* 91, 1966, cols. 801ff.

—⁓ 'Das sogenannte apodiktisch formulierte Recht und der Dekalog', *KuD* 11, 1965, 49ff. = *Studien zur alttestamentlichen Theologie und Geschichte*, BZAW 115, 1969, 120ff.

E. Gerstenberger, *Wesen und Herkunft des 'apodiktischen' Rechts*, WMANT 20, 1965

H. Gese, 'Psalm 50 und das alttestamentliche Gesetzesverständnis', in *Rechtfertigung*, FS E. Käsemann, 1976, 57ff.

J. Halbe, *Das Privilegrecht Jahwes Ex 34, 16–26*, FRLANT 114, 1975, esp. 43ff., 506ff.

G. F. Hasel, see IIIc above

F. Hesse, ' "Gebot und Gesetz" und das Alte Testament', *ELKZ* 13, 1959, 117ff.; see also III, 3

E. Hirsch, *Das Alte Testament und die Predigt des Evangeliums*, 1936

F. Horst, *Das Privilegrecht Jahwes*, FRLANT 45, 1930 = *Gottes Recht. Studien zum Recht im AT*, TB 12, 1961, 17ff.

A. Jepsen, 'Berith. Ein Beitrag zur Theologie der Exilszeit', in *Verbannung und Heimkehr*, FS W. Rudolph, 1961, 161ff.

E. Kinder and K. Haendler (eds.), *Gesetz und Evangelium, Beiträge zur gegenwärtigen theologischen Diskussion*, WdF 142, 1968

H.-J. Kraus, 'Freude an Gottes Gesetz. Ein Beitrag zur Auslegung der Psalmen 1, 19B und 119', *EvTh* 10, 1950/1951, 337ff.

E. Kutsch, 'Berit – Verpflichtung', *THAT* 1971, 339ff.

— *Verheissung und Gesetz. Untersuchungen zum sogenannten 'Bund' im Alten Testament*, BZAW 131, 1973

G. Liedke, *Gestalt und Bezeichnung alttestamentlicher Rechtssätze*, WMANT 39, 1971

D. J. McCarthy, *Old Testament Covenant*, 1973

M. Noth, *Das System der zwölf Stämme Israels*, BWANT 4, 1, 1930
— 'Die mit des Gesetzes Werken umgehen, die sind unter dem Fluch', in *In Piam memoriam A.v.Bulmerincq*, 1938, 127ff. = *Gesammelte Studien zum AT*, TB 6, 1960, 155ff.
— 'The Laws in the Pentateuch', in *The Laws in the Pentateuch and other Essays*, ET 1966, 1ff.
— 'Das Amt des "Richters" Israels', in *FS A. Bertholet zum 80.Geburtstag*, 1950, 404ff. = *Gesammelte Studien zum AT* II, TB 39, 1969, 71ff.
— 'Das alttestamentliche Bundesschliessen im Lichte eines Mari-Textes', *Gesammelte Studien zum AT*, TB 6, 1957, 142ff.
R. Numelin, *Intertribal Relations in Central and South Africa*, Societas Scientiarum Fennica. Commentationes Humanorum Litterarum 32, 3, 1963
L. Perlitt, *Bundestheologie im Alten Testament*, WMANT 36, 1969
H. Graf Reventlow, 'Kultisches Recht im AT', *ZThK* 60, 1963, 267ff.
A. A. van Ruler, *Die christliche Kirche und das Alte Testament*, BEvTh 23, 1955
R. Smend, 'Das Nein des Amos', *EvTh* 23, 1963, 404ff.
— 'Zur Frage der altisraelitischen Amphiktyonie', *EvTh* 31, 1971, 623ff.
J. J. Stamm, 'Jesus Christ and the Old Testament', ET in C. Westermann (ed.), *Essays on Old Testament Interpretation*, 1963, 200ff.
T. C. Vriezen, 'Theocracy and Soteriology', ET in *Essays on Old Testament Interpretation*, 211ff.
M. Weinfeld, 'BERIT', *TWAT* I, 1973, cols. 781ff. (with further bibliography)
C. Westermann, 'Genesis 17 und die Bedeutung von berit', *TLZ* 101, 1976, cols. 161ff.
E. Würthwein, 'Der Sinn des Gesetzes im AT', in *Wort und Existenz. Studien zum AT*, 1970, 39ff.
W. Zimmerli, 'Das Gesetz im AT', *TLZ* 85, 1960, cols. 481ff., cited from *Gottes Offenbarung, Gesammelte Aufsätze*, TB 19, 1963, 249ff.
— *The Law and the Prophets*, ET 1965
— 'Erwägungen zum "Bund"', in *Wort, Gebot, Glaube*, FS W. Eichrodt, ATANT 59, 1970, 171ff.

V *The Old Testament as the Document of an Alien Religion*

F. Baumgärtel, see IIIc above
R. Bultmann, 'The Significance of the Old Testament for the Christian Faith', ET in *The Old Testament and Christian Faith*, ed. B. W. Anderson, 1964, 8ff.
— 'Prophecy and Fulfilment', ET in C. Westermann (ed.), *Essays on Old Testament Interpretation*, 1963, 50ff.
— 'The Significance of the Idea of Freedom for Western Civilization', ET in *Essays Philosophical and Theological*, 1955, 305ff.

F. Delitzsch, *Das babylonische Weltschöpfungsepos*, ASGW. PH 17,2, 1896
— *Babel and Bible*, ET 1903
— *Die grosse Täuschung*, 1920–1921
H. Donner, 'Das Problem des Alten Testaments in der christlicher Theologie. Überlegungen zu Begriff und Geschichte der alttestamentlichen Einleitung', *Beiträge zur Theorie des neuzeitlichen Christentums*, ed. H. J. Birkner and D. Rössler, FS W. Trillhaas, 1968, 37ff.
G. W. F. Hegel, *Early Theological Writings*, ET by T. M. Knox, 1948.
V. Herntrich, *Völkische Religion und Altes Testament*, 1933
F. Hesse, see IIIc above
E. Hirsch, see IVB above
P. Jensen, *Das Gilgamesch Epos in der Weltliteratur*, I, 1906
— *Mose, Jesus, Paulus*, 1909
— *Gilgamesch-Epos, Judäische Nationalsagen, Ilias und Odyssee*, 1924
A. Jeremias, *Das Alte Testament im Lichte des alten Orients*, [2]1966
O. Keel, *Feinde und Gottesleugner. Studien zum Image des Widersachers in den Individualpsalmen*, SBM 7, 1969
F. X. Kugler, *Im Bannkreis Babels, Panbabylonistische Konstruktionen und religionsgeschichtliche Tatsachen*, 1910
E. Schader, *Studien zur Kritik und Erklärung der biblischen Urgeschichte, Gen. I–XI*, 1863
— *Die Keilinschriften und das Alte Testament*, [3]1901
F. D. E. Schleiermacher, *Brief Outline on the Study of Theology* ET 1966
— *Speeches on Religion to its Cultured Despisers*, ET reissued 1958
— *The Christian Faith*, ET 1928
W. Vischer, see IIIc above
H. Winckler, *Die babylonische Geisteskultur in ihren Beziehungen Zur Kulturentwicklung der Menschheit*, 1907

VI *The Old Testament as a History Book*

VIA *On the problem of history and salvation history*

B. Albrektson, *History and the Gods. An Essay on the Idea of Historical Manifestations in the Ancient Near East and in Israel*, CB. OT 1, 1967
K. Barth, *Church Dogmatics*, I, 2, *The Doctrine of the Word of God*, ET 1956, 70ff.
J. T. Beck, *Einleitung in das System der christlichen Lehre oder propaedeutische Entwicklung der christlichen Lehrwissenschaft*, 1838 ([2]1870)
E. Bloch, *Tübinger Einleitung in die Philosophie* I, II, 1963/1964
R. Bultmann, *History and Eschatology*, 1957
R. G. Collingwood, *The Idea of History*, 1949
O. Cullmann, *Christ and Time*, ET 1951
— *Salvation in History*, ET 1967

C. Dietzfelbinger, *Heilsgeschichte bei Paulus?*, TEH 126, 1965

G. Ebeling, 'The World as History', in *Word and Faith* 2 ET 1963, 363ff.

J. Fangmeier, 'Heilsgeschichte?', in J. Fangmeier, M. Geiger, *Geschichte und Zukunft*, ThSt 87, 1967, 5ff.

E. Fuchs, 'Christus das Ende der Geschichte', in *Zur Frage der historischen Jesus*, 1960 (²1965), 79ff.

H. Gese, 'Psalm 22 und das NT', *ZThK* 65, 1968, 1ff., cited from *Vom Sinai zum Zion. Alttestamentliche Beiträge zur biblischen Theologie*, BEvTh 64, 1974, 180ff.

— 'Erwägungen zur Einheit biblischer Theologie', *ZThK* 67, 1970 417ff., cited from *Vom Sinai zum Zion*, 11ff.

— 'Anfang und Ende der Apokalyptik, dargestellt am Sacharjabuch', *ZThK* 70, 1973, 20ff., cited from *Vom Sinai zum Zion*, 202ff.

H. G. Geyer, 'Zur Frage der Notwendigkeit des ATs', *EvTh* 25, 1965, 207ff.

F. Hesse, 'Die Erforschung der Geschichte Israels als theologische Aufgabe', *KuD* 4, 1958, 1ff.

— 'Bewährt sich eine "Theologie der Heilstatsachen" am Alten Testament? Zum Verhältnis von Faktum und Deutung', *ZAW* 81, 1969, 1ff.

— *Abschied von der Heilsgeschichte*, ThSt 108, 1971

— 'Zur Profanitätder Geschichte Israels', *ZThK* 71, 1974, 262ff.

J. C. K. von Hofmann, *Weissagung und Erfüllung im Alten und im Neuen Testament* I, 1841; II, 1844

— *Biblische Hermeneutik*, ed. von Hofmeister and Volck, 1888

M. Honecker, 'Zum Verständis der Geschichte in G. von Rads *Theologie des ATs*', *EvTh* 23, 1963, 143ff.

E. Käsemann, 'Justification and Salvation History in the Epistle to the Romans', in *Perspectives on Paul*, ET 1971, 6off.

G. Klein, 'Röm.4 und die Idee der Heilsgeschichte' (1963), in *Rekonstruktion und Interpretation, Gesammelte Aufsätze zum NT*, 1969, 170ff.

— *Theologie des Wortes Gottes und die Hypothese der Universalgeschichte*, BEvTh 37, 1964
'Heil und Geschichte nach Römer IV', *NTS* 13, 1966–1967, 43ff.

— 'Individualgeschichte und Weltgeschichte bei Paulus' (1964), in *Rekonstruktion und Interpretation*, 180ff.

— 'Bibel und Heilsgeschichte. Die Fragwürdigkeit einer Idee', *ZNW* 62, 1971, 1ff.

R. Knierim, 'Offenbarung im Alten Testament', in *Probleme alttestamentlicher Theologie*, FS G. von Rad, 1971, 206ff.

K. Koch, *The Rediscovery of Apocalyptic*, SBT II 22, 1972

G. Krüger, *Geschichte und Tradition*, 1948

F. Lang, 'Christuszeugnis und Biblische Theologie', *EvTh* 29, 1969, 523ff.

G. E. Lessing, *Die Erziehung des Menschengeschlechts* (1780), in G. E. Lessing, *Gesammelte Werke* 8, ed. P. Rilla, 1968

K. Löwith, *Meaning in History*, 1949.

F. Mildenberger, *Gottes Tat im Wort. Erwägungen zur alttestamentlichen Hermeneutik als Frage nach der Einheit der Testamente*, 1964

J. Moltmann, *Theology of Hope*, ET 1967

W. Pannenberg (ed.), *Revelation as History*, ET 1969
— *Theology and the Philosophy of Science*, ET 1976

H. D. Preuss, 'Das Alte Testament in der Verkündigung der Kirche', *DtPfrBl* 68, 1968, 73ff.

R. Rendtorff, 'Hermeneutik des Alten Testaments als Frage nach der Geschichte', *ZThK* 57, 1960, 27ff.
— '"Offenbarung" im Alten Testament', *TLZ* 85, 1960, cols. 833ff.
— 'The Concept of Revelation in Ancient Israel', ET in W. Pannenberg (ed.), *Revelation as History*, 1969, 23ff.
— 'Geschichte und Wort im Alten Testament', *EvTh* 22, 1962, 621ff.
— 'Geschichte und Überlieferung', in FS G. von Rad, 1964, 81ff.

K. Schwarzwäller, *Das Alte Testament in Christus*, ThSt 84, 1966

E. Stauffer, *New Testament Theology*, ET 1963

K. G. Steck, *Die Idee der Heilsgeschichte – Hofmann – Schlatter – Cullmann*, ThSt 56, 1959

P. Stuhlmacher, 'Neues Testament und Hermeneutik', *ZThK* 68, 1971, 121ff., cited from *Schriftauslegung auf dem Wege zur biblischen Theologie*, 1975, 9ff.
— 'Das Bekenntnis zur Auferweckung Jesu von den Toten und die Biblische Theologie', *ZThK* 70, 1973, 365ff. = op. cit., 128ff.
— 'Historische Kritik und theologische Schriftauslegung', op. cit., 59ff.

P. Vielhauer, 'Paulus und das AT', in *Studien zur Geschichte und Theologie der Reformation*, FS E. Bizer, 1969, 33ff., esp. 43ff.

C. Westermann, *Das Alte Testament und Jesus Christus*, 1968
— (ed.), *Essays on Old Testament Interpretation*, see IIIc above

G. E. Wright, *God Who Acts*, SBT 8, 1952

W. Zimmerli, 'Das Wort des göttlichen Selbsterweises (Erweiswort), eine prophetische Gattung', in *Mélanges Bibliques rédigés en l'honneur de André Robert*, 1957, 154ff., cited from *Gottes Offenbarung, Gesammelte Aufsätze*, TB 19, 1963, 120ff.
— '"Offenbarung" im AT', *EvTh* 22, 1962, 15ff.
— 'Promise and Fulfilment', ET in C. Westermann (ed.), *Essays on Old Testament Interpretation*, 1963, 89ff.

VIB. *On the discussion of typology*

H. Braun, 'Das Alte Testament in Neuen Testament', *ZThK* 59, 1962, 16ff.

R. Bultmann, 'Prophecy and Fulfilment', see IVB above

W. Eichrodt, 'Is Typological Exegesis an Appropriate Method?', ET in C. Westermann (ed.), *Essays in Old Testament Interpretation*, 1963, 224ff.

E. Fuchs, *Hermeneutik*, see IB above

F. Michaeli, 'La "typologie" biblique', *FV* 50, 1952, 11ff.

H. D. Preuss, see VIA above

G. von Rad, 'Typological Interpretation of the Old Testament', ET in C. Westermann (ed.), op. cit., 17ff.

N. H. Ridderbos, 'Typologie', *VoxTh* 1961, 149ff.

T. Schieder, 'Der Typus in der Geschichtswissenschaft', *StGen* 5, 1962, 228ff.

R. Wittram, *Das Interesse an der Geschichte*, KVR 59–61, ³1968, esp. ch. 4, 'Vergleich, Analogie, Typus'

H. W. Wolff, 'The Hermeneutics of the Old Testament', in Westermann, op. cit., 160ff.

— 'The Understanding of History in the OT Prophets', in Westermann, op. cit., 336ff.

VII *The Old Testament as Part of the Christian Canon*

James Barr, *Old and New in Interpretation*, 1966

F. Beisser, 'Irrwege und Wege der historisch-kritischen Bibelwissenschaft', *NZSTh* 15, 1973, 192ff.

E. Bloch, *Atheismus im Christentum*, 1968

E. Brunner, 'Die Bedeutung des Alten Testaments für unseren Glauben', *ZZ* 8, 1930, 30ff.

R. Bultmann, 'The Significance of the Old Testament for the Christian Faith', see V above

H. H. von Campenhausen, 'Das AT als Bibel der Kirche', see IIB above

G. Ebeling, 'The Significance of the Critical Historical Method', see IB above

— 'The Meaning of "Biblical Theology"', ET in *Word and Faith*, 1963, 79ff.

H. Geyer, 'Zur Frage nach der Notwendigkeit des Alten Testaments', *EvTh* 25, 1965, 207ff.

H. Grass, *Christliche Glaubenslehre* II, ThWiss 12,2, 1974, 92ff.

A. H. J. Gunneweg, 'Über die Prädikabilität alttestamentlicher Texte', *ZThK* 65, 1968, 389ff.

— 'Sola Scriptura', *WPKG* 65, 1976, 2ff.

A. Jepsen, 'Kanon und Text des ATs', see IIA above
Wissenschaft vom Alten Testament, AVTRW 1, 1958, abbreviated ET 'The Scientific Study of the Old Testament', in Westermann, 246ff.

W. Joest, 'Überlegungen zum Thema Theologie und Wissenschaft', *KuD* 19, 1973, 150ff.

E. Käsemann, 'Vom theologischen Recht historisch-kritischer Exegese', *ZThK* 64, 1967, 259ff.

— (ed.), *Das Neue Testament als Kanon. Dokumentation und kritische Analyse zur gegenwärtigen Diskussion*, 1970

M. Kähler, *Dogmatische Zeitfragen I. Zur Bibelfrage*, 1907, esp. 126ff., 266ff.

H. D. Preuss, 'Das Alte Testament in der Verkündigung der Kirche', see VIA above

H. H. Rowley, *The Relevance of the Bible*, 1942
— *The Rediscovery of the Old Testament*, 1946
— *The Authority of the Bible*, 1949
— *The Unity of the Bible*, 1953
W. Schmithals, 'Über die Bedeutung der Exegese für Theologie und Kirche', in W. Schmithals and J. Beckmann, *Das Christuszeugnis in der heutigen Gesellschaft*, EZS 53, 1970, 43ff.
W. Schrage, 'Theologie und Christologie bei Paulus und Jesus auf dem Hintergrund der modernen Gottesfrage', *EvTh* 36, 1976, 121ff.
K. Schwarzwäller, *Das Alte Testament in Christus*, see VIA above
E. Würthwein, 'Vom Verstehen des ATs', see IIIc above

For further bibliographical details with comments see:
W. H. Schmidt, ' "Theologie des Alten Testaments" ', IIIc above
E. Würthwein, 'Zum Theologie des Alten Testaments', IIIc above

INDEX OF NAMES AND SUBJECTS

INDEX OF BIBLICAL REFERENCES

OLD TESTAMENT

APOCRYPHA

NEW TESTAMENT